Katharine Gibbs
HANDBOOK
OF
BUSINESS
ENGLISH

Katharine Gibbs
HANDBOOK
OF
BUSINESS
ENGLISH

MICHELLE QUINN

MACMILLAN PUBLISHING COMPANY
New York

COLLIER MACMILLAN PUBLISHERS
London

Copyright © 1982 by Katharine Gibbs School, Inc.

Macmillan Publishing Company
866 Third Avenue, New York, N.Y. 10022

Collier Macmillan Canada, Inc.

Library of Congress Catalog Card Number: 82-48356

Printed in the United States of America

20   19   18   17   16   15   14   13   12   11

Library of Congress Cataloging in Publication Data

Main entry under title:
Katharine Gibbs handbook of business English.

Includes index.
1. English language—Grammar—1950–   2. English language—Usage.   3. Commercial correspondence.
I. Katharine Gibbs Schools.
PE1112.K3   1982   808'.066651   82-48356
ISBN 0-02-543180-3

TABLE OF CONTENTS

FOREWORD

There is a notion abroad that important secretarial positions are few in number; that most secretarial positions are primarily stenographic and mechanical. On the contrary there is today a great and unsatisfied demand for secretaries of a high type in positions that offer opportunities of fascinating interest and rapid advancement in business, professional, and journalistic fields.

The business training that will prove a recognized password into these fields must be more than facility with notebook and typewriter; it must represent a working knowledge of the principles and practices of modern business and professional life

> —*Katharine M. Gibbs*
> Founder
> The Katharine Gibbs School

When Katharine M. Gibbs wrote these words in 1922, she expressed the educational philosophy that still guides the Katharine Gibbs School today in each of its locations. It was her firm belief that the finest secretarial training not only teaches technical skills but also teaches the principles and theories that underlie those skills.

This emphasis on understanding basic principles is reflected in the Katharine Gibbs English curriculum. We at the Gibbs School believe that a true mastery of the English language requires a thorough understanding of its structure. To use the language fluently and well, one must know not only that a given sentence is correct but also understand *why*.

The *Katharine Gibbs Handbook of Business English* is the handbook used by Gibbs students in their English courses. As such, the book covers all aspects of English grammar, style, and usage with the same thoroughness that has made the Gibbs curriculum famous.

As any person in business will attest, a mastery of good English is probably the most valuable tool one can have in a business career.

> Eleanor Vreeland
> President
> The Katharine Gibbs School

PREFACE

Over the years business people have consistently telephoned the Katharine Gibbs School nearest their offices to ask an "English question." How to decide between *who* and *whom*, whether to capitalize a title after a name, how to form the possessive of a noun in the name of an organization or a publication—these are just a few of the problems that confront the careful writer and the conscientious secretary. Discussing such specific questions has often led to more general requests. Callers have asked for help with basic grammar and writing rules. They have expressed the need for a reference book that is written in clear, simple language; that includes model letters as well as current trends in written business English; and that is available to everyone in the business world, not just to Gibbs students and graduates. The *Katharine Gibbs Handbook of Business English* is the answer to these requests.

A totally new book, not just a revision, the *Katharine Gibbs Handbook of Business English* covers the content, mechanics, and format of nontechnical written business communications. Whether the production equipment is a standard typewriter or the latest in word-processing systems, the letter that is ready for a signature must illustrate the qualities of effective business writing and incorporate the correct and current rules of style, grammar, punctuation, and usage. The *Katharine Gibbs Handbook of Business English* gives clear, detailed coverage to each of these topics.

The author gratefully acknowledges the guidance and support of Eve Rouke, *Director of Education for the Katharine Gibbs Schools;* the dedication and editorial expertise of Rosanna Hansen and Curtis Cox; the confidence of Kathleen Achorn, *former director of the Katharine Gibbs School, Norwalk, Connecticut* and of Jean Bailey, *Secretarial Studies Dean, Katharine Gibbs School, Norwalk, Connecticut;* the recommendations of Sister Barbara Dewey, SSND, *English Instructor, Katharine Gibbs School, Norwalk, Connecticut;* Sister Joan Dineen, SSND, *Head of the English Department, Girls Catholic High School, Malden, Massachusetts;* Anita W. Hardie, *Secretarial Studies Dean, Katharine Gibbs School, Montclair, New Jersey;* Thomas J. McGowan, *Customer Service Representative, United States Postal Service, Stamford, Connecticut;* Geraldine C. Pelegano, *Head of the English Department, Wolcott High School, Wolcott, Connecticut;* Jane Porter, *Liberal Arts Dean, Katharine Gibbs School, Norwalk, Connecticut;* the special efforts of the Katharine Gibbs Advisory Committee: Patricia Bosze, *Norwalk, Connecticut;* Dorothy Bloodgood Kennedy, *Huntington, New York;* Deborah R. Naclerio, *New York, New York;* and Patricia F. St. Pierre, *Montclair, New Jersey;* the definitions for the "Glossary of Word-Processing Terms" contributed by Eileen Tunison, *Editor of* Today's Office, *Garden City, New York;* the secretarial assistance of Mary Doukas, Mary Fletcher, and Karen Kaechele; and the patience of family and friends, especially that of Lorraine, John, Maureen, and Patty, who lived with every comma, period, and exclamation point.

CHAPTER I
NUMBERS, CAPITALIZATION, AND ABBREVIATIONS

PART I—NUMBERS

PART II—CAPITALIZATION

PART III—ABBREVIATIONS

NUMBERS

Numbers are an essential part of every business communication. Every business letter includes, at the least, the numbers involved in the date and in the addresses. Time, measurements, and prices are also common parts of a business message. A number that is expressed incorrectly or ambiguously may result in costly misunderstanding. For example, there is a great difference between "three million-dollar contracts" (three contracts) and "$3 million contracts" (each contract is worth $3 million).

In general, numbers should be written in a style that is appropriate to their particular context. Following are the three basic styles of expressing numbers in business writing.

Formal Style

Formal circumstances require formal writing. A graduation diploma, an invitation to a state dinner, and an official announcement or proclamation are usually written in formal style. In addition, high-level executive correspondence uses the formal style of expressing numbers to avoid giving them an emphasis that is not intended. In formal writing, all numbers are spelled out.

Technical Style

Many businesses are involved in communicating specialized (technical) information. Scientific, technological, and building industries use numbers in countless situations. In technical writing, numbers are expressed in figures.

Nontechnical Business Style

Business correspondence can certainly contain technical references. It can also on occasion be intentionally formal. The more formal the style, the less frequently figures will appear.

Because most contemporary writers agree that reading numbers expressed in figures is easier and faster, they tend to favor the use of figures wherever feasible. However, the ordinary business letter, memorandum, or report will observe the following rules of nontechnical business English.

BASIC RULES

■ Always spell out a number that begins a sentence, or rephrase the sentence so that the number falls within it.

> Ten thousand copies were printed in June.
>
> In June we had 10,000 copies printed.

■ If no special rule applies . . .

Spell out numbers under 11 and numbers that are to be de-emphasized.

> The contract has been in effect for seven years.

Write in figures numbers starting with 11 and numbers that require special emphasis.

> The warehouse has shipped 12 cartons.

■ Be consistent. Having decided how to express a particular number, adhere to that style throughout a given text.

SPECIAL RULES

Abbreviations

Always use figures with abbreviations. (Although abbreviations seldom appear in nontechnical business writing, an occasional technical reference may require their use.) In addition, except at the beginning of a sentence, the words *number* and *numbers* are always abbreviated and capitalized before a figure.

> She ordered Nos. 14 and 15.
>
> Number 23 is missing.
>
> He used 35-mm film.

Addresses

Within a sentence write out house, building, and street numbers under the number 11.

> He moved to Six East Fourth Street.

Use figures starting with the number 11.

> Nelson's Bookstore is at 12 East 54th Street.

All street names through Ninety-ninth Street may be written out.

> ACCEPTABLE: . . . 12 East Fifty-fourth Street.

ZIP Codes are written in figures without commas. They are typed a single space after the state when they are part of an address within a sentence.

> She lives at 6399 Lakeland Avenue, El Toro, CA 92630. Please forward her mail to that address.

In an address that appears on an envelope or is set off within a letter, use a double space between the state and the ZIP Code.

> Please forward this order to me at the following address:
>
> 6399 Lakeland Avenue
> El Toro, CA   92630

Advertising and Sales

For quick reading, for ease of comprehension, and for emphasis, numbers in advertising and sales writing are almost always expressed in figures.

> At Kramer's you can have 2 for the price of 1!

Ages and Anniversaries

In general, express the age of a person or thing in words.

> When she was eleven years old, her family moved to Europe.

> That fifteen-year-old house needs extensive renovation.

Use figures . . .

In significant statistics

> Inoculation is necessary for children between 2 and 6 years of age.

Immediately following a name

> John Rowe, 43, suffered a stroke.

In an expression of age that includes months and days. (Do not use internal punctuation.)

> He gave his age as 50 years 6 months 13 days.

In general, write out ordinal numbers (*first, second, third,* and so forth) used with anniversaries.

> Shortly after their twelfth anniversary, they were able to buy a home.

Use figures when . . .

More than two words would be needed to express the number

> In the year 2001 our country will celebrate its 225th anniversary.

Special emphasis is desired.

> I don't believe that you are celebrating your 50th anniversary!

Consecutive Numbers

When two numbers that are expressed the same way come together in a sentence, use a comma to separate them.

> Of the seven, two were disqualified.

> In 1980, 200 workers went on strike.

When two numbers precede and modify a noun, write out the first number unless the second number is significantly shorter.

> She bought twelve 20-cent stamps.

> > BUT

> She bought 200 twenty-cent stamps.

Credit Terms

Numbers in credit terms are expressed almost exclusively in figures.

> PREFERRED: Their terms were 2 percent 10 days, net 30 days.

> ACCEPTABLE: Their terms were 2 percent ten days, net thirty days.

Dates

Use cardinal figures (*1, 2, 3,* and so forth) when a date follows a month.

> on June 2

> on Tuesday, June 2,

Use either ordinal numbers (*first, second,* and so forth) or figures with ordinal endings (*1st, 2nd, 3rd, 4th,* and so forth) when a date appears either before a month or alone.

> on the second of June

> on the 2nd of June

> since the 3rd [or third]

Current usage does not require a comma after a year or between a month and year. It is important, however, to be consistent within a given text.

> on June 2, 1982,

> on June 2, 1982 (current usage)

> in June, 1982,

> in June 1982 (current usage)

Foreign or military correspondence usually shows the date as a cardinal figure written before the month and year without commas.

> on 2 June 1982

Decimals

Numbers with decimals are expressed in figures. To prevent misreading, place a zero before a decimal that does not have a whole number unless the decimal itself begins with zero.

We drove 23.321 miles on one gallon of gasohol.

He found a discrepancy of 0.3 percent.

Her measurement was .004 inch shorter than mine.

Fractions

In general, spell out common fractions.

She covered three fourths of the lesson.

Use figures if the fraction . . .

Would be long and awkward and has a two-digit denominator

3/16   5/32   17/64

Is used in a technical context

six ¼-pound weights

Needs emphasis

to divide them by 3/4

Is used with a whole number.

7½ inches

In typing, do not mix fractions that appear on the typewriter keyboard with those that do not. Leave one space between a whole number and a fraction; leave no space before or after the diagonal bar.

The room is 27 3/4 feet long.

Use a hyphen in a fraction before a noun.

She waited one-half hour.

Do not use a hyphen . . .

In a fraction that stands alone

I ate one half.

In a fraction that precedes an *of* phrase.

I ate one half of the pie.

Indefinite Numbers

Express indefinite numbers in words.

a few thousand students

cost them millions

hundreds of books

Law and Finance

In legal or financial correspondence and documents, express important numbers in words followed by confirming figures enclosed in parentheses.

A check for twenty-five thousand dollars ($25,000) will be drawn today.

Military and Political Divisions

Express military and political divisions in words.

> the Third Armored Battalion
> the Sixteenth Congressional District

Money

Use figures for exact and approximate amounts beginning with 1 cent. Write out the word *cent(s)*.

> I remember when a postage stamp cost 5 cents.

Use the dollar sign with exact and approximate amounts beginning with $1. Repeat the dollar sign before amounts in succession.

> Their dresses sell for $25.60 and $34.25.

An even number of dollars is written without a decimal point and two zeros except in a tabulation that includes amounts expressed in dollars and cents.

> He pays me $20 a week.   BUT $11.56
>   20.00

A sum of money may combine with one or more words to form a one-thought modifier of a following noun. Hyphenate accordingly.

> a $50-a-month raise
> an 18-cent stamp
> a one-half-cent increase

The words *cent(s)* and *dollar(s)* become possessive nouns when they are followed by the word *worth*.

> Five dollars' worth of supplies
> about 2 cents' worth

When a sum of money expressed with the dollar sign precedes *worth*, no possessive is shown.

> He bought $5 worth of supplies.

Sums of money in round numbers with seven or more digits may be expressed in three ways. The first column is usually preferred.

> | $1 million | 1 million dollars | $1,000,000 |
> | $25 billion | 25 billion dollars | $25,000,000,000 |
> | $3.2 million | 3.2 million dollars | $3,200,000 |

Numbers as Numbers

When referring to a number as a number, use figures. Do not underscore or italicize the figure.

> Many people consider 7 a lucky number.

Numbers for Identification

When you identify an object by giving it a number, the number is always written in figures. The noun preceding the number is capitalized.

>She will meet us at Gate 6.

>The dictating equipment is in Room 12.

Because the words *line, sentence, verse, paragraph,* and *page* represent small units, capitalizing them before a number is optional.

>The figures to which I referred are on page 6.

>OR

>. . . Page 6.

Percentages

Use figures starting with 1 percent.

>We had a 2 percent increase in sales last month.

Use decimals or write out numbers under 1 percent. Do not use fractions such as ½ or ⅓.

>He predicts a 0.5 percent tax increase.

>Their price estimates are one-third percent lower this month.

Do not put a hyphen between the word *percent* and the number that precedes it.

>They gave us a 15 percent discount on our purchases.

Do not use the percent symbol (%) except in technical and statistical material.

Ratio and Proportion

Express ratios and proportions in figures.

>The votes were 2 to 1 in favor of expansion.

>Mix the dry ingredients with the liquid in proportions of 3 to 1.

Related Numbers

Numbers used in a similar way within a text should be expressed in the same way. If one number is expressed in figures, all related numbers should be expressed in figures.

>Of the 18 students present, only 6 completed the work.

>They have cakes that feed 10, 20, or 30 people.

>We will have 7-, 10-, and 12-minute timings.

The fact that a number at the beginning of a sentence must be written as a word does not affect the expression of the numbers which follow it.

>Seven-, 10-, and 12-minute timings are on this week's schedule.

Numbers that are unrelated (not used in a similar way within a text) should be expressed according to the individual rules that apply to them.

> I told those 12 students they could have five more days to finish their projects.

Roman Numerals

Do not use periods after Roman numerals except when they enumerate main topics in an outline.

> Volume III   Edward VIII   BUT   IV. Social Needs

Round Numbers

Round numbers that would require only two words may be expressed in words.

> There were two hundred people present.

With millions and billions . . .

Use a combination of figures and words.

> They expect 3 million people to see that show.

Use figures with related numbers below a million or with a number that cannot be expressed in a combination.

> They expected 1,000,000 people, but only 800,000 attended.

Symbols

Symbols appear infrequently in business writing except as technical references. However, except at the beginning of a sentence, the dollar sign symbol always appears before exact amounts of money starting with $1.

> We agree that $200 is a fair price.

> Two hundred dollars seems a fair price.

Telephone Numbers

In general, telephone numbers are written in figures with the Area Code in parentheses followed by a space and with a hyphen after the exchange.

> PREFERRED: (203) 568-1400

> ACCEPTABLE: Area Code 203 568-1400

> 203 568-1400

> 203 LOwell 8-1400 (*used infrequently today*)

Temperature

Temperature readings are usually expressed in figures (except zero) with the word *degrees*.

> The temperature was 85 degrees when he started out.

> It will be zero degrees tomorrow.

Time

Clock time   Use figures with A.M. (a.m.) and P.M. (p.m.).

> The meeting will begin at 8:30 A.M. (or 8:30 a.m.)

NOTE: In printed material, A.M. and P.M. are set in small capitals.

Noon and midnight can be used alone or with the figure 12.

> I studied from 9:30 A.M. until midnight.
> We finished at 12 noon.

According to current usage time may be written in words or in figures when used with *o'clock* or when hours and minutes are expressed.

> They made a reservation for eight (or 8) o'clock.
> We were in our seats by seven-thirty (or 7:30).

Express precise time in figures with a colon between the hour and the minutes.

> The show begins at 8:15 P.M.
> > BUT
> She will arrive about four-thirty this afternoon.

When time is expressed in words, a hyphen separates the hour from the minutes unless the minutes contain a hyphen.

> They started at seven-thirty (or 7:30).
> They started at seven forty-five (or 7:45).

Special years   Years that have academic or historical significance may be expressed in abbreviated figures.

> the Class of '81   the Spirit of '76

Decades may be expressed in several ways.

> the 1970s   the seventies   the nineteen-seventies
> the mid-1960s   the mid-sixties

Centuries may be expressed in words or in figures.

> the 1600s   the sixteen hundreds
> the 21st century   the twenty-first century

Weights and Measures

Express numbers in figures.

> We bought 5 feet of wire.

Write out units of weight and measurement except in technical or tabular matter.

> STANDARD: inch, foot, yard, pint, quart
> METRIC: gram, liter, meter

When writing a metric measurement of five or more figures, separate the figure into groups of three by counting from right to left and using a single space. When writing a standard measurement of five or more figures, separate the figure into groups of three by using a comma. (A comma may be used to separate a four-digit figure, although current usage tends to omit it.)

36 850 grams	OR	36,850 gallons	
2145 grams		2,145 gallons	OR 2145 gallons

When a figure combines with a noun to form a one-thought modifier of a following noun, use a hyphen.

He is now driving a 6-ton truck.

When the unit of measurement (inch, foot, and so forth) in two compounds is expressed only once, a hyphen followed by a space (a suspended hyphen) follows the first number.

a 3- by 5-inch card

OR

a 3-inch by 5-inch card

a card 3 by 5 inches

When dimensions, measurements, or weights are expressed in several words, treat the construction as a unit, and do not use punctuation between the items.

That container holds 6 gallons 3 quarts 1 pint.

PART II

CAPITALIZATION

Capitalization is used to make a word stand out: to give it importance, to distinguish it from other words in a sentence or outline, to show respect, to signal the reader that a new sentence is beginning.

The basic rules of capitalization are agreed upon by most writers of English. This is not true, however, of special rules: Individuals, organizations, and circumstances often contribute variations to conventional style. Nevertheless, today's business writers follow these general guidelines:

- Use capital letters deliberately and sparingly.
- If your office or company has a preference regarding capitalization, follow it.
- Be consistent within a text.

BASIC RULES

Capitalize proper nouns as well as adjectives derived from them (proper adjectives) and well-known nicknames and descriptive names substituting for them.

A proper noun is the name of a *particular* person, place, or thing.

Proper Noun	Proper Adjective
Italy	Italian language
America	American citizen
Canada	Canadian province

Proper Noun	Descriptive Name or Nickname
Abraham Lincoln	Honest Abe
the Rocky Mountains	the Rockies
New York City	the Big Apple
Europe	the Continent
Rome	the Eternal City
New Jersey	the Garden State

Capitalize the pronoun *I*.

> She suggested that I read her report first.

Capitalize the first word of a sentence.

>He said he would have no difficulty with the assignment.

>The meeting was long but worthwhile.

When writing the name of a person, an organization, or a publication, make every effort to learn the correct style or individual preference. (Ask directly, or check a letterhead or company literature.)

>He wants the check made out to Texaco Inc.

SPECIAL RULES

Special rules govern the use of capitals in the following cases:

Addresses p. 14
Brand Names and Trademarks p. 14
Buildings p. 15
Calendar Terms p. 15
Courses of Study p. 15
Direct Address p. 16
First Words p. 16
Hyphenated Words p. 17

Laws and Treaties p. 17
Organizations p. 17
Parts of a Letter p. 19
Place Names p. 19
Special Words p. 21
Time Zones p. 21
Titles of Honor and Position p. 21
Titles of Works p. 22

Addresses

Street addresses   Capitalize and spell out all important words (including house, building, and street numbers through ten). Write out the words *Avenue, Lane, Road,* and *Street.*

>She has moved to One Linden Road in Malden.

>His office is at 416 Avenue of the Americas.

City or town   Capitalize and write out the name in full (including the words *Fort, Mount, Point,* and *Port*). Abbreviate the word *Saint* (St.) only when the abbreviation is actually written that way in the geographical name.

>Mount Kisco   Fort Lee
>
>St. Louis   St. Petersburg

State   For a mailing address use the two-letter ZIP Code abbreviation written in capitals and without periods. (*See pages 170ff for use with envelope address; see page 155 for use with inside address.*) When not giving a specific mailing address, write the name of the state in full with an initial capital.

>She attended the Katharine Gibbs School in Norwalk, Connecticut.

>Please mail the booklets to me at the following address:
>
>5739 Cheena
>Houston, TX   77035

Brand Names and Trademarks

Capitalize a brand name but not the common noun that follows it. The trademarked name of a commercial product is a proper noun; the name of the general class into which the product falls is a common noun.

Xerox	Kleenex	Campbell soup	Ford cars
Vaseline	Coca-Cola	Lux soap	Crest toothpaste

NOTE: Through popular usage certain words originally derived from proper nouns have lost their specialized meaning and are not capitalized. When in doubt, consult a dictionary.

> manila paper   morocco leather   venetian blinds

Buildings

Capitalize the names of buildings, but do not capitalize the word *building* when it is used alone, even in a specific reference, or when it is written in the plural following two or more proper nouns.

> While in New York, I visited the Chrysler Building and the Empire State Building. These buildings . . .
>
> **BUT**
>
> While in New York, I visited the Chrysler and the Empire State buildings. These buildings . . .
>
> The meeting will take place at the Southern New England Telephone Company building.

NOTE: Monuments such as the Statue of Liberty and the Eiffel Tower are capitalized according to the rule for buildings.

Calendar Terms

Capitalize the names of holidays, holy days, days of the week, and months of the year. Capitalize such words as *day* and *week* only when they are part of the name of a holiday. Do *not* capitalize the names of seasons unless they are personified.

> National Secretaries' Week   Labor Day
> Christmas Eve   New Year's Day
> Veterans Day   Washington's Birthday
>
> **BUT**
>
> in the fall   this winter

Courses of Study

Capitalize names of languages and specific course titles.

> He failed French but passed Spanish.
>
> My favorite English course was entitled The Short Story in Twentieth-Century American Literature.

NOTE: Do *not* capitalize general areas of study: biology, history, and so forth.

> Because I love biology and history, I registered for Biology 201 and Principles of American Government.

Direct Address

Capitalize names used in direct address. Do *not* capitalize the words *madam, sir, ladies,* and *gentlemen* when used alone in direct address.

> I assure you, gentlemen, that we will meet the deadline.

> They told you, Mr. Albert, that the book was not available.

First Words

In addition to capitalizing the first word of every sentence, capitalize the first word of . . .

An independent clause following a colon

> Our department store has one policy: The customer is always right.

An independent clause within quotation marks

> He closed by saying, "Everything else is irrelevant."

An independent question inserted in a sentence

> We discussed the question Is coal really the answer? at last night's meeting.

Each item in a tabulation or in a topical outline

> Television Today
>
>   I. Introduction
>   II. Programs
> III. Commercials
> VI. Conclusion

Material that begins an enumeration on the line following a colon

> He had these two proposals to make:
>
>   1. That all the members . . .
>   2. That the minutes . . .

A sentence enclosed in parentheses when it follows the sentence to which it refers. (When a sentence enclosed in parentheses is *within* the sentence to which it refers, capitalize the first word only if it is a proper noun or other word that is ordinarily capitalized.)

> I have enclosed the catalog you requested. (The price list is on page 48.)

> I have enclosed a catalog (the price list is on page 48) that lists all the articles about which you inquired.

Hyphenated Words

Capitalize proper nouns and proper adjectives in hyphenated compounds.

> the East-West games
>
> American-Italian relations
>
> the McEnroe-Borg duel

Do not capitalize the word following the hyphen when it is neither a proper noun nor a proper adjective except in a heading or in the title of a work.

> an Ohio-based company
>
> among English-speaking people
>
> the book *English Among English-Speaking People*

Do not capitalize a prefix or a suffix added to either a proper noun or a proper adjective except in a heading or in the title of a work.

> She interviewed ex-President Carter.
>
> President-elect Mason will speak to us at 2 P.M.
>
> I just finished reading *Life in Post-Elizabethan England*.

Laws and Treaties

Capitalize official and accepted titles (proper nouns). Do not capitalize an incomplete title or a common noun (act, bill, and so forth) even in a specific reference.

> Social Security Act . . . that act
>
> the Nineteenth Amendment . . . that amendment

Organizations

Capitalize the important words in the full name of all organizations (business, civic, educational, governmental, political, professional, religious, and social). Do not capitalize the articles *a, an,* and *the;* prepositions of fewer than four letters; or the conjunctions *and, or, but, nor.*

> I will send a copy of this report to the Sony Corporation of America.
>
> Mail your check to The Savings and Loan Association.

Capitalize the article *the* when it precedes a title only if it is part of the official name of an organization.

> We placed an ad in *The New York Times*.

Verify and follow the style preference of an organization with regard to capitalization, spelling, punctuation, and the use of ampersands and abbreviations.

> Use your charge card at Lord & Taylor.

Do not capitalize the common noun at the end of an organization name when using this noun in place of the full name. Such words include *association, board, club, college, committee, company, corporation, league,* and *university.*

> She attends Manhattanville College in New York. The college offers an excellent liberal arts program.

NOTE: In formal documents such words may be capitalized.

> We have officially approved the enclosed policy for the Mobil Oil Credit Corporation. This agreement will enable the Corporation to limit its liability.

Also capitalize such words when the following three conditions are present simultaneously:

- The full name has already been mentioned
- The article *the* precedes the word
- The writer wishes to give the word special importance or the word has special importance to the readers (usually members of the organization itself).

> Fifty-two members of the Tucson Women's Club were present. Mrs. Tracy invited the Club members . . . [minutes of the meeting]

> We are happy to welcome you as an employee of the General Electric Corporation. We assure you that the Corporation . . .

Departments   Capitalize the name of an organization's department or division on an envelope, in the inside address, and in the signature block.

> Macmillan Educational Company
> A Division of Macmillan Publishing Co., Inc.

Within a sentence the name of a department or division is usually not capitalized except by employees of the organization or in the shortened form of the name.

> Please leave this information with Mrs. Clark in the Personnel Department. [for an interoffice memorandum]

> I have already spoken to Miss Andrews in Accounting.

Government agencies   Capitalize the words *federal* and *government* only when they are part of an official name.

> She works for the Federal Bureau of Investigation.

> He contends there are too many federal regulations.

> You can order these pamphlets from the United States Government Printing Office.

> He objects to all government regulations.

> Providing that information is a free service of the federal government.

Parts of a Letter

Salutation   Capitalize the first word and any nouns or titles in the salutation of a letter.

> Dear Professor Albert:

Complimentary close   Capitalize the first word only.

> Sincerely yours,

Envelope, inside address, return address, and signature block Capitalize all names and all titles, whether the titles precede or follow the names.

> Mr. John Delaney, President

Attention and subject lines   Capitalize the first word and all important words. Do not capitalize articles, conjunctions, and prepositions of fewer than four letters.

> Attention: Mr. John Delaney, President
>
> Subject: Sales Figures for 1982

In care of   Spell out with an initial capital for *In* unless it is necessary to use *c/o* because of space.

> Miss Barbara Allen
> In care of Ms. Louise Craig
>
> Ms. Louise Craig
> c/o Mr. Bartholomew Burton-Longfellow

Place Names

Capitalize words that designate parts of the world or regions of a continent or country.

Europe	the Middle East
the Atlantic Ocean	the Indian Ocean
Tropic of Capricorn	the Tropics
the Continent (Europe)	the Orient
Upper Michigan	the Low Countries

NOTE: Descriptive adjectives that are not specifically part of a regional name are *not* capitalized.

> northern New York   southern Korea   BUT   South Korea

Capitalize the popular descriptive names of specific regions and localities.

the Deep South	Back Bay (Boston)
the Great Plains	Foggy Bottom (Washington)
the Loop (Chicago)	the West Side (New York)

Capitalize such directions as *North, South, East, West,* and *Central* when they are used as names of sections of the United States or are used in descriptive titles of parts of the world or of national divisions.

the East	the South	the West Coast
the Midwest	the Middle West	the Northwest
East Germany	South Korea	North Dakota
Southeast Asia	Central Asia	Central America

NOTE: Do *not* capitalize the words *north, south, east, and west,* and *central* in either noun or adjective form when they refer to directions or are not part of a commonly accepted title.

> Our winds come from the south.

> Iron was discovered in eastern Nebraska.

The current trend in nontechnical business English is to lower-case nouns and adjectives derived from the words *north, south, east,* and *west* when they are used generally.

> She enjoyed her hosts' southern hospitality.

> He found that some midwesterners have difficulty adjusting to life in the East.

Capitalize words designating national, regional, or local political divisions when they follow a place name and are an official part of it.

> Washington State

> Fairfield County

> Kansas City

NOTE: Lower-case such words as *city, county,* and *state* when they *precede* a proper noun and are not used as part of an official name.

> The city of New York consists of five boroughs.

> The delegates from the state of Maine have not arrived.

Capitalize the names of mountains, lakes, rivers, islands, and so forth. A generic topographical term (*mountain, island, ocean*) used as part of a name is also capitalized.

> Rocky Mountains

> Lake Michigan

> Amazon River

> the Philippine Islands

NOTE: Do not capitalize a topographical term that is written in the plural following two or more proper nouns.

> the Ohio and Mississippi valleys

> Westchester and Fairfield counties

Special Words

Capitalize references within a sentence to notations on bills, letters, packages, and signs. These notations are often used with such words as *labeled*, *marked*, and *stamped*.

>Someone stamped "Paid" on the attached bill.

>He posted a "No Smoking" sign in each office.

Time Zones

When a time zone refers to an area of a country, the words are usually capitalized. When using an abbreviation, type in full capitals with no spaces and with or without periods.

>Make the call at 1 P.M. Eastern Standard Time (or EST or E.S.T.).

NOTE: The term *daylight-saving time*, which does not refer to a specific area of a country, is not capitalized.

Titles of Honor and Position

Capitalize titles of honor, position, and public office when the titles *precede* a name (unless the name is in apposition and is set off by commas).

>I spoke to Dean Marcus about that matter.

>I spoke to the dean, James Marcus, about that matter.

>She is the dean of women at a college in the South.

Capitalize titles that refer to high-ranking officials, whether the title precedes, follows, or substitutes for the name of the specific person holding office, as with . . .

Officials of foreign and international governing bodies

>While in Rome, they had an audience with the Pope.

>Margaret Thatcher, Prime Minister of England, visited Canada.

The President, Vice-President, Cabinet members, members of the United States Congress, Supreme Court justices, state governors, and lieutenant governors.

>I had asked to speak with the Senator from Iowa, but any senator could have answered my questions.

>The Secretary of Defense will meet with the President this afternoon.

Other titles used alone, after, or in place of a name are usually not capitalized unless the writer wishes to show special respect or importance (within an organization or in a local publication).

>Your appointment is at 2 P.M. with Mrs. Colby, Dean of Secretarial Studies. (within an organization)

Capitalize the word *president* in any general reference to a President of the United States.

>He has read the biographies of every United States President.

NOTE: Do not capitalize *ex, elect, former,* and *late* when used with a title, whether or not the title is capitalized.

> President-elect Johnson will preside at tomorrow's meeting.

Titles of Works

Capitalize the first word, the last word, and all other important words in the titles of publications, broadcasts, and similar media.

Do not capitalize articles, conjunctions, and prepositions of fewer than four letters.

Capitalize *the* only if it is the first word of the official title.

These rules of capitalization apply in particular to . . .

Titles of chapters in books and of articles, columns, essays, poems, and short stories in books, magazines, and newspapers

Titles of reports, radio and television programs, plays, motion pictures, musical compositions, and works of art

Titles of lectures and speeches.

NOTE: The use of quotation marks to indicate titles is generally limited to short compositions such as short stories, short poems, and chapters or sections within a publication. In a typed manuscript the titles of the publications themselves are underscored. In printed material these titles are italicized.

Similarly, the title of a television or radio series is underscored, but the title of one episode in a series is enclosed in quotation marks. See the following examples.

> Books: Contemporary Business Writing; The American West
>
> Magazines: Newsweek; U.S. News & World Report
>
> Newspapers: The New York Times; The Wall Street Journal
>
> Columns: "Wall Street Analysis"
>
> Chapters: "You and Your Vocabulary"
>
> Articles: "Word Processing in Today's Office"
>
> Reports: "Advantages of a Four-Day Workweek"
>
> Television programs: Newswatch; Sixty Minutes; Maverick, "Shady Deal at Sunny Acres" (episode)
>
> Movies and plays: Gone With the Wind; Othello
>
> Works of art: Michelangelo's Pietà
>
> Songs: "Moon River"
>
> Major musical works: Messiah
>
> Poems: "The Death of the Hired Man"
>
> Major poetical works: The Canterbury Tales

PART III

ABBREVIATIONS

An abbreviation is a shortened form of a written word or phrase. The use of abbreviations is generally restricted to technical writing, tabular matter, and statistical material. Abbreviations also occur frequently in such business documents as catalogs and standard forms, where the aim is to convey information in the smallest amount of space. However, in other types of nontechnical business writing, use abbreviations sparingly.

BASIC RULES

When an abbreviation that may be unfamiliar to the reader is used for the first time, give the full expression first, and follow it by the abbreviation in parentheses.

> The Bureau of Indian Affairs (BIA) announced that . . .

In all subsequent references use the abbreviation alone.

> The BIA further announced . . .

Never begin a sentence with an abbreviation. The exceptions to this rule are *Ms., Mrs., Mr., Dr.,* and their respective plurals.

Be consistent when using abbreviations within a given text. Do not abbreviate a word in some sentences and spell it out in other sentences.

Check a dictionary or other reliable reference work for the acceptable form or forms of an abbreviation. When a word can be abbreviated in more than one way, choose one form and use it consistently.

Plurals of Abbreviations

Form the plurals of abbreviations that contain capital letters by adding a lower-case *s* (CPAs, Ph.D.s, Drs.). Form the plurals of lower-case abbreviations that contain internal periods by adding '*s* (c.o.d.'s). (*See Plurals page 201.*)

NOTE: The following abbreviations form their plurals by doubling:

> pp. (pages)   vv. (verses)   ff. (and those following)

Punctuation and Spacing of Abbreviations

When a single word is abbreviated, it requires a period after it.

> Ms.   Dr.   Inc.   Nos.   Sr.

In general, do not use periods within or after abbreviations written in all capital letters. Notable exceptions are academic degrees and abbreviations used with time.

> IBM   UN   ITT   CBS   IQ

If an interrogative or exclamatory sentence ends with an abbreviation, type the question mark or exclamation point immediately after the abbreviation or its period. (No space should be left between the abbreviation and the final punctuation mark.)

> Does she work for RCA?
>
> It's already 4 A.M.!

If a declarative or imperative sentence ends with an abbreviation, the final period of the abbreviation is also the period that terminates the sentence.

> I'll meet you at 6 A.M.

Capitalization and Hyphenation

When a word is abbreviated, it is usually capitalized or hyphenated according to the same rules that would apply if it were written out in full.

Jan.	January	Co.	Company
ft-tn	foot-ton	p.m.	post meridiem

EXCEPTIONS:	B.C.	before Christ
	A.D.	anno Domini
	PTA	Parent-Teacher Association

SPECIAL RULES

The following rules offer guidance on specific kinds of abbreviations. The rules are listed in alphabetical order by topic.

Academic Degrees and Religious Orders

Express abbreviations of academic degrees and religious orders with a period after each element and without any interior spacing. (*Check the Reference Sections "Abbreviations and Acronyms" page 211 or a dictionary for abbreviations not included here.*)

B.A.	M.D.	Ph.D.	Litt.D.	O.S.B.
B.S.	R.N.	LL.B.	D.D.S.	S.J.
M.A.	D.D.	J.D.	M.B.A.	S.N.D.

Use commas to set off these abbreviations when they follow a name.

> Sara Tucker, M.D., addressed the committee.

When a personal name is followed by an academic degree, do not use the titles *Miss, Mrs., Ms., Mr.,* or *Dr.* before the name.

> Benjamin Jones, M.D.
>
> OR
>
> Dr. Benjamin Jones
>
> BUT NOT
>
> Dr. Benjamin Jones, M.D.

Other titles may precede a person's name provided that the information conveyed does not repeat the information given in the degree.

> Professor Diane Baroni, Ph.D.
>
> Vice-President Stephen R. Levine, M.B.A.

Acronyms and Other Shortened Forms

An acronym is a shortened form made up of the initial letters of the words that make up a complete term. For example, the acronym NATO is made up of the first letters of *North Atlantic Treaty Organization.*

Acronyms are written in all capitals and without punctuation. They are pronounced as words (ZIP or SALT) rather than letter by letter (YMCA). Since acronyms have been purposely coined to replace the longer terms they represent, they are appropriate for use in all but the most formal business writing.

> | UNESCO | United Nations Educational, Scientific, and Cultural Organization |
> |--------|--|
> | BASIC | Beginner's All-purpose Symbolic Instruction Code |
> | ZIP | Zone Improvement Plan |
> | SALT | Strategic Arms Limitation Talks |

Some acronyms are so commonly used that they have become words in their own right and no longer require capitalization or punctuation.

> laser scuba sonar

Some words have shortened forms that are not abbreviations or acronyms. These shortened forms do not require either capitalization or punctuation.

> memo lab co-op info
>
> phone stereo exam math

Compass Directions

Compass directions are spelled out rather than abbreviated except in the following special cases.

When referring to the actual points of the compass or a directional bearing determined by those points, use capital letters with no spaces or periods.

> N   E   SW   NNW
> S   W   NE   SSE
>
> Her instructions are to fly compass bearing WSW from Pierre, South Dakota.

In addresses spell out compass directions that are part of a street name.

> 45 North State Street
>
> OR
>
> 45 State Street North

However, abbreviate two-syllable directions that indicate a quadrant or section of a town or city. Separate the quadrant abbreviation from the street name with a comma, and type the abbreviation with periods but without internal spaces.

> 45 State Street, N.W.

Courtesy Titles

Always abbreviate these courtesy titles when they precede a person's full name or surname:

> Mr.   Mrs.   Ms.
> Messrs.   Mmes.   Mss. or Mses.

Use the title *Ms.* when the woman is known to prefer it or when her marital status is unknown.

In general, spell out other titles used with personal names.

> Professor Jonathan Hall   Senator George McGovern

Honorable is a courtesy title often used before the full name of a person who is or has been an elected or appointed government official. The title *Honorable* should not be used before a surname standing alone but must be used with an intervening first name, an initial or initials, or another title. Furthermore, *Honorable* must be capitalized and is usually spelled out. It is often preceded by the article *the*, which is capitalized except within a sentence.

> We are pleased to announce that the Honorable Elizabeth Holtzman will address our conference.

It is acceptable, though less formal, to use the abbreviation *Hon.* in an envelope address or in tabular matter.

Reverend is a courtesy title used before the full name or additional title of a person who is a member of the clergy. Do not use *Reverend* with only a surname. *Reverend* must be capitalized and is usually spelled out. It is often preceded by the article *the,* which is capitalized except within a sentence.

> The preacher today is the Reverend Dr. Martha Elting.

> The charity was founded by the Reverend Harrison K. Blackbull.

> **BUT NOT**

> . . . Reverend Blackbull

It is acceptable, though less formal, to use the abbreviation *Rev.* in an envelope address or in tabular matter.

> Rev. H. K. Blackbull
> 1347 Hawthorne Ave.
> Amityville, MA   01201

Lengthy religious, military, and honorary titles should always be spelled out in formal correspondence but may be abbreviated in informal correspondence.

> Brigadier General John Jones   Brig. Gen. John Jones

> Lieutenant Commander Preston Smith   Lt. Comdr. Preston Smith

(See pages 156f. for the use of titles in addresses; pages 157f. for the use of titles in salutations.)

Dates

In most contexts the days of the week should be capitalized and spelled out. When they must be shortened for reasons of space, use these standard abbreviations:

Sun.	Tues.	Thurs.	Sat.
Mon.	Wed.	Fri.	

If space does not allow for the standard abbreviations, use the following forms with no periods:

> Su   M   Tu   W   Th   F   Sa

In general, the names of the months should be capitalized and spelled out. When they must be abbreviated, do so as follows:

Jan.	Feb.	Mar.	Apr.	May	June
July	Aug.	Sep.	Oct.	Nov.	Dec.

If space does not allow for the standard abbreviations, use the following forms with no periods:

> Ja   F   Mr   Ap   My   Je   Jl   Au   S   O   N   D

Always abbreviate A.D. (*anno Domini*) and B.C. (before Christ). The year is written after A.D. and before B.C.

> A.D. 1963   384 B.C.

Geographical Terms

Names of countries and national or geographic groupings are usually spelled out in text. If the repetition of such names becomes awkward, it is sometimes permissible to use well-known abbreviations. Abbreviations may be used in lists and tabular matter. These abbreviations are usually styled with periods and no interior spacing.

U.A.R.	B.W.I.	U.K.
U.S.A.	U.S.S.R.	N.A.

The names of states, territories, and possessions of the United States should be spelled out except in addresses and tabular matter. In tabular matter use the abbreviations shown at the left of each column. For envelope addresses, use the approved ZIP Code abbreviations shown at the right of each column. (*See pages 170ff. for a fuller discussion of envelope addresses.*)

Ala., AL	Idaho, ID	Mont., MT	R.I., RI
Alaska, AK	Ill., IL	Nebr., NE	S.C., SC
Ariz., AZ	Ind., IN	Nev., NV	S.Dak., SD
Ark., AR	Iowa, IA	N.H., NH	Tenn., TN
Calif., CA	Kans., KS	N.J., NJ	Tex., TX
Colo., CO	Ky., KY	N.Mex., NM	Utah, UT
Conn., CT	La., LA	N.Y., NY	Vt., VT
Del., DE	Maine, ME	N.C., NC	Va., VA
D.C., DC	Md., MD	N.Dak., ND	V.I., VI
Fla., FL	Mass., MA	Ohio, OH	Wash., WA
Ga., GA	Mich., MI	Okla., OK	W.Va., WV
Guam, GU	Minn., MN	Oreg., OR	Wis., WI
Hawaii, HI	Miss., MS	Pa., PA	Wyo., WY
	Mo., MO	P.R., PR	

NOTE: Alaska, Guam, Hawaii, Idaho, Iowa, Maine, Ohio, and Utah are never abbreviated except in envelope addresses.

The word *Saint* in geographical names is often (but not always) abbreviated. Check a dictionary or atlas to be sure.

St. Louis   St. Petersburg   St. Paul

The abbreviation *Ste.* is derived from *Sainte*, a French word in the feminine gender meaning *Saint*.

Sault Ste. Marie

The words *Mount, Point, Fort,* and *Port* should not be abbreviated except in lists and tabular matter.

In lists of addresses and tabular matter the following may be abbreviated.

Ave.	Blvd.	Pl.	Dr.
Bldg.	St.	Sq.	Rd.

Latin Abbreviations

In all but the most informal texts, it is usually best to avoid the following Latin abbreviations by using their English equivalents.

i.e.   (*id est*), that is

e.g.   (*exempli gratia*), for example

c. or ca.   (*circa* or *circiter*), approximately

etc.   (*et cetera*), and so forth

NOTE: The abbreviation *etc.* or its English equivalent *and so forth* should be used only when the unwritten elements of a series are known to the reader.

The child could recite her numbers up through 100: 1, 2, 3, 4, and so forth.

Organization and Company Names

Many well-known companies and other organizations are referred to by their initials. When these abbreviations are used, spell out the first usage, followed by the abbreviation in parentheses. Type these abbreviations in capitals without periods or interior spaces.

AMA	YWCA	IBM
AT&T	SEC	NAACP

A spokesman for the American Medical Association (AMA) said that smoking is definitely dangerous to one's health. Later in the conference AMA officials . . .

In writing the name of a company or organization, abbreviate only those words that the company itself abbreviates.

Company, Co.	Limited, Ltd.
Corporation, Corp.	Manufacturers, Mfrs.
Incorporated, Inc.	Manufacturing, Mfg.

Many companies today omit the comma before such words or abbreviations as *Limited* and *Ltd.*, *Incorporated* and *Inc.*

Personal Names

The abbreviations *Jr.* and *Sr.* are used only with a person's full name. A courtesy title such as *Mr.* or *Dr.* may precede the name.

Alan Blake Jr.

OR

Mr. Alan Blake Jr.

BUT NOT

Mr. Blake Jr.

In current usage a comma is not used before *Jr.* and *Sr.* unless it is known that the person prefers it. If the comma style is used, the abbreviation must also be followed by a comma, which is dropped if the name becomes possessive.

Warren B. Young, Jr., has invited us to lunch at the Algonquin.

Alfred Gill, Sr.'s memorandum of April 3 has created quite a stir.

Do not abbreviate first names. Although the person may sign his letters *Chas.* or *Edw.*, such names should be spelled out in any typed reference.

Professional Designations

The abbreviation *Esq.* for *Esquire* may be used by lawyers of either sex in place of the title *Attorney at Law*. Follow the lawyer's preference when it is known. Never use a courtesy title when *Esq.* or *Attorney at Law* follows the name.

Lorraine A. Murphy, Esq., is an associate at Barnes, Barnes & Withers.

Type the abbreviation *CPA* without periods when it is the only abbreviation following a person's name. If, however, it is used in conjunction with other professional designations or degrees, use periods for consistency.

David Johnson, CPA, is the new person you've all seen in the accounting department.

BUT

Dina Caswell, B.A., M.B.A., C.P.A.

Symbols

Use a dollar sign ($) with exact and approximate amounts of money.

She owes me $6.25.

I foresee a capital investment of about $15 million in this project.

Sums of money referred to as *a dollar, a hundred dollars, several dollars* are spelled out.

The repairs will cost about a hundred dollars.

The ampersand (&) should be used only when it is part of the official title of a company or publication.

American Telephone & Telegraph

Do not use a comma before an ampersand or before the words *and Company.*

Time and Time Zones

When time is expressed in numerals, the abbreviations a.m. and p.m. (or a.m. and p.m.) are used. Both upper-case and lower-case styles are correct; choose one of these styles and be consistent.

The meeting will be in my office at 4 P.M.

In printed texts, these abbreviations are printed in small capitals.

2 A.M.   4 P.M.

Time zones, when abbreviated, may be typed in either of two acceptable styles: (1) capital letters without periods or interior spaces; (2) capital letters with periods after each letter and no interior spaces. The standard time zones may therefore be abbreviated as follows:

EST or E.S.T.	Eastern Standard Time
CST or C.S.T.	Central Standard Time
MST or M.S.T.	Mountain Standard Time
PST or P.S.T.	Pacific Standard Time

When daylight-saving time is in force, these forms are used:

EDT or E.D.T.	Eastern Daylight Time
CDT or C.D.T.	Central Daylight Time
MDT or M.D.T.	Mountain Daylight Time
PDT or P.D.T.	Pacific Daylight Time

Weights and Measures

Units of measure may be abbreviated in highly technical or tabular matter. The trend is to delete the periods after all unit abbreviations.

in	inch	mm	millimeter
ft	foot	cm	centimeter
yd	yard	kl	kiloliter

(*For a listing of common abbreviations, see pages 211ff.*)

CHAPTER II

PARTS
OF SPEECH

Ideas are expressed in words. Words, in turn, have names that describe the way they are used. The eight classifications of words according to function are called the eight parts of speech.

Many words are able to perform a variety of functions and may be used as more than one part of speech.

VERB: She *is working* hard.

NOUN: She enjoys *working* hard.

ADJECTIVE: She has a good *working* relationship with her colleagues.

The table below summarizes the names and functions of the eight parts of speech.

Parts of Speech	Function	Examples
Verb	Expresses action, helps make a statement	transcribes, has, is, am, lies
Noun	Names a person, place, thing, or idea	woman, oven, Madison, compassion
Pronoun	Takes the place of a noun	he, who, them, it
Adjective	Modifies by describing, identifying, or limiting a noun or a pronoun	young, clever, three
Adverb	Modifies the meaning of a verb, a verbal, an adjective, or another adverb by answering the questions How? When? Where? Why? and To what degree?	quickly, very, quite
Preposition	Connects by showing the relationship between a noun or a pronoun and some other word in the sentence	over, with, from, between
Conjunction	Connects by joining words, phrases, or clauses to each other	and, or, if, because
Interjection	Expresses strong feeling	Help! At last!

Verbals are closely related to the eight parts of speech. They are formed from verbs but are used as other parts of speech—namely, as nouns, adjectives, and adverbs.

Verbals	Function	Examples
Participle	*Adjective*—modifies a noun or a pronoun	hurrying, completed
Gerund	*Noun*—names an action	typing, processing
Infinitive	*Noun*—names an action *Adjective*—modifies a noun or a pronoun *Adverb*—modifies a verb, an adjective, or another adverb	to understand, to have accomplished

VERBS

A verb is a word that . . .

Expresses action (mental or physical)

> MENTAL: They *pondered* that question all morning.

> PHYSICAL: She *covered* the typewriters.

Helps make a statement.

> He *has* the encyclopedia.

> The report *is* incomplete.

Relationship to Subject

Every sentence has two parts: a subject (what the sentence is talking about) and a predicate (what the sentence is saying about the subject). The verb is the principal and sometimes the only word in the predicate. It is also the key to finding the subject. When the question Who? or What? is asked of the verb, the answer will always be the subject of the sentence.

> Their plan failed.

(The predicate is the verb *failed*. What failed? Plan. *Plan* is the subject.)

> Their plan to open a new office failed because of the expense involved.

(The predicate is *failed because of the expense involved*. The verb is *failed*. What failed? *Their plan to open a new office* is the complete subject. *Plan* is the subject word.)

Voice

The voice of a verb indicates whether the subject of the verb is the doer of the action (*active voice*) or the receiver of the action (*passive voice*).

The passive voice is always made up of at least two words—a form of the verb *be* and the past participle of another verb.

The students <u>repeated</u> the rule five times.

(Active voice. Who repeated? *Students.* Students performed the action.)

The <u>rule</u> was <u>repeated</u> five times by the students.

(Passive voice. What was repeated? *Rule.* The rule received the action performed by the students.)

Transitive Verbs

A transitive verb is one that expresses an action which "crosses over" to a receiver.

Direct object If a verb is in the active voice and has a receiver, the receiver is called the direct object and is always in the objective case. By asking What? or Whom? after the subject and verb, one will always find the direct object if there is one.

He presented his *budget* last night.

(Transitive. Active voice. He presented What? *Budget* is the direct object.)

Indirect object If a transitive verb in the active voice has a direct object, it may also have an indirect object. The indirect object is the person or thing (to) or (for) whom something is done, given, or told. The words *to* and *for* are understood, not expressed. The indirect object is always in the objective case.

She gave *me* the new budget figures.

(She gave the figures [to] *me*.)

Subject receives action All passive voice verbs are transitive. In some cases the subject receives the action.

Our new *letterhead* was designed by Ann Ames.

(Transitive. Passive voice. What was designed? *Letterhead*. Letterhead, the subject, received the action.)

Subject receives results In other passive voice sentences, the subject receives the results of the action.

Kevin was awarded the second prize.

(Transitive. Passive voice. The subject *Kevin* received the results of the action—namely, the awarding of the second prize.)

Retained object When a passive voice verb has a complement, the complement is called a retained object. The object remains an object whether the sentence is written in the active or in the passive voice.

I gave that customer a *refund*.

(Active voice. *Refund* is the direct object.)

That customer was given a *refund*.

(Passive voice. *Refund* is the retained object.)

Intransitive Verbs

An intransitive verb is one that has *no receiver* of action. Intransitive verbs include the following:

Verbs that express state of being or condition

> She *was standing* near the telephone.

Action verbs without a receiver

> They *will fly* to Chicago tomorrow.

Linking verbs link the subject to a noun or a pronoun (predicate nominative) that equals it or an adjective (predicate adjective) that describes it.

> That meal was delicious.   (delicious meal)
>
> Carol is our new secretary.   (Carol = secretary)

The most common linking verbs are *appear, be, become, feel, grow, keep, look, remain, seem, smell, sound, stay,* and *taste.* Many of these verbs can also be used as action verbs.

> LINKING: She *has grown* quite tall.
>
> ACTION: We *grow* tomatoes every summer.
>
> LINKING: The sauce *smells* good.
>
> ACTION: I can *smell* the sauce.

Principal Parts and Tenses

Every verb has four principal parts—the present, the present participle, the past, and the past participle.

The tense of a verb indicates the time that the verb is expressing. The four principal parts of a verb are used to form the six tenses (or times) of that verb.

Present	Present Participle	Past	Past Participle
work	working (with a form of *be*)	worked	worked (with *has, have,* or *had*)

The present participle and the past participle are used with one or more auxiliary (helping) verbs in a verb phrase (a verb of more than one word).

Auxiliary Verbs

am	been	has	must
is	can	have	shall
was	could	had	will
were	do	may	should
be	does	might	would
being	did		

The parts of a verb phrase may be separated from each other in a sentence.

> *Have* you *read* that report?
>
> She *had* thoroughly and painstakingly *reviewed* all the data before speaking.

The chart below shows the six tenses a verb can have. Each tense, in turn, has a progressive form, which is used to emphasize the progression of the action at the time indicated. In addition, the present and the past have an emphatic form composed of *do, does,* or *did* plus the present form of the verb. The emphatic form emphasizes the performance of the action expressed by the verb.

Tense		Progressive	Emphatic
Present	I write	I am writing	I do write
Present Perf.	I have written	I have been writing	
Past	I wrote	I was writing	I did write
Past Perf.	I had written	I had been writing	
Future	I shall (will) write	I shall (will) be writing	
Future Perf.	I shall (will) have written	I shall (will) have been writing	

Formal writing retains the use of *shall* with *I* and *we* to express future time. Informal writing uses *shall* and *will* interchangeably to express future time with *I* and *we.*

Present denotes present time, a habitual action, an accepted truth.

> PRESENT: I hear footsteps.
>
> HABITUAL: He travels to Boston by train.
>
> ACCEPTED TRUTH: Haste makes waste.

Present perfect identifies an action that began in the past and was completed in the present, *or* an action that began in the past and is still continuing.

> COMPLETED: I *have finished* all my homework.
>
> CONTINUING: She *has worked* here since 1978.

Past denotes an action that both occurred and was completed in the past.

> Yesterday she *wrote* to several senators.

Past perfect identifies an action as having occurred in the past before another past action or event.

> He *had spoken* with them before he made his decision.

Future denotes an action that will occur at some time in the future.

> Next week they *will paint* all our offices.

Future perfect identifies an action that will occur at some time in the future *before* another future action or event.

He *will have gathered* all the data by the time we arrive.

Irregular Verbs

As shown by the principal parts of the verb *work* on page 38, a regular verb has the following endings: *d* or *ed* (added to the present to form the past and the past participle) and *ing* (added to the present to form the present participle).

Many verbs in English are irregular. The chart below shows the principal parts of frequently used irregular verbs.

Present	Past	Past Participle with *has*, *have*, or *had*	Present Participle with a form of *be*
am	was	been	being
arise	arose	arisen	arising
awake or wake	awaked or awoke waked or woke	awaked, waked	awaking, waking
become	became	become	becoming
begin	began	begun	beginning
bid (offer)	bid	bid	bidding
bid (invite)	bade	bidden	bidding
bring	brought	brought	bringing
build	built	built	building
buy	bought	bought	buying
choose	chose	chosen	choosing
come	came	come	coming
dive	dived or dove	dived	diving
do	did	done	doing
draw	drew	drawn	drawing
drive	drove	driven	driving
eat	ate	eaten	eating
fall	fell	fallen	falling
feel	felt	felt	feeling
fit	fitted or fit	fitted	fitting
fly	flew	flown	flying
forbid	forbade	forbidden	forbidding
forego	forewent	foregone	foregoing
forget	forgot	forgotten or forgot	forgetting
give	gave	given	giving
go	went	gone	going

Present	Past	Past Participle with *has, have,* or *had*	Present Participle with a form of *be*
have	had	had	having
know	knew	known	knowing
lay (to place)	laid	laid	laying
lead	led	led	leading
learn	learned	learned	learning
leave	left	left	leaving
lend	lent	lent	lending
let	let	let	letting
lie (to recline)	lay	lain	lying
lie (to tell a falsehood)	lied	lied	lying
lose	lost	lost	losing
make	made	made	making
mean	meant	meant	meaning
meet	met	met	meeting
pay	paid	paid	paying
plead	pleaded or pled	pleaded or pled	pleading
prove	proved	proved or proven	proving
read	read	read	reading
ride	rode	ridden	riding
ring	rang	rung	ringing
rise	rose	risen	rising
run	ran	run	running
see	saw	seen	seeing
seek	sought	sought	seeking
sell	sold	sold	selling
show	showed	shown or showed	showing
sing	sang	sung	singing
sink	sank or sunk	sunk	sinking
sit	sat	sat	sitting
speak	spoke	spoken	speaking
steal	stole	stolen	stealing
take	took	taken	taking
teach	taught	taught	teaching
tell	told	told	telling
think	thought	thought	thinking
throw	threw	thrown	throwing
wear	wore	worn	wearing
wring	wrung	wrung	wringing
write	wrote	written	writing

Mood

The mood of a verb refers to the manner in which a verb expresses action, condition, or state of being. Every verb has three moods—the *indicative*, the *imperative*, and the *subjunctive*.

Indicative makes a statement or asks a question.

> He left early.
>
> Did he leave early?

Imperative gives a command or makes a request. The subject *you* is usually understood, not expressed.

> Tell them to lock the door when they leave.
>
> Please close the door as you leave.

Subjunctive indicates that an action or a condition does not exist in reality. The action or condition is wished for or is dependent on an unrealized factor. Use the subjunctive after *wish*, *as if*, and *as though*.

> She wishes she *were* able to type faster.

(The reality is that she is not able to type faster.)

> If I *were* you, I wouldn't include that paragraph.

(I'm not you.)

The subjunctive follows a verb or an expression indicating demand, necessity, or suggestion.

> It is necessary that you *be* ready by 2 P.M.
>
> He suggested that she *take* the material home.

Using the subjunctive involves using a special form of the verb in the following instances:

The present tense of the verb **be**

Present Indicative		Present Subjunctive	
I am	we are	(required that) I be	we be
you are	you are	(required that) you be	you be
he is	they are	(required that) he be	they be

The past tense of the verb **be**

Past Indicative		Past Subjunctive	
I was	we were	(if) I were	(if) we were
you were	you were	(if) you were	(if) you were
he was	they were	(if) he were	(if) they were

The present tense form of every verb in the third person singular (the form used with a singular noun and with all singular pronouns except *I* and *you*).

Present Indicative	Present Subjunctive
he works	(suggested that) he work
she finishes	(demanded that) she finish
it happens	(is necessary that) it happen

Subject-Verb Agreement

Frequent errors in the use of verbs occur because of the writer's failure to follow this rule:

A verb must always agree with its subject in person and in number.

Person refers to the fact that the subject can be . . .

First Person: The speaker—*I, we*

Second Person: The person spoken to—*you*

Third Person: The person or thing spoken about—*he, she, they, them, it*

Number refers to the fact that the subject can be singular (one person or thing) or plural (more than one person or thing).

The *report is lying* on the desk.

The *reports are lying* on the desk.

Several circumstances governed by the rule of subject-verb agreement require special attention.

Amounts   A plural noun denoting *one amount* or unit (distance, measurement, money, quantity, weight) is singular and takes a *singular verb*.

Twenty-two feet is the measurement he quoted.

Change in order   In normal sentence order the subject precedes the verb. When this order is changed, take the time to find the subject in the sentence, and then make sure the verb agrees with it. The words *here* and *there* are never subjects.

Does she understand the importance of today's meeting?

Here are the four copies you requested.

There go my chances for a raise.

In the top middle drawer are two new typewriter ribbons.

Collective nouns name a group or a collection of people or things. Because the group or collection is usually thought of as a single unit, a collective noun usually takes a singular verb.

The jury is ready with its verdict.

My family has arrived from Florida.

When it is clear that the individual members are thought of as acting separately, use a plural verb.

My family are still arguing with each other about vacation plans.

To avoid using a collective noun with a plural verb, substitute the word *members*.

The members of my family are still arguing about vacation plans.

Compound subject A compound subject joined by *and* that names two or more persons, places, or things is always plural and takes a plural verb.

The director and her staff are in the conference room.

A compound subject joined by *and* that names one person is always singular and takes a singular verb.

His friend and partner works across the hall. (one person)

BUT

His friend and his partner work across the hall. (two persons)

When the two nouns joined by *and* form a unit, the subject is singular and takes a singular verb.

Ham and eggs is my favorite dish, but spaghetti and meatballs runs a close second.

When two or more subject words are joined by *or* or *nor*, the verb agrees with the subject word that is closer (closest) to it.

Either Ann or Carol has the other copy.

Neither Robert, Paul, nor I am responsible for the delay.

John or his partners have the original document.

Indefinite pronouns Refer to indefinite pronouns on pages 50 and 51 to confirm which indefinite pronouns are always singular (and therefore take singular verbs) and which are always plural (and take plural verbs).

Neither of you *appreciates* the time she has devoted to you.

Both of these students *have* interviews this afternoon.

All, any, most, none, and *some.* The "of" phrase (expressed or understood) following these words determines whether they are singular or plural. If the noun after *of* is singular, the indefinite pronoun preceding *of* is singular.

All the money *has* been received.   (all of the money)

None of the absenteeism *has* been explained.

Some of his testimony *was* incredible.

If the noun after *of* is plural, the indefinite pronoun preceding *of* is plural.

All the members *are* enthusiastic. (all of the members)

None of those patterns *are* available now.

Some of the apartments *have* been leased.

Intervening phrases The subject of a verb is *never* found in a prepositional phrase. A phrase that intervenes (comes between) a subject and a verb does not affect agreement.

> *Carol,* as well as her friends, *is* happy to be able to help you.
>
> The *books* on top of the file in your office *have* excellent statistics.

Names of business firms; organizations; publications; artistic, literary, and musical works are singular.

> *General Motors is* the company for which he works.
>
> I think *The New York Times has* the best crossword puzzle.
>
> *Merrill Lynch, Pierce, Fenner & Smith has* one of its many offices there.
>
> Holbein's *The Ambassadors hangs* in London's National Gallery.

Percentages, portions, fractions The "of" phrase (expressed or understood) following these amounts determines whether they are singular or plural. They are singular if the noun following *of* is singular; they are plural if the noun following *of* is plural.

> *Three fourths* of the students *were* absent yesterday.
>
> *Three fourths* of the cake *was* left untouched.

Relative pronouns A relative pronoun (*see pages 49f.*) is singular when the word to which it refers is singular.

> Mr. Warren is the *executive who is* responsible for our campaign.

A relative pronoun is plural when the word to which it refers is plural.

> Each of the young *women who are* waiting has taken the aptitude test.

each, every, many a, no, such a These words always indicate a singular subject and take a singular verb.

> *Each clerk and each bookkeeper* has received a copy of the schedule.
>
> *Every car, tractor, and trailer carries* this identification.
>
> *Many a long hour was spent* compiling this information.
>
> *No city and no county is* free to levy a tax of that kind.
>
> *Such an outflow and depletion* of our resources *calls* for immediate scrutiny.

the number This expression always requires a singular verb.

> *The number* of books she needs *is* overwhelming.

a number This expression always requires a plural verb.

> *A number* of people *have questioned* that decision.

NOUNS

A noun is a word that names a person, place, thing, or idea. Nouns are divided into two major classifications—proper and common.

Proper Nouns

A proper noun is the name of a particular person, place, or thing. A proper noun is always capitalized.

> Robert Redford
>
> Mexico City
>
> the Empire State Building

Common Nouns

A common noun is the general name of a person, place, or thing. Common nouns can be classified as follows:

Concrete nouns are common nouns that name something that can be known by the senses.

> book   flower   river

Abstract nouns are common nouns that name a quality or an idea.

> gentleness   evil   devotion

Collective nouns are common nouns that name a group of persons, places, or things.

> jury   nation   flock

Compound Nouns

Compound nouns are nouns that have two or more words. Some compound nouns are proper nouns; some are common nouns.

> Atlantic City   sales tax   brother-in-law

PRONOUNS

A pronoun is a word used in place of a noun or of another pronoun. The noun or pronoun that is being replaced is called the *antecedent*. The use of pronouns avoids the monotony and awkwardness that would result from constantly repeating the same word.

> Mary finished all Mary's typing before Mary went home.
>
> Mary finished all *her* typing before *she* went home.
>
> Will everyone please cover everyone's typewriter.
>
> Will everyone please cover *her* typewriter.

Person

First person refers to the person(s) speaking.

> I   mine   we   ours
>
> my   me   our   us

Second person refers to the person(s) spoken to.

> you   your   yours

Third person refers to the person(s) or thing(s) spoken about.

he	his	its	their
she	her	him	theirs
it	hers	they	them

Number

The number of a pronoun refers to the fact that a pronoun is singular or plural. A pronoun always agrees in number with its antecedent.

Does *everyone* have *her* lunch?

Gender

The gender of words refers to their grammatical classification according to sex distinction.

Gender	Sex	Examples
masculine	male	John, man, he
feminine	female	Sally, women, her
common	either	citizen, student
neuter	none	house, machines, it

When a common noun is the antecedent, the question of which pronoun to use frequently arises. A writer can do one of the following:

Refer to both sexes.

I hope every teacher will send me his/her recommendations.

I hope every teacher will send me his or her recommendations.

Make the antecedent plural.

I hope all the teachers will send me their recommendations.

Eliminate the pronoun.

I hope every teacher will send me recommendations.

Case

The case of a noun or a pronoun indicates how the noun or pronoun functions in relationship to other words in the sentence. In English the three cases are the *nominative,* the *objective,* and the *possessive.* Pronouns, unlike nouns, change form when they change case.

NOMINATIVE: *I* called Mary.

OBJECTIVE: Mary called *me.*

POSSESSIVE: She has *my* books.

Personal Pronouns

Personal pronouns, with the exception of *it,* refer to persons. They change form as they change case.

	Nominative	Possessive	Objective
First person singular	I	my, mine	me
Second person singular	you	your, yours	you
Third person singular	he, she, it	his, her, hers, its	him, her, it
First person plural	we	our, ours	us
Second person plural	you	your, yours	you
Third person plural	they	their, theirs	them

Compound Personal Pronouns

Compound personal pronouns have two uses:

They are *reflexive* when they *receive* the action of the verb and *refer* to the person or thing being talked about.

> *Ann* prepared *herself* for the interview.

They give *emphasis* to another noun or pronoun in the sentence.

> *Carol* completed the project *herself.*
>
> *Roger himself* said we could order that material.

Singular	Plural
myself	ourselves
yourself	yourselves
herself	themselves
himself	
itself	

A compound personal pronoun must always have an antecedent within the sentence.

> INCORRECT: He spoke to Ann and myself.
>
> CORRECT: He spoke to Ann and me.

Interrogative Pronouns

Interrogative pronouns ask questions. The pronoun *who* changes form as it changes case.

Nominative	Possessive	Objective
who	whose	whom
what		what
which		which

> *Who* has already completed the assignment?
>
> *Whom* do you want to see?
>
> *Whose* typewriter needs a new ribbon?
>
> *Which* typewriter needs a new ribbon?
>
> *What* did he want?

Relative Pronouns

Relative pronouns introduce a clause. The pronouns *who* and *whoever* change form as they change case.

Nominative	Possessive	Objective
who, whoever	whose, whosever	whom, whomever
that		that
what, whatever		what, whatever
which, whichever		which, whichever

> I don't know *who* completed the assignment.
>
> He wants to interview the student *whom* you recommended.
>
> She interviewed those students *whose* reports had been completed.
>
> They give help to *whoever* needs it.

which, that, who   The relative pronoun *which* usually refers to things but may also refer to a collective noun, a group of persons acting as a unit.

Referring to something inanimate:

> The Harcourt *Building, which* is on Maple Street, has been sold.

Referring to a collective noun:

> The Maxwell *Company, which* has an office in this building, is a brokerage firm.

The relative pronoun *that* refers to things, although it is sometimes used in an impersonal reference to people.

Referring to things:

> Is the *dictionary that* you selected thumb-indexed?

Impersonal reference:

> The *candidate that* wins this election will need the full support of the party.
>
> (Also correct: The *candidate who* . . .)

The relative pronouns *who* and *whom* refer to persons.

> Mr. Bell is the man *who* I believe is chairperson.

who, whom   The pronoun *who* (nominative case) has the following uses:

Subject of a verb

> She is the secretary who answered the telephone.
>
> Who answered the telephone?

Complement of a linking verb

> I don't know who she is. (She is who?)
>
> Who is she?

Complement of a linking infinitive that does not have a subject. (*See Infinitives, pages 65f.*)

> Who did he pretend to be? (He pretended to be who?)

The pronoun *whom* (objective case) has the following uses:

Direct object of a verb

> Miss Granger is the secretary whom we employed. (We employed her.)
>
> Whom did you call? (You called her.)

Object of a preposition

> She is the secretary *to whom* I gave the letter.
>
> *To whom* did you give the letter?

Subject of an infinitive (*See Infinitives, pages 65f.*)

> She is a person whom we believe to be very capable.
>
> (We believe her to be very capable.)
>
> Whom did you ask to do that job?
>
> (You asked her to do that job.)

Complement of an infinitive. (*See Infinitives, pages 65f.*)

> He is the one whom we wish to interview.
>
> (We wish to interview him.)
>
> Whom do you wish to interview?
>
> (You wish to interview him.)

NOTE: In choosing between *who* or *whom*, put the sentence or clause to which *who* or *whom* belongs in subject-verb-complement order. Substitute *he* or *him* (she or her) for *who* or *whom*. If he (she) is correct, use *who*. If him (her) is correct, use *whom*.

Demonstrative Pronouns

Demonstrative pronouns point out particular persons, places, or things. They change spelling in the plural.

> **Singular   Plural**
>
> this   these
>
> that   those
>
> *That* is not the book I recommended to you.
>
> *These* are much too expensive for our budget.

Indefinite Pronouns

Indefinite pronouns substitute for an unidentified person, place, or thing or for an indefinite number of persons, places, or things. When they indicate possession, they do so by adding *'s.*

Always Singular

another (another's)	everything
anybody (anybody's)	neither (neither one's)
anyone (anyone's)	no one (no one's)
anyone else (anyone else's)	one another (one another's)
anything	one (one's)
each	other (other's)
each one (each one's)	somebody (somebody's)
each other (each other's)	someone (someone's)
either (either one's)	someone else (someone else's)
everyone (everyone's)	something

> *Neither* of the accountants finished *his* report.
>
> Does *either* of you need help?

Written as one word, *anyone, everyone,* and *someone* denote persons and are the equivalent of *anybody, everybody,* and *somebody.*

> *Anyone* is free to express *his* opinion.
>
> *Everyone* has *her* own job to do.

Any one, every one, and *some one* denote persons or things before *of* and a plural noun.

> We have many orders but shall ship *every one* (of them) this week.
>
> *Any one of the secretaries* is willing to help.

The word *one* is used in an *impersonal* reference. Pronouns referring to *one* should be third person singular personal pronouns. The pronoun *you* should be used only in direct *personal* reference.

> IMPERSONAL: *One* may obtain *her* credit card at this office.
>
> PERSONAL: *You* must apply for *your* application form by mail.

Always Plural

both	several
few	many
others (possessive: others')	

> *Many* of the students have already left for the day.
>
> *Few* understand the importance of his message.

ADJECTIVES

Adjectives modify a noun or a pronoun by *describing, limiting,* or *identifying* it. Adjectives usually answer one of these questions: Which one? What kind? How many?

> That *tweed* suit would be perfect for work.

(Describes. Answers What kind?)

> I will need at least *three* copies of that report.

(Limits. Answers How many?)

> Do you want *this* pen?

(Identifies. Answers Which one?)

Proper Adjectives

Proper adjectives are derived from proper nouns and are capitalized.

> The *French* and *American* flags have different designs but the same colors.

Coordinate and Noncoordinate Adjectives

Coordinate adjectives modify the same noun equally and separately. If the word *and* is placed between the adjectives or the adjectives are reversed, the sentence will still read smoothly. It is important to recognize coordinate adjectives because commas must be used to separate them from each other. Do not use a comma after the adjective that immediately precedes the noun.

> He is the most *intelligent, articulate* student in his class.

Noncoordinate adjectives do not modify a noun equally and separately. If *and* is used between them or they are reversed, the sentence will sound awkward.

> I bought a *new brown* coat.

Nouns as Adjectives

A word that is usually classified as a noun because it names a person, place, or thing becomes an adjective when it performs the function of an adjective—that is, when it *describes* a noun.

> NOUN: She is working in her *office.*
>
> ADJECTIVE: They are familiar with all our *office* machines.

Pronouns as Adjectives

Indefinite, relative, and interrogative pronouns are used as adjectives when they *identify* or *limit* the meaning of a noun.

> ADJECTIVE: *Either* approach would be suitable.
>
> PRONOUN: *Either* would be acceptable.

Compound Adjectives

Compound adjectives consist of two or more words that are combined, with or without hyphens, to form a one-thought modifier.

> Your shipments will be delivered in *first-class* condition.
>
> Here is a *lifetime* gift.

Articles

Although *a, an,* and *the* have their own grammatical name (articles), they are classified with adjectives because of their function, which is to modify a noun or a pronoun.

The indefinite articles *a* and *an* are placed before an object when the reference is not to any particular one.

> Have you found *a site* for your new office?

The definite article *the* refers to a particular object.

> Where is *the site* of your new office?

Placement of Adjectives

Adjectives may precede the noun or pronoun they modify.

> ADJECTIVE PRECEDING A NOUN: *Fresh* produce is always shipped promptly.

> ADJECTIVE PRECEDING A PRONOUN: *Eager* for a promotion, he worked with energy and determination.

Adjectives may follow the word modified.

> The company needs young men *capable* of providing leadership. (capable men)

> All produce, *fresh* or *frozen,* is dispatched immediately. (fresh or frozen produce)

Adjectives may follow a linking verb or a verbal.

> Miss Collins feels *bad about the oversight.*

> We commend you on being *diplomatic.*

Adjectives may be objective complements following a direct object.

> This light bulb will make the room *brighter.*

> Be sure to keep the paper *straight.*

Comparison of Adjectives

Comparison refers to the change in the form of an adjective when it is used to compare the quality of a noun or a pronoun with a similar quality in one or more other nouns or pronouns. Most adjectives have three degrees of comparison—the *positive,* the *comparative,* and the *superlative.*

Positive degree is the simple form of an adjective and is used when no comparison is intended.

> The blue rug is *wide.*

> The paper produced a *clear* copy.

Comparative degree is used when two items are compared with each other. It is formed by adding *r* or *er* to all one-syllable and a few two-syllable adjectives. *More* or *less* is placed before most adjectives of more than one syllable.

> The blue rug is *wider* than the red one.
>
> Her house is the *more modern* of the two.
>
> That color is *less flattering* than the other one.

Superlative degree is used to compare three or more items. It is formed by adding *st* or *est* to all one-syllable and to some two-syllable adjectives. *Most* or *least* is placed before most adjectives of more than one syllable.

> The gray rug is the *widest* of the three.
>
> Of the five rugs the red is the *most colorful.*
>
> This rug is the *least durable* of all the rugs that we stock.

Table of Sample Comparisons

Positive	Comparative	Superlative
cheap	cheaper	cheapest
fast	faster	fastest
happy	happier	happiest
thoughtful	more thoughtful	most thoughtful
beautiful	more beautiful	most beautiful
perfect	(more nearly) perfect	(most nearly) perfect
good*	better	best
well*	better	best
much*	more	most
many*	more	most

* Irregular comparisons

NOTE: Some adjectives cannot be compared. They are complete in their simple form, the positive degree. The only comparison possible is formed by using *more nearly* or *most nearly* before the positive degree. Such adjectives include the following:

correct	inferior	straight
different	perfect	unique
empty	round	wrong
full	square	

In the comparison of adjectives, three areas deserve special attention:

other, else   When comparing a person, place, or thing with the group or class of which it is a member, use the word *other* or the word *else* in the second part of the comparison.

> That rug is wider than *any other rug* in stock.
>
> Mr. Boles has been more outspoken than *anyone else* in the group.

BUT

Detroit, Michigan is larger than *any city* in Iowa.

(Detroit is not a city in Iowa.)

all   When an item is compared in the superlative with all members of the same class or group, *all* is used.

This dictionary is the *best of all* I have used.

Of all the courses I took, Principles of American Government was the *hardest*.

NOTE: Only nouns with comparable qualities can be compared.

CORRECT: Our *profits* are higher than *they* were last year.

Our *profits* are higher than *those* of last year.

Our *profits* are higher than *last year's*. (last year's profits)

INCORRECT: Our *profits* are higher than *last year*.

(Illogical comparison. *Profits* and *year* are not comparable.)

ADVERBS

An adverb modifies a verb, a verbal, an adjective, or another adverb. An adverb usually answers one of these questions: How? When? Where? To what degree?

He finished that project *quickly*. (How)

She went *downtown*. (Where)

She enunciates *very* distinctly. (To what degree)

Independent Adverbs

Independent adverbs are those used to modify the sentence thought. They are usually separated from the rest of the sentence by a comma.

Yes, I will finish by 3 P.M.

No, she didn't leave a forwarding address.

Truthfully, I wasn't happy about your decision.

Interrogative Adverbs

An interrogative adverb at the beginning of a sentence asks a question.

How did you arrive at that conclusion?

When will you finish that report?

Where did you put the carbon paper?

Why didn't you mail that letter?

Relative Adverbs

A relative adverb introduces an adjective clause and modifies the verb in that clause.

This is the house *where* I was born.

(*Where I was born* modifies house; *where* modifies *was born*.)

Nouns Used as Adverbs

Words that are usually nouns become adverbs when they modify a verb or a verbal and answer the questions When? Where? or To what degree?

> I am ready to go *home*. (Where)
>
> She went *downtown* this afternoon. (Where)
>
> The room measures *12 feet* in length. (To what degree)
>
> The meeting took place *Monday*. (When)

Correlative Adverbs

Correlative adverbs are used in pairs as the connectives for adverbial clauses.

> Miss Lacey is *as* cooperative *as* she can be.
>
> I am *so* tired *that* I can't think.

Placement of Adverbs

Such adverbs as *almost, also, even, exactly, just, merely, nearly, only, scarcely,* and *too* should be placed before the word they modify in order to avoid ambiguity.

> We painted *only two* offices.
> (We didn't paint more than two.)
>
> *Only we* painted the offices. (Nobody else helped paint them.)
>
> We *only painted* the two offices.
> (We didn't do anything else.)

Comparison of Adverbs

The rules for forming the comparative and superlative degrees of adverbs are the same as those for adjectives.

Positive	Comparative	Superlative
hard	harder	hardest
clearly	more (or less) clearly	most (or least) clearly
early	earlier	earliest
skillfully	more (or less) skillfully	most (or least) skillfully
ill*	worse	worst
little*	less	least
much*	more	most
well*	better	best

* Irregular comparisons

NOTE: Some adverbs cannot be compared. They are already complete, attain their highest degree, in the simple form. Such adverbs include the following:

completely	perfectly
conclusively	scarcely
hardly	universally

ly Adverbs

The suffix *ly* is often added to an adjective to form an adverb.

Adjective	Adverb
bad	badly
direct	directly
easy	easily
real	really
sure	surely

NOTE: *ly* is not always an adverbial ending.

Some adverbs do not end in *ly*.

fast	very
here	too
near	well
there	

Some adjectives end in *ly*.

friendly
lovely
kindly

PREPOSITIONS

A preposition is a word that connects by showing the relationship between a noun or a pronoun and some other word in the sentence.

I bought the flowers *from her*.

I bought the flowers *for her*.

I brought the flowers *to her*.

She brought the flowers *with her*.

Prepositional Phrases

A preposition is always used with at least one other word—namely, the noun or pronoun it is relating to another word in the sentence. The noun or pronoun that follows the preposition is the *object* of the preposition and is always in the objective case.

The preposition, the object of the preposition, and any words that modify the object make up the *prepositional phrase*.

Placement and Usage

Avoid ending a sentence with a preposition if such an ending is unnecessary and awkward.

> AVOID: Whom are you talking to?
>
> PREFERRED: To whom are you talking?

Use a preposition at the end of a sentence when doing so sounds natural and when such placement provides the desired emphasis.

> AVOID: I don't know about what this is.
>
> PREFERRED: I don't know what this is about.
>
> AVOID: I know for whom this is but not about what it is.
>
> PREFERRED: I know whom this is for but not what it is about.

When the same preposition is correct for two different words that are joined by *and, or, but, nor,* the preposition is placed after the second word.

> He has *respect* and *admiration* for the chairman.
>
> She has an *appreciation* and a *knowledge* of music.

When each word requires a different preposition, both prepositions must be inserted.

> He has neither the *aptitude for* nor an *interest in* politics.
>
> We have *confidence in* and *respect for* your abilities.

Do not add prepositions to words that are complete and sensible without prepositions.

> INCORRECT: Where were you at?
>
> CORRECT: Where were you?
>
> INCORRECT: Where are you going to?
>
> CORRECT: Where are you going?
>
> INCORRECT: The tickets are inside of the envelope.
>
> CORRECT: The tickets are inside the envelope.
>
> INCORRECT: The cartons fell off of the truck.
>
> CORRECT: The cartons fell off the truck.

Commonly Used Prepositions

about	as	beyond	in	off
above	at	by	inside	on
across	before	but (*except*)	into	onto
after	behind	concerning	less	out
against	below	despite	like	outside
along	beneath	during	minus	over
amid	beside (*at the side*)	except	near	past
among	besides (*in addition*)	for	notwithstanding	plus
around	between	from	of	regarding

since	to	unlike	via
through	toward	until	with
throughout	under	up	within
till	underneath	upon	without

Compound Prepositions
(sometimes called phrasal prepositions)

according to	by reason of	in regard to	pertaining to
ahead of	contrary to	in spite of	referring to
along with	except for	instead of	regardless of
apart from	for the sake of	in view of	relating to
as to	in accordance with	irrespective of	relative to
aside from	in addition to	on account of	together with
because of	in connection with	out of	with respect to
by means of	in place of	owing to	

Idiomatic Prepositions

accompanied

by a person	She was accompanied by her husband.
with a thing	Please accompany your report with charts.

account

for an action	He hasn't accounted for his whereabouts.
to a person	You will have to account to your supervisor.

adapt

for (made suitable for)	The building was adapted for storage purposes.
from (patterned after)	That play was adapted from a novel.
to (change to meet a new situation)	She quickly adapted to the routine.

agree

in (be alike or similar)	They agree in their basic philosophies.
on or *upon* (to come to a common understanding)	The city and the union have agreed on one major issue.
with (concur with a person; correspond to)	Our sales figures agree with yours.

angry

with a person	He was very angry with the negotiators.
at or *about* a situation	He was very angry at the intrusion.

authority

for (refers to one who is the source of a statement or idea)	Who is the authority for those statistics?
on (refers to one who has a claim to be believed)	He is an authority on nuclear physics.
over (denotes power to command)	She has authority over all the salespeople.

compare

to (to liken; to represent as similar)

Oak is often compared to iron because of its strength and endurance.

with (to bring into comparison; to show resemblance or difference)

Compare this amount with the amount on your check.

correspond

to (agree with; resemble; be equivalent to)

Be sure the number on your check corresponds to that on the stub.

with (to communicate by writing)

My attorney has been corresponding with them for some time.

differ

from (to be unlike something else)

California differs from Florida in many respects.

in, over, about (to disagree)

We seldom differ about office procedures.

with (to be in disagreement with a person)

The stockholders differed with the board members about bonus plans.

different

from (NOT different than)

The number on the check is different from that on the stub.

disappointed

by or *in* (someone)

We were disappointed by your representative when he canceled the meeting.

with (something)

Were you disappointed with the verdict?

liable

for (an action)

The company is liable for the acts of its agents.

to (someone)

They were liable to their employer for loss of time.

speak, talk

to (implies a monologue)

I will talk to you later about your behavior. (You will listen.)

with (implies an exchange of ideas and opinions)

She wants to speak with me about next week's seminar.

Miscellaneous Idiomatic Prepositions

absolve *from*	appreciation *of*	comply *with*	desist *from*
abstain *from*	or *for*	conducive *to*	deter *from*
accede *to*	appreciative *of*	conform *to*	devoid *of*
acquiesce *in*	aptitude *for*	connect *with*	dissuaded *from*
acquit *of*	at variance *with*	conversant *with*	identical *with*
adverse *to*	aversion *to*	deficient *in*	in compliance *with*
agreeable *to*	coincident *with*	dependent *on*	in conformity *with*
analogous *to*	compatible *with*	or *upon*	incongruous *with*

incorporated *in*	monopoly *of*	occasion *on* which	provided *for* (not *to*)
independent *of*	necessity *of* or *for*	(not *in* which)	retroactive *to* (not *from*)
indifferent *to*	need *of* or *for*	persistent *in*	worthy *of*
instill *into*	negligent *of*	preparatory *to*	
interested *in*	oblivious *of*	prerequisite *to*	

CONJUNCTIONS

A conjunction is a word that connects by joining words, phrases, and clauses to each other.

CONNECTS WORDS: Carol *and* Ann will attend the convention.

CONNECTS PHRASES: Today I went to the bank *and* to the library.

CONNECTS CLAUSES: Last week we went to New York, *and* next week we are going to Boston.

Coordinate Conjunctions

A coordinate conjunction joins words, phrases, or clauses of the same kind.

INCORRECT: She likes swimming and to fish.

CORRECT: She likes swimming and fishing.
She likes to swim and to fish.

Coordinate Conjunctions

and   or   but   nor

The house is small *but* comfortable.

Correlative Conjunctions

Correlative conjunctions are used in pairs.

both . . . and   not only . . . but also
either . . . or   not only . . . but
neither . . . nor

He bought *not only* a desk *but also* a cabinet.

Subordinate Conjunctions

A subordinate conjunction connects a dependent clause to an independent clause and shows the relationship between the two.

Commonly Used Subordinate Conjunctions

after	because	since	until
although	before	than	when, whenever
as	if	that	where, wherever
as if	in order that	though	while
as though	provided that	unless	

After I had finished filing, I began to type.

You may stop in for a visit *whenever you are in the area.*

Conjunctive Adverbs

A conjunctive adverb connects two independent thoughts by showing the relationship between them.

Commonly Used Conjunctive Adverbs

accordingly	furthermore	moreover	then
also	hence	nevertheless	therefore
besides	however	otherwise	thus
consequently	likewise	still	yet

I wanted to be there; *however,* we had an emergency here.

We received the grant money; *therefore,* you may go ahead with your plans.

INTERJECTIONS

An interjection is a word that expresses strong feeling. It is followed by an exclamation point or a comma, depending upon the emphasis intended.

Well, try a different approach!

Help! We can't balance our books without your payment of the enclosed bill.

VERBALS

Closely related to the parts of speech are the three verbals: the *participle,* the *gerund,* and the *infinitive. Verbals come from verbs; they are not verbs.* They cannot combine with a noun or a pronoun to express a complete thought. However, verbals do retain the three properties of a verb:

They can express action, possession, or state of being.

They can have subjects, objects, and adverbial modifiers (verbal phrases).

They have tense and voice.

Participles

A participle is a verbal adjective. Its purpose is to describe or to identify a noun or pronoun by *picturing* its action or state of being.

The students *studying for exams* missed the party.

(Identifies students. Participle.)

The students *studied* for exams and missed the party.

(States action. Verb.)

Hurrying to class, Ann lost her wallet.

(Pictures Ann. Participle.)

Ann *hurried* to class and lost her wallet.

(States Ann's action. Verb.)

Participial forms

	Present	Past	Perfect
Active	helping	—	having helped
Passive	being helped	helped	having been helped

The present participle describes action that occurs *at the same time* as that of the main verb.

> *Dashing* down the stairs, the student dropped her books.

The past and the perfect participles describe action that occurred *before* that of the verb.

> *Having finished* her work, she decided to write a letter.

Usage   A participle can be *necessary* or *unnecessary* to the identification of the noun or pronoun it modifies. A participle that is *necessary* to the identification of the word that it modifies is often called a *restrictive* participle.

*N*ecessary participle   *N*o commas

*U*nnecessary participle   *U*se commas

*A*n introductory participle   *A* comma follows

> The students *waiting in the lobby* are freshmen.

(Necessary. No punctuation.)

> The New York–New Haven express, *having been delayed in Stamford,* will not arrive until 7:30 P.M.

(Unnecessary. Use commas.)

> *Standing in the doorway,* she watched him walk away.

(Introductory. A comma follows.)

Participial absolutes   A participial absolute consists of a noun or a pronoun (subject of the participle) plus a participle and is *grammatically independent* of the rest of the sentence. Its only real relationship to the rest of the sentence is one of thought (content). Use commas to separate or set off participial absolutes.

> *Weather permitting,* we will go to the beach.

> I think they did very well, *all things being considered.*

Placement   A participle should *precede* or *follow* the noun or the pronoun that it modifies. The relationship between the participle and the word that it modifies should be appropriate, logical, and absolutely clear to the reader.

When a participle is not in its proper place in a sentence, it is said to "dangle."

> DANGLING: *Having studied hard,* the test was easy to pass.
>
> CORRECT: *Having studied hard,* I passed the test with ease.
>
> DANGLING: The dog grabbed the bone *running across the lawn.*
>
> CORRECT: *Running across the lawn,* the dog grabbed the bone.

Independent participial phrases An independent participial phrase usually begins with an expression such as *allowing for, considering, granted that,* or *speaking of* and is used to name a general action without reference to a specific performer or receiver of the action indicated.

> *Granted that stock prices are low,* the economy seems buoyant.

> *Speaking of British sportswear,* the fall collection at Harrod's is attractive.

Avoid the following errors in the use of participles:

Participial phrases beginning with *being that* and *being as,* used in place of adverbial clauses beginning with *because* or *since,* are NEVER acceptable.

> INCORRECT: Being that I was sick, I stayed home.

> CORRECT: Because I was sick, I stayed home.

> INCORRECT: Being that you're free now, let's discuss that project.

> CORRECT: Since you're free now, let's discuss that project.

Do *not* use participial phrases to begin the opening or closing sentences of a business letter.

> WEAK: Having received your letter of March 4 . . .

> STRONG. PREFERRED: Thank you for your letter of March 4.

> WEAK: Trusting that you will investigate the matter . . .

> STRONG. PREFERRED: I trust you will investigate the matter at once.

Do *not* use a participial phrase to express purpose or result. A participle is an adjective. Expressing purpose and result is the work of an adverb.

> INCORRECT: We studied for 15 hours, assuring that we would do well.

> CORRECT: We studied for 15 hours because we wanted to do well.

Gerunds

A gerund is a verbal noun; it names an action.

> *Swimming* is an excellent form of exercise.

> She enjoys *playing* tennis and golf.

Gerund forms

	Present	**Perfect**
Active	telling	having told
Passive	being told	having been told

The present forms of the gerund name an action that occurs *at the same time* as the action of the verb.

> *Telling* her the answers *is* not helping her.

The perfect forms of the gerund name an action that occurred *before* the action of the verb.

> His *having told* the story many times *prepared* him for their questions.

With the possessive case In general, use the possessive case before a gerund. A gerund names an action. The possessive noun or pronoun before the gerund answer the question Whose action?

> *His working* so erratically was his downfall.

> I appreciate *your calling* but not *your reversing* the charges.

With the objective case Use the objective case before a gerund when . . .

The gerund has a compound subject

> I don't like *you and Paula staying out so late.*

Other words separate the gerund from its subject

> I don't understand *a student of her caliber dropping that course.*

A possessive form does not exist.

> I hated to see *that happening.*

When it does not seem clear whether an *ing* verbal is a participle or a gerund, follow these guidelines:

If the emphasis is on the *ing* verbal, the verbal is a gerund. Use the possessive case before it.

> I don't like *Ann's cooking.* (Emphasis is on *cooking.*)

> *His talking* distracted the class. (Emphasis is on *talking.*)

If the emphasis is on the person performing the action of the *ing* verbal, the verbal is a participle.

> Look at that picture of *me standing* next to Paul. (Emphasis is on *me.*)

> I saw *him running* down the street. (Emphasis is on *him.*)

Placement A frequent error in the use of the gerund occurs with an introductory prepositional-gerund phrase. In this case the doer of the action must follow immediately after the comma that follows such a phrase. Failure to do so results in a prepositional-gerund phrase that "dangles."

> DANGLING: *By studying hard, the test* was easy to pass.

> CORRECT: *By studying hard, I* passed the test with ease.

> DANGLING: *After hearing the weather report, the picnic* was postponed by the Smiths.

> CORRECT: *After hearing the weather report, the Smiths* postponed the picnic.

Infinitives

An infinitive is a verb form, usually preceded by *to*, that is used as a verbal noun, a verbal adjective, or a verbal adverb.

> NOUN: *To win* the gold medal is her goal.

> ADJECTIVE: The play *to see* this year is *Evita.*

> ADVERB: *To succeed* at Gibbs, you must work hard.

Infinitive forms

	Present	**Perfect**
Active	to see	to have seen
Passive	to be seen	to have been seen

The present forms of the infinitive express action that occurs at *the same time* as that of the main verb.

> We *were* glad *to see* you yesterday.

The perfect forms of the infinitive express action that occurred before that of the verb.

> I *am* proud *to have been associated* with your firm.

Without *to*   The sign of the infinitive, the word *to*, is omitted in certain constructions and after certain verbs, such as *dare, feel, hear, help, let, make, need, please, see,* and *watch*.

> I wanted to run and hide. (to hide)
>
> We didn't dare repeat that story. (to repeat)
>
> She offered to file those papers and type the report. (to type)
>
> Will you let me help you? (allow me to help)
>
> They made us leave. (to leave)
>
> He helped her do the budget. (to do)
>
> This machine does everything but talk. (except to talk)
>
> Please sign the enclosed card. (Be willing to sign)

Subjects and complements   The subject of the infinitive is always in the *objective case*.

> We asked *her to help* us.
>
> She invited *me to attend* the next meeting.

The *complement* following an infinitive presents a problem only when the infinitive is *to be*. In that instance, observe these two rules:

If *to be* has its own subject, the complement following *to be* is in the objective case.

> Many persons believed *him to be me*.
>
> We supposed the *guilty ones to be them*.

If *to be* does *not* have its own subject, the complement following *to be* is in the *nominative case*.

> Would you like *to be she*?
>
> I was thought *to be he*.

Infinitive absolute phrases   Infinitive absolute phrases are made up of a noun or a pronoun in the nominative case (subject of the infinitive) plus an infinitive or an infinitive phrase. The relationship of an absolute phrase to the rest of a sentence is one of content only; it is grammatically independent.

> That work will cost $15,000, *we to pay only one third.*

> Tomorrow we will decide on a date, *you and she to be notified of our decision.*

Split infinitive A split infinitive occurs when one or more adverbs separate *to* from the verb. Such a split can cause an awkward construction and prevent the adverb(s) from functioning most effectively.

In general, do not split an infinitive.

> I decided *not to take* that course.

> They wanted *to discuss* the plan *privately.*

> We hope *to finish promptly* at 4 P.M.

When splitting the infinitive in a particular sentence is necessary to provide naturalness of expression, clarity, and logical adverbial emphasis, do so.

> She wants *to really work* at solving that problem.

> It was a mistake *to even consider* their proposal.

> We hope *to more than triple* our profits this year.

Placement An introductory infinitive phrase should immediately precede the word that it modifies.

> INCORRECT: *To succeed* at Gibbs, *hard work* is necessary.

> CORRECT: *To succeed* at Gibbs, *students* must work hard.

> INCORRECT: *To finish that report,* about five more *hours* will be needed.

> CORRECT: *To finish that report,* I will need about five more hours.

NOTE: Use an infinitive, not the conjunction *and,* after *try, come,* and *be sure.*

Incorrect	Correct
Try and finish that project.	*Try to finish* that project.
Come and see me soon.	*Come to see* me soon.
Be sure and tell her the news.	*Be sure to tell* her the news.

CHAPTER III
SENTENCE STRUCTURE

This chapter deals with the basic unit of thought, the sentence. It clearly distinguishes sentences from other word groups—namely, phrases, dependent clauses, and independent clauses. In addition, it explains the classifications of sentences according to structure and purpose.

PHRASES

A phrase is a group of words that . . .

- **does not have a subject-verb combination**
- **acts as a single part of speech—noun, verb, adjective, or adverb**
- **cannot stand alone to express a complete thought.**

There are three main classifications of phrases: verb phrases, prepositional phrases, and phrases containing verbals—that is, gerunds, participles, and infinitives. (*For more on verbals see pages 62ff.*)

Verb Phrases

I know she *will have finished* those letters by now.

(The verb phrase *will have finished* is composed of the main verb *finished* and the helping verbs *will* and *have*. The verb *will have finished* expresses one action.)

Prepositional Phrases

From Here to Eternity is an excellent movie.

(The prepositional phrase *From Here to Eternity* is used as a noun. It names the movie.)

Please give me the file *on the Taylors*.

(The prepositional phrase *on the Taylors* is used as an adjective. It tells *which* file.)

She is *in Cleveland* today.

(The prepositional phrase *in Cleveland* is used as an adverb. It tells *where* she is today.)

Verbal Phrases

Finishing that report by 5 P.M. will be quite a task.

(*Finishing that report by 5 P.M.* is a gerund phrase used as a noun to *name* an action.)

The person *working on that report* will be exhausted.

(*Working on that report* is a participial phrase used as an adjective. It tells *which* person will be exhausted.)

She left the meeting early *to work on a report*.

(*To work on a report* is an infinitive phrase used as an adverb. It tells *why* she left.)

CLAUSES

A clause is a group of words that has a subject and a verb and is used as part of a sentence. Clauses are classified grammatically as dependent or independent.

Dependent Clauses

A dependent clause is a group of words that . . .

- **has a subject-verb combination**
- **acts as a single part of speech—noun, adjective, or adverb**
- **cannot stand alone to express a complete thought.**

That she was the person best qualified for the job was obvious.

(*That she was the person best qualified for the job* is a noun clause. It is the subject of the sentence because it tells *what* was obvious.)

The person *who is best qualified for the* job is Marcia Adams.

(*Who is best qualified for the job* is an adjective clause. It tells *which* person Marcia Adams is.)

We chose Marcia *because she was the best qualified applicant.*

(*Because she was the best qualified applicant* is an adverbial clause. It tells *why* we chose Marcia.)

To determine whether a clause is dependent or independent, read every word in the clause as one unit; then decide whether that unit expresses a complete thought. Always include the first word of the clause, such as the words *that, who,* and *because* in the preceding examples.

Independent Clauses

An independent clause is a group of words that . . .

- **has a subject-verb combination**
- **is used as a part of a sentence**
- **could stand alone to express a complete thought but doesn't. It is joined to another clause, dependent or independent.**

She will type while I file.

(*She will type* is an independent clause joined to a dependent clause.)

She will type, and *I will file.*

(*She will type* and *I will file* are two independent clauses joined to each other.)

SENTENCES

A sentence is a group of words that . . .

- **has at least one subject-verb combination**
- **stands alone to express a complete thought**
- **begins with a capital letter and concludes with the appropriate end punctuation.**

Every sentence has two basic parts—the subject and the predicate. As the following table illustrates, each of these parts may consist of one or more words, phrases, or dependent clauses.

The Sentence

Subject	**Predicate**
What or whom the sentence is talking about; found by asking Who? or What? of the verb.	What the sentence is saying about the subject.
Essential Element	**Essential Element**
Subject word—noun; pronoun; word, phrase, or clause used as a noun.	*Verb*—word expressing action or helping to make the statement.
Additional Elements	**Additional Elements**
Adjective modifiers—words, phrases, or clauses.	*Adverbs*—words, phrases, or clauses.
Adverbial modifiers—modifying adjectives, verbals, or other adverbs.	*Adjectives*—modifying complements.
	Complements
	Direct object—found by asking What? or Whom? after the subject and verb.
	Indirect object—person or thing (to) or (for) whom or which something is done, given, or told.
	Predicate adjective—after a linking verb to describe the subject.
	Predicate nominative—noun or pronoun after a linking verb that equals the subject.

Independent Elements
Absolute constructions—participial or infinitive. *See page 63 and page 66.*
Interjections—exclamations of strong feeling. *See page 62.*
Transitional and independent expressions. See pages 95 ff.

Sentences by Structure

Sentences are classified according to structure as simple, compound, complex, and compound-complex. (*See table on page 78.*)

Simple   A simple sentence has one subject and one verb, either or both of which may be compound (may have two or more separate parts).

The number of words in a sentence does not affect its structural classification, although it may affect the ease with which it can be read and understood. A simple sentence, regardless of its length, has one subject-verb combination.

> Joe is checking the invitations.

(One verb—*is checking*. One subject—*Joe*.)

> Joe is checking and mailing the invitations.

(One verb, compound—*is checking, (is) mailing*. One subject—*Joe*.)

> Joe and Pat are checking and mailing the invitations.

(One verb, compound—*are checking, (are) mailing*. One subject, compound —*Joe, Pat*.)

Compound   A compound sentence is one that contains at least two independent clauses. Therefore, a compound sentence always has two or more subject-verb combinations.

The independent clauses of a compound sentence may be joined by a . . .
Comma and a coordinate conjunction

> and   or   but   nor

> Joe is checking the invitations, and Pat is mailing them.

Comma and correlative conjunctions

> both . . . and   not only . . . but also
> either . . . or   not only . . . but
> neither . . . nor

> Either we shall build a new factory, or we shall remodel the present one.

Semicolon.

> Joe is checking the invitations; Pat is mailing them.

> Joe is checking the invitations; however, Pat is mailing them.

Complex   A complex sentence has one independent clause and one or more dependent clauses.

> Roger will file those papers after I have checked them.

(*Roger will file those papers* is an independent clause. *After I have checked them* is a dependent clause.)

> After I make one more call, I will check those papers so that you can file them.

(*I will check those papers* is an independent clause. *After I make one more call* and *so that you can file them* are dependent clauses.)

There are three types of dependent clauses in complex sentences—adjective, adverbial, and noun clauses. Each type can be recognized by the function the clause performs in the sentence to which it belongs. Certain connecting words are a part of dependent clauses and usually begin each type of dependent clause.

Adjective Clause Connectives

Adjective clauses begin with the following connective words:

Relative pronouns: who   whom   which   that

Relative adjective: whose

Relative adverbs: when   where   why

> Houston is the city *where we will hold next year's convention.*

Who, whom. In deciding whether to use *who* or *whom,* consider only the dependent clause to which the pronoun belongs. The correct use of *who* and *whom* is determined by how the pronoun functions within the clause of which it is a part. (*For more on* who, whom, *see page 197.*)

> We have hired the person *whom you recommended.*

That, which. In general, *that* is used when the adjective clause provides information necessary to the meaning or the identification of the noun or the pronoun that it modifies.

> We need a duplicator *that is small* and *that will produce legible copies.*

Which is used when the adjective clause is unnecessary to the identification of the noun or the pronoun that it modifies.

> Duplicator 236, *which is small* but *which produces legible copies,* is our choice.

When a sentence contains a noun clause or an adverbial clause beginning with the word *that,* a necessary adjective clause should begin with the word *which.*

> We said *that* the duplicator *which we need* must be small.

> We are glad *that* the duplicator *which* Mr. Branton ordered is portable.

(*For more on the correct usage of* that, which, *and* who, *see page 196.*)

Adverbial Clause Connectives

Adverbial clauses often begin with one of the following connective words.

after	before	that
although	if	though
as	in order that	unless
as long as	now that	until
as if	provided that	when, whenever
as often as	since	where, wherever
as soon as	so that (in order that)	whereas
as though	so . . . that	while
because	than	

We are happy *that you enjoyed our presentation.*

Because you have given us such excellent service in the past, we are once again requesting your help.

He has more time and money invested in that project *than we.* (than we have invested)

You work as quickly *as she.* (as she does)

Noun Clause Connectives

Noun clauses usually begin with one of the following connectives.

Indefinite relative pronouns

who   which   what   that

whoever   whichever   whatever

Whatever you decide will be all right with the committee.

Indefinite relative adjectives

whose   which   whatever

I don't know *whose decision it was.*

Indefinite relative adverbs

where   when   why   how

Do you know *where the meeting will be held?*

Compound-complex   A compound-complex sentence has at least two independent clauses (compound) and at least one dependent clause (complex).

Your résumé indicates excellent qualifications, and we would like to arrange an interview time when we call you Monday.

(*Your résumé indicates excellent qualifications* is an independent clause. *We would like to arrange an interview time* is an independent clause. *When we call you on Monday* is a dependent clause.)

Elliptical sentences   An elliptical sentence is a sentence from which one or more words have been omitted that the reader can fill in easily and naturally. Whether a sentence is elliptical or not does not in any way affect its classification according to purpose or structure.

An elliptical adverbial clause with only the subject expressed frequently follows the conjunctions *than* and *as.*

She did more work on that project than I. (than I *did*)

We are as eager to complete this project as you. (as you *are*)

In imperative sentences *you* is usually the implied subject.

Read that file before deciding. (*you* read)

Give a copy of that memo to Barbara. (*you* give)

Additional examples of elliptical sentences:

> Kathy completed the typing; Maureen, the filing. (Maureen *completed* the filing.)
>
> While there, he discussed the problem with Senator Burns. (While *he was* there)
>
> Had you been here, you would have met Alan Arthur. (*If* you had been here)
>
> This morning I interviewed four applicants; this afternoon, three. (This afternoon *I interviewed* three.)

Sentences by Purpose

Sentences are divided into four classifications according to the writer's purpose, and they are punctuated according to those classifications.

Declarative   A declarative sentence states a fact.

> She will type while I file.
>
> I wonder whether she received our letter of August 28.

Imperative   An imperative sentence makes a request or gives a command. The subject of an imperative sentence may be implied.

> Close the door. (gives a command)
>
> Please return the enclosed card. (makes a request)

Interrogative   An interrogative sentence asks a question.

> Do you plan to attend Tuesday's seminar?

Exclamatory   An exclamatory sentence is one in which the writer expresses strong feeling. Exclamatory sentences are seldom used in business writing except in advertising and sales.

> You may have already won $50,000!

("Words and Word Groups," table, page 78.)

Words and Word Groups

(A Summary of Structural Relationships)

Words	Phrase	Dependent Clause	Independent Clause	Sentence
Parts of Speech Verb	a group of words	a group of words	a group of words	a group of words
Noun Pronoun Adjective Adverb Preposition	does *not* have a subject-verb combination	has a subject-verb combination	has a subject-verb combination	has a subject-verb combination
Conjunction Interjection	used as a part of speech: noun verb	used as a part of speech: noun adjective	used as a part of a sentence	begins with a capital letter and concludes with end
Verbals Participle Gerund Infinitive	adjective adverb	adverb		punctuation
	Cannot stand alone to express a complete thought	*Cannot* stand alone to express a complete thought	*Could* stand alone to express a complete thought but doesn't	*Does* stand alone to express a complete thought

CHAPTER IV
PUNCTUATION

Punctuation has a dual purpose: to facilitate the reading and ensure the clarity of a written message. Originators, producers, and proofreaders should be aware of punctuation, but readers of the finished document should not. Proper punctuation is an inconspicuous part of smooth, clear, natural writing. In accordance with current trends, use punctuation sparingly, deliberately, and correctly.

The correct use of punctuation depends on understanding the functions of words and the structure and the functions of phrases, clauses, and sentences.

APOSTROPHES

The apostrophe (') will show possession, form contractions of words, and form some plurals.

Apostrophes and Possession

Possessive endings are added to nouns to show authorship, ownership, or possession. Such possessive forms will use apostrophes. Possessive forms can usually be replaced by an *of,* a *by,* or a *belonging to* phrase.

Hemingway's *A Farewell to Arms*	*A Farewell to Arms* by Hemingway
my parents' home	the home of my parents
Clare's locker	the locker belonging to Clare

Singular possession Most singular common or proper nouns are made possessive by adding an apostrophe and *s* ('s).

the student's schedule	Roger's car
the witness's story	Charles's absence

If a singular noun ends in *s* and the resulting possessive form would sound awkward or be hard to pronounce, many writers choose one of the following ways to show singular possession.

Change the possessive noun to an *of* or *by* phrase:

> The appeal of Mr. Cousins (instead of Mr. Cousins's appeal)

OR

Add just an apostrophe ('):

> Mr. Cousins' appeal (instead of Mr. Cousins's appeal)

To a singular or plural compound noun, written with or without hyphens, add an apostrophe and *s* ('s) at the end of the compound.

> the editor in chief's decision
>
> her sisters-in-law's homes

When the word *the* precedes a singular proper noun, the noun becomes a proper adjective (answering the question Which one? or Which ones?) and is not possessive.

> the Burns home   the Nixon tapes

Plural possession   If a plural common noun ends in *s*, add just an apostrophe ('). If a plural common noun ends in a letter other than *s*, add an apostrophe and *s* ('s).

> those nurses' uniforms   the men's cars
>
> three students' reports   both children's toys

To a plural proper noun, add just an apostrophe (').

> the Coles   the Coles' invitation
>
> the Denbys   the Denbys' apartment
>
> the Joneses   the Joneses' garden

Possession in elliptical constructions   When the object owned is not expressed but is clearly understood (elliptical possessive), show possession as if the object were expressed.

> an average as good as his sister's (sister's average)
>
> one week's vacation this year and two weeks' next year (two weeks' vacation)

Joint and separate possession   When ownership or possession is shared, the last individual named carries the sign of the possessive.

> Nancy and Tom's stores   (stores owned jointly by Nancy and Tom)
>
> Miss Oliver and Mrs. Tyler's   (one shop owned by both persons)
> shop

When ownership or possession is separate, each individual named carries the sign of the possessive.

> John's and Tom's shoes   (shoes owned separately)
>
> Men's, women's, and children's   (clothes for each group)
> clothes

Miss Prince's and Miss Norris's   (parents of each person)
parents

When joint possession is expressed by a possessive noun and a possessive pronoun, only the noun will carry the apostrophe.

Jack's and her assignment   Dad's and my conversation

Organization and publication names Always follow a known or accepted preference for showing possession within the names of organizations and publications.

Child's Restaurant   *Reader's Digest*

Ladies' Home Journal   Women's Clubs of America

Within the name of an organization or publication, a regularly formed plural will often not show possession.

American Bankers Association   *Consumers Digest*

Other possessives Although possession is usually not attributed to inanimate objects, usage has established the use of the possessive with expressions of time, distance, and value and with certain idiomatic expressions.

a moment's delay   your money's worth

in harm's way   the sun's rays

a stone's throw   the water's edge

Appositives and such designations as *Jr., Sr., 2d, 2nd,* and *II* carry the sign of the possessive if they follow a noun that would otherwise be possessive.

Dr. John Marcus Jr.'s office   Mary, my friend's, apartment

Contractions

In a contraction, the shortened form of words or phrases, an apostrophe will stand in place of omitted letters.

don't (do not)   I'm (I am)

o'clock (of the clock)   you're (you are)

Plurals of Numbers, Symbols, Letters, Abbreviations, and Words Used as Words

Numbers, symbols, capital letters, abbreviations that end with a capital letter, and words referred to as words are made plural by the addition of *s* if no confusion results.

average in the 90s   several ?s   no ands, ifs, or buts

some size 14s   three CPAs   the three Rs

To form the plural of *A, I,* and *U,* add an apostrophe and *s* (*'s*) to avoid misreading.

A's (not As)   I's (not Is)   U's (not Us)

An apostrophe and *s* are preferably used to form the plurals of lower-case letters and of lower-case abbreviations with internal periods.

> Cross your t's   too many c.o.d.'s

A lower-case *s* without an apostrophe is used to form the plural of the abbreviation for doctor, esquire, and number.

> Drs.   Esqs.   Nos.

BRACKETS

Brackets [ ] are used as secondary parentheses, and they also enclose information inserted within quoted material. Brackets are always used in pairs.

Within quotations   Use brackets to enclose additions, corrections, or explanations that are inserted within quoted material.

> Our Cleveland distributor writes: "Our stock is down to three dozen sets of UHF strips [he means VHF], and we must have another shipment at once."

With *sic*   Use brackets to enclose the Latin word *sic*, meaning "thus," after an error in quoted material to indicate that the error is in the original. Most often used in literary contexts, *sic* is rarely used or appropriate in business.

> Mr. Hart said in his letter: "The staff is well qualified to make an analyses [*sic*] of prevailing wage rates."

As secondary parentheses   Use brackets as secondary parentheses (parentheses within parentheses).

> Remote Control Commander 600 is not standard equipment on Model 8976 (see Catalog 94 [Summer, 19___] for separate pricing).

COLONS

The colon (:) is a mark that alerts the reader to expect the explanation, quotation, list, or enumeration that will follow.

For emphasis   When the wording of a sentence leads the reader to expect an explanation, use a colon (or dash) to give emphasis to the word or words that provide the explanation. (*See Dash on page 100.*)

> We prize one quality above all others: integrity.

Between clauses   Use a colon before an independent clause that completes the thought expressed in the preceding independent clause.

> Our department store has one policy: The customer is always right.

After an introduction to a tabulation   Use a colon after the introduction to a tabulation. Capitalize the first word of each tabulated item. (*See page 110 for end punctuation with lists and topical outlines.*)

Our secretaries' duties may be summed up under these headings:

1. Opening and blue-penciling mail
2. Answering the telephone and making appointments
3. Taking dictation and transcribing letters, memoranda, and reports
4. Taking the minutes at small conferences.

After an introduction to a run-on enumeration   If the items are independent clauses, the first word of the first clause is capitalized; otherwise, the items are not capitalized unless they would be capitalized in any case.

Our company has two objectives: (1) It hopes to serve the public interest by making superior television available, and (2) it hopes to create a greater knowledge of our capabilities, products, services, and contributions to society and to the economy.

You attest to these facts when you endorse a check: (a) that the check is genuine and valid, (b) that you have received value for it, (c) that if necessary, you will pay for it yourself.

After a formal introduction   Use a colon after a formal introduction to a quotation. *Spoke thus, said in part, as follows, the following,* and *stated* are examples of formal introductions to quotations.

The President continued as follows: "Much will depend on you, the citizens of our nation, who . . . ."

To introduce long quotations   Use a colon after the introduction to a quotation that is longer than one sentence.

Our architect, Mr. Wells, wrote: "When one specifies such quality products, an $80,000 house will rise in cost by $10,000. The additional cost will result in increased monthly mortgage payments."

Additional uses of the colon:

After the salutation of a letter

Dear Mr. Dexter:	Ladies:
Dear Sir:	My dear Mr. Allen:

After a subject introduction (*See page 159.*)

Subject: Forthcoming Stockholders' Meeting

Between the hours and minutes in expressing exact time

appointment at 11:30 A.M.

Between the dictator's and the typist's initials

RBA:JC   LH:CD   IMS:jk   BD:gl

Between the title of a book and a subtitle

Thomas Jefferson: Private Letters

Between the name of the city of publication and the name of the publisher when reference is made to a publication in a footnote

> [1]Athena Theodore, ed., *The Professional Woman*. (Cambridge, Mass.: Schenkman Publishing Company, Inc., 1971), p. 74.

Between the act and the scene of a play.

> Act II: 3

COMMAS

The comma is a punctuation mark that facilitates reading in two ways: It separates introductory, nonessential, and interruptive material from the main thought; it clarifies the relationship of words, phrases, and clauses to each other.

Introductory Words, Phrases, and Dependent Clauses

Introductory words, phrases, and dependent clauses should be separated from the rest of the sentence by a comma. Certain words, phrases, and dependent clauses are introductory when they precede the subject of the sentence or clause that contains the word they modify. In some cases an introductory independent expression does not modify one word but is a comment on the thought expressed in the sentence or clause. (*See Transitional and Independent Expressions pages 95ff.*)

Introductory adverbial clauses   Use a comma after an introductory adverbial clause that precedes the subject of an independent clause, the subject of a noun clause, or the subject of another adverbial clause.

> While Mr. Clark was in Washington, he addressed the Press Club. (independent clause)
>
> We have agreed upon the terms of the contract, and if signatures are obtained this week, work can begin on April 1. (independent clause)
>
> We believe that unless conditions change radically, we shall exceed last year's record. (noun clause)
>
> If after you have read the manual, you would like to have a salesman call, please telephone this office. (adverbial clause)

Sometimes an introductory adverbial clause is elliptical. In an elliptical clause one or more words are unstated but clearly implied. Introductory elliptical clauses are followed by a comma.

> While there, he interviewed several applicants. (While he was there, . . .)
>
> Should you be detained, please telephone me. (If you should be detained, . . .)
>
> Were Miss Adams here, she would be able to give you those answers. (If Miss Adams were here, . . .)

Introductory prepositional phrases   Although a comma is acceptable after any introductory prepositional phrase, the comma is necessary if the phrase contains five or more words.

Because of certain major design changes, we expect better gasoline mileage.

In addition to her responsibilities in that department, she also recruits seniors.

Always place a comma after an introductory prepositional phrase that contains a verb or a verbal.

Before signing, we read the contract carefully.

From what she told us, the location is excellent.

Sometimes an introductory prepositional phrase is elliptical—that is, it appears without a preposition. Punctuate such phrases as you would any other introductory prepositional phrase.

The day you were here, we discussed that question. (On the day . . .)

Introductory participial phrases   Use a comma after an introductory participle or participial phrase.

Mr. Hudson said that based on last month's earnings, the figures indicate an encouraging trend.

Having been elected, Miss Sheehy expressed her appreciation to the members.

Introductory infinitive phrases   Use a comma after an introductory infinitive or infinitive phrase.

To qualify, one must be a high school graduate.

To prepare the minutes accurately, the secretary must listen attentively.

Introductory adjectives   Use a comma after one or more introductory adjectives that precede an article, a personal pronoun, an indefinite pronoun used as an adjective, or a proper noun.

Tired and frustrated, the strikers turned away.

Always ambitious, he will certainly succeed.

Eager to do well, many students attended the workshop.

Dignified and diplomatic, Mr. Law is my first choice.

Introductory adverbs   The use of a comma after short introductory adverbs—for example, *hence, then, thus, still, yet*—is a matter of taste. The trend today is to omit that comma.

He is a perfectionist; *thus* he is a demanding employer.

Introductory transitional and independent expressions   Use a comma after an introductory transitional or independent expression. A transitional expression shows the relationship between a preceding and a following idea. (*See Transitional and Independent Expressions, pages 95ff.*)

> First, *The Herald* owes its success primarily to its dedicated staff. Second, *The Herald* goes into nearly every home in this state.

An independent expression is a writer's comment on the sentence thought.

> In my opinion, our company should strive to achieve stability of employment.

Do not punctuate introductory independent or transitional expressions that are intended to give emphasis to the sentence thought.

> Of course Mr. Mills will reply to your letter.

Introductory admonition Use a comma after a short admonition when the connective *that* is unexpressed.

> Remember, the customer is always right.
>
> Don't forget, curtailment of production may have far-reaching consequences.
>
> Just think, we have almost reached our goal!
>
> Recall too, we have a backlog of unfilled orders.

Introductory noun clauses Use a comma after a noun clause that is used as a direct object when the clause precedes the subject of the sentence.

> That the market will rise soon, he firmly believes.

Compound Sentences

The independent clauses in a compound sentence are usually joined by the coordinate conjunctions *and, or, but,* or *nor.*

Two independent clauses In general, use a comma before a coordinate conjunction joining two independent clauses.

> Our headquarters is in Nashville, but our refineries are in the North.

Short independent clauses A comma before the coordinate conjunction is optional if either or both of the independent clauses in any compound sentence contain fewer than four words.

> Sign the enclosed card, and mail it today.
>
> > OR
>
> Sign the enlosed card and mail it today.

NOTE: Do not place a comma before a coordinate conjunction when it joins two predicates that have the same subject.

> Mr. Chapin completed the report on Tuesday and presented it to the district supervisor. (Mr. Chapin completed and presented)

NOTE: A sentence in which *please* governs two infinitives with the *to* not expressed should not be punctuated as a compound sentence. (*See Infinitives pages 65ff.*)

> Please complete the attached form and return it by June 15.

(For use of the serial comma in a series of independent clauses, see Series page 93.)

(To punctuate a compound sentence that does not contain a coordinate conjunction or that does contain either a punctuated independent clause or an elliptical independent clause, see Semicolons page 114.)

Nonessential Elements

Nonessential elements need commas to set them off from the main ideas of sentences. A general rule used in determining whether an element is nonessential or essential is this: If you can remove an element from a sentence without substantially changing the meaning of the sentence, then the element is nonessential.

Nonessential adverbial clauses Use a comma before an adverbial clause that follows an independent clause if the information in the adverbial clause is clearly unnecessary to the thought expressed in the independent clause.

> NONESSENTIAL: I don't like him, although he's compassionate. (His compassion does not change my dislike for him.)

> ESSENTIAL: I like him because he's compassionate. (His compassion is essential to my liking him.)

An adverbial clause that falls between the subject and the predicate of the sentence is nonessential and should be set off by commas. Place commas before and after the dependent clause.

> Ms. Sherman, when told about her promotion, seemed surprised.

Essential and nonessential adjective clauses Use a comma or a pair of commas to set off a nonessential adjective clause, one that is unnecessary to the identification of the noun or pronoun it modifies.

> Mr. John Haven, whom you have just met, will preside. (Mr. John Haven will preside.)

> **BUT**

> The young man whom you have just met will preside. (Which young man? The adjective clause is essential.)

In general, an adjective clause introduced by *that* is necessary to the identification of the noun or pronoun that it modifies. Therefore, it is not set off by commas. An adjective clause introduced by *which*, however, is usually unnecessary to the identification of the noun or pronoun that it modifies and is therefore set off by commas.

> We need a duplicator that will produce legible copies.

> Duplicator 234, which produces the clearest copies, is our choice.

NOTE: When a sentence includes a noun clause or an adverbial clause beginning with *that*, an essential adjective clause will begin with *which*. No commas are needed.

We said that the duplicator which we need must be small.

We were glad that the duplicator which Mr. Branton ordered is portable.

Adjective clauses beginning with the following and similar expressions are always considered nonessential and are set off by commas.

a copy of which	either of which (whom)
a few of which (whom)	many of which (whom)
a number of which (whom)	most of which (whom)
a sample of which	neither of which (whom)
any of which (whom)	one of which (whom)
both of which (whom)	several of which (whom)
contact with which (whom)	reference to which (whom)
each of which (whom)	some of which (whom)

The annual report, a copy of which you should have received, contains all of the necessary information.

Nonessential participial phrases   Use a comma or a pair of commas to set off a nonessential participial phrase, one that is unnecessary to the identification of the noun or pronoun it modifies.

Mr. Ames, addressing the meeting, said that profits were excellent.

Thank you for your letter of September 10, inviting us to attend next month's seminar.

BUT

The man addressing the meeting is Mr. Ames.

Thank you for your letter inviting us to attend next month's seminar.

With nonessential adjectives   Commas set off nonessential adjectives that follow the noun or pronoun they modify.

The speaker, undismayed, continued his presentation.

Those trees, young and old, retard erosion.

BUT

We are seeking students willing and able to assume responsibility.

(*For a series of nonessential adjectives after a noun, see Dashes page 100.*)

With coordinate adjectives   Use a comma to separate coordinate adjectives that can be read smoothly with the word *and* between them or can be reversed without affecting the meaning of the sentence.

New, interesting projects were undertaken.

BUT

Mr. Blair requested several extra blank tax forms.

Series

A series consists of three or more words, phrases, or clauses. In general, use a comma to separate items in a series.

Words, phrases, and dependent clauses in series   When three or more words, phrases, or dependent clauses occur consecutively and only the last two are connected by *and, or, but,* or *nor,* use a comma after each item in the series. The final serial comma is placed before the conjunction.

> Write, telephone, or visit your dealer today.
>
> We looked in the file, on her desk, and behind the bookcase.
>
> The booklet tells you what to take with you, what to leave at home, and how to handle foreign money.

NOTE: The comma before the conjunction is considered optional if its omission would not cause misreading. In business writing, however, this comma is required.

When *and, or,* or *nor* join all the items in a series of words, phrases, or dependent clauses, no commas are used.

> This design is available in gold and in silver and in platinum.

When a company name consists of a series, use the punctuation preferred by that company.

> Putney, Twombley, Hall and Hirson

A series of independent clauses   A series of independent clauses, the last two of which are joined by a coordinate conjunction, is treated like any other series: Use a comma after each clause; place the last comma before the conjunction.

(For a punctuated series see Semicolons page 114.)

> These Perma-Glaze utensils are inexpensive, they are not affected by heat or cold, and they are chip-proof.

Parenthetical Elements

Parenthetical elements either interrupt the flow of the main idea or add an idea to the end of the sentence. In either case, parenthetical elements should be set off by commas.

Interrupting prepositional phrases   When a prepositional phrase beginning with one of the following expressions separates the subject from the verb, place commas before and after the phrase.

accompanied by	besides
along with	but not
and not	in addition to
as well as	including

instead of	plus
minus	rather than
never	seldom
no less than	together with
not	yet not

Mr. Webb, along with his two aides, inspected the installation.

Please ask whether the furniture, together with the carpeting, was delivered today.

BUT

I asked them to deliver the furniture together with the carpeting.

For clarity use commas to set off a short interrupting phrase ending with *after, before,* or *since.*

We were familiar with the layout because, a short time before, we had inspected the construction work.

He took advantage of the trial offer, and ever since, he has been a regular subscriber.

A prepositional phrase that breaks the continuity of the sentence thought is set off by commas.

The dividend will, for the time being at least, remain at 75 cents.

When a prepositional phrase begins with *as* and the object of the preposition refers to the noun or pronoun that the phrase follows, such a phrase is set off by commas.

Jack Poole, as project manager, accepted the award.

Additional prepositional phrases   When a prepositional phrase beginning with one of the following words is added to the end of a sentence, use a comma to set off the phrase from the rest of the sentence.

despite	perhaps
especially	possibly
in spite of	preferably
irrespective of	probably
particularly	regardless of

The geologists will continue the survey, regardless of the weather.

Please call me at the office, preferably after three o'clock.

When a prepositional phrase beginning with *such as* provides additional but nonessential information about the preceding noun or pronoun, set off such a phrase with a comma or a pair of commas.

I have ordered all the filing supplies, such as guides, folders, and labels.

Our science courses, such as biology and chemistry, require three hours of laboratory work each week.

When the prepositions *concerning, pertaining to, regarding, referring to,* and *relating to* mean "about," the phrases they introduce are considered essential to the words they modify. Therefore, they are not set off by commas.

Thank you for your letter of May 7 concerning our summer flight schedule.

Mr. Tate's letter referring to changes in your policy will receive immediate attention.

Interrupting infinitive phrases   When an infinitive phrase parenthetically interrupts a sentence, set it off with commas.

The meeting, to be sure, was not as productive as it could have been.

Additional infinitive phrases   Use a comma or a pair of commas to set off a nonessential infinitive phrase that is added to the end of a sentence.

Positions are available in such departments as research, advertising, and accounting, to name just a few.

You did more than we expected, to say the least.

Interrupting clauses   Many parenthetical elements are short clauses. Use commas to set off such clauses when they interrupt the main idea of a sentence.

Mr. Lansing will, we believe, return on the first or second day of May.

American Electronics has, as you know, enlarged its old plant.

The advertising program, Mrs. Burden says, begins on June 15.

When a short independent clause follows the connective for an adjective clause, the independent clause is essential to the meaning of the sentence and is not punctuated.

Mr. Niven is the man who I believe won the nomination.

Independent expressions   Independent expressions such as *needless to say* or *so to speak* should be set off with commas when they interrupt a sentence or are added to the end of one.

Her recommendation, so to speak, was not helpful.

She was delighted with your report, needless to say.

Transitional and Independent Expressions

Transitional expressions are words or phrases that make logical connections between sentences. An independent expression is a writer's comment on the sentence thought. When they are used within a sentence, place commas before and after them.

Common Transitional and Independent Expressions

accordingly	generally speaking	most of all
actually	however	nevertheless
as a result	in addition	no
at any rate	in any case	obviously
besides	in any event	of course
best of all	in brief	on the contrary
consequently	in conclusion	on the other hand
evidently	in essence	on the whole
finally	in other words	otherwise
first (first of all)	in short	second, secondly
for example	in summary	strictly speaking
for instance	in the first (second) place	therefore
for one thing	indeed	truthfully
fortunately	likewise	unfortunately
furthermore	more than that	yes

Mr. Byrnes, on the other hand, found several errors.

No department, furthermore, will escape the reductions in the budget.

Commas with *and so forth, inclusive,* and *respectively* Use a comma or a pair of commas to set off the words *and so forth, inclusive,* and *respectively.*

Pages 419 to 423, inclusive, were deleted, were they not?

For the offices of governor and lieutenant governor, we nominated Mrs. Crane and Mr. Archer, respectively.

Commas omitted for emphasis Do not use commas to set off transitional expressions that are intended to give emphasis to the sentence.

She will in any event attempt to convince them.

Appositives

An appositive is a word or group of words that is placed next to a noun or pronoun for the purpose of identifying, renaming, or explaining it. An appositive can be a noun, a pronoun, or a phrase or clause acting as a noun.

Nonessential appositives A nonessential appositive is one that is unnecessary to the identification of the noun or pronoun that precedes it. Use a comma or a pair of commas to set off a nonessential appositive.

I discussed the matter with Miss Clay, my attorney.

I spoke to Miss Clay, my attorney, about the matter.

Essential appositives   An appositive is essential when it is necessary to identify the noun or pronoun that precedes it. Do not set off essential appositives with commas.

> She quoted from the essay "Self-Reliance" by Emerson.
>
> His friend Tony won the championship.

Optional commas with appositives   When a common noun is followed by a proper noun in apposition, the punctuation of the appositive is optional. However, the meaning of the sentence may be ambiguous.

> His agent Mr. Clifton telephoned this morning. (Commas around Mr. Clifton might indicate that he is the only agent.)

To ensure clarity, put the proper noun first and make the common noun the appositive.

> Mr. Clifton, his agent, telephoned this morning.

Appositives beginning with *or*   An appositive beginning with *or* explains or defines the noun it follows. Always set off such appositives with commas.

> Micrology, or attention to petty details, characterizes far too many supervisors.

Appositives for emphasis   When the writer wants to emphasize an appositive that the reader has been led to expect, use a dash or a colon instead of a comma.

> We prize one quality above all others—integrity. (most emphatic)
>
> We prize one quality above all others: integrity. (less emphatic)
>
> We prize one quality, integrity, above all others. (least emphatic)

Punctuating appositives for clarity   Use parentheses to set off an appositive that could be misread if commas were used.

> Mrs. Bailey (the new dean) and I attended the seminar. (Only two people attended the seminar.)

Absolute Phrases

An absolute phrase is composed of a noun or pronoun in the nominative case followed by a participle or an infinitive. It is grammatically independent of the rest of the sentence. Use a comma or a pair of commas to set off absolute phrases.

> He said that, weather permitting, we will hold the ceremony outdoors.
>
> The excavation work will cost $2,500, we to pay one third.

Direct Quotations

Quotation marks enclose the exact words of a writer or speaker. Use a comma or a pair of commas to set off a direct quotation from the rest of the sentence.

> Mr. Decker said, "The board will meet tomorrow at 10 A.M."
>
> "The educational value of the film," he continued, "is remarkable."

If the direct quotation is a question or an exclamation, a question mark or an exclamation point instead of a comma follows the quotation.

> "Will the board meet tomorrow at ten?" Mr. Decker asked.
>
> "These rules are killing me!" the student exclaimed.

A quotation that acts as the subject of a sentence is not set off with commas.

> "Be prepared" was his motto.

Use a colon instead of a comma to introduce a long quotation.

> She summed up her lecture with these comments: "Zen stresses the gradual change and fading of all things. Out of this awareness arose the concept of nothingness . . . ."

Indirect quotations do not use quotation marks and are usually expressed in noun clauses beginning with *that*. Commas are not used with indirect quotations.

> She said that Zen stresses the gradual change of all things.

Contrasting and Limiting Ideas

Commas are used with contrasting and limiting ideas to mark an abrupt shift in the flow of a sentence.

Contrasting   Use a comma or a pair of commas to set off a contrasting idea that begins with *not, never,* or *seldom.*

> She ordered dark, not light, beer.
>
> She ordered dark beer, not light.
>
> *National Outlook* is available only by subscription, never on newsstands.

Limiting   Use a comma or a pair of commas to set off a limiting idea that begins with *but.* This rule does not apply to the correlative conjunctions *not only . . . but* or *not only . . . but also.*

> The club will be open on Sunday, but only for members.
>
> BUT
>
> The secretary represents not only her executive but also her company.

Degree-Result Clauses

Unless degree-result clauses are very short, use a comma to separate them from each other.

> The higher the salary, the greater the responsibility.

She agrees that the sooner we subscribe for that service, the more value we will derive from it.

BUT

The sooner the better.

The more the merrier.

Abbreviated Titles After Names

Use commas to set off abbreviations after names.

Ms. Helen Hancox, Ph.D., was the main speaker at the assembly.

The current trend is to omit the commas before and after *Jr.* and *Sr.*

George Wendell Jr. will attend the luncheon.

Dates, Numbers, and Addresses

Commas with dates   Commas are usually necessary to separate the items that comprise dates, numbers, and addresses. There are, however, notable exceptions.

Use commas to separate a day of the week from the date.

On Friday, April 4, he will meet with the other directors.

Use a comma to separate the date from the year.

On May 7, 1981 her campaign began.

NOTE: Although some writers still use a comma after the year, the current trend is to omit that comma.

When only the month and year are given, no punctuation is necessary.

His contract will end in June 1984.

With dates for years consisting of five or more digits, put a comma after the digit representing thousands.

25,000 B.C.

BUT

1100 B.C.

Commas with numbers   In general, use commas to mark thousands and millions in numbers.

1,350,000

76,000

Do not use commas in the following instances.

1700 Park Avenue	Post Office Box 1832
page 2382	License RC 2309
Room 1543	in the year 2000
telephone MAin 5-5000	Model 8765
Life Insurance Policy 233256	

Use a comma to separate two unrelated numbers. It is better, however, to place them far enough apart to avoid any misreading.

> In 1980, 1,500,000 letters were received by the commission.
>
> **BUT**
>
> In 1980 the commission received 1,500,000 letters.

Commas with addresses Place a comma between a city and state.

> Our representative in Albany, New York will call you.

Use commas to separate the items in an address when it appears in a sentence.

> They moved to 90 Locust Street, Savannah, Georgia soon after World War II.

Commas for Clarity

Use commas to prevent the possibility of misreading.

> To George, Washington was a challenging city.
>
> Whatever is, is right.
>
> Whoever protests, protests in vain.

DASHES

The dash (—) is a strong punctuation mark, usually marking a dramatic shift in thought within a sentence. It should not be used casually as an easy substitute for the comma. In writing, a dash is about twice as long as a hyphen. In typing, it is indicated by two hyphens (--).

To show a sudden shift in thought Use dashes to set off a word, phrase, or clause that creates a sudden shift in the flow of a sentence thought.

> Can he—indeed, should he—attempt to scale that mountain?
>
> She's generous—too generous!

To set off punctuated adjectives Use a dash or a pair of dashes to set off a punctuated series of adjectives following the noun modified.

> These apartments—modern, comfortable, and attractive—are renting well.
>
> We insure all your shipments of produce—fresh, frozen, or dried.

To set off a punctuated appositive Use a dash or a pair of dashes to set off an appositive that already contains punctuation.

> Telephone calls to moving vehicles—cars, trains, trucks, and planes—are made through a mobile service operator.
>
> A mobil service operator will call all moving vehicles—cars, trains, trucks, and planes.

Such appositions may often be introduced by *namely, for example, for instance,* and *that is.*

> The secretary orders all office supplies—for example, notebooks, paper, pens, and typewriter ribbons.
>
> A small piece of luggage—for instance, a fabric flight bag—is all that a passenger may carry onto the plane.

With summary words   Use a dash before a noun or a pronoun that follows and summarizes a list of two or more words, phrases, or clauses.

> Enthusiasm and imagination—*these* are the qualities that our employees must have.

For emphasis   Use a dash to set off an emphatic word that begins a sentence.

> Money—that's all they ever talk about.

When the wording of a sentence leads the reader to an emphatic conclusion, use a dash (or a colon) instead of a comma. (*See Colons, pages 86ff.*)

> We prize one quality above all others—integrity.

With credit lines and dates   Use a dash before a name in a credit line.

> Ask not what your country can do for you but what you can do for your country.   —John F. Kennedy

Use a dash to indicate an open-ended date.

> in 19—
>
> Richard Milhous Nixon (1913—)

In manuscript preparation (the em dash)   In preparing manuscript for typesetting, dashes are customarily marked $\frac{1}{M}$ to distinguish them from hyphens.

ELLIPSES

An ellipsis is an omission in text. Use three periods (. . .) to indicate that words have been omitted from material that is being quoted directly. If the ellipsis falls at the end of a declarative sentence, use four periods.

> He drew in breath, stopped midway . . . , stretched, and died.
> —Leo Tolstoy
>
> The thousand injuries of Fortunato I had borne as best I could. . . .
> —Edgar Allan Poe

EXCLAMATION POINTS

The exclamation point (!) expresses emotion. It can be used after any word, phrase, clause, or sentence that expresses strong feeling. Use this mark of punctuation with restraint.

> Congratulations on your promotion!

HYPHENS

A hyphen (-) is generally half the length of a dash. Unlike dashes, hyphens function solely within words, where they have three main uses: They assist in forming certain kinds of compound words, they are used to separate base words from certain prefixes and suffixes, and they are used to mark the division of a word between lines of writing.

Hyphens to Form Compound Words

A hyphen is sometimes part of the spelling of a compound word. Used in this way, the hyphen brings together two or more words either to express a new idea or to form a temporarily convenient adjective.

> the only cure-all
>
> the blue-gray shade
>
> the New York-Boston shuttle

Stylistic guides and dictionaries often differ about whether to use a hyphen in a particular compound word. Many words that until recently were routinely hyphenated appear in the latest dictionaries as unhyphenated words. The best rule of thumb concerning hyphens is to use a reliable dictionary and to follow it consistently. If the dictionary does not enter a compound noun, spell it as separate words. The rules that follow should serve to familiarize you with the concepts involved in hyphenating compound words.

Compound nouns   Certain compound nouns are always hyphenated.

> brother-in-law   a two-year-old
>
> father-in-law   a light-year
>
> mother-in-law   by-products
>
> sister-in-law   jack-in-the-box

Compound adjectives   Use a hyphen to connect most compound adjectives that come directly before a noun.

> an up-to-date newsletter   a hang-dog expression
>
> an after-hours club   the duty-free shop

A compound adjective composed of *well* and a participle is always hyphenated before a noun.

> a well-fitting suit   a well-founded suspicion
>
> a well-known author   well-made shoes

In other positions in a sentence the use of the hyphen is optional when *well* and the past participle can be reversed with smoothness and without change in sentence thought.

> That author is well known in Detroit. (is known well)

In each of the following *well* combinations, the hyphen is retained because *well* and the past participle cannot be reversed without changing the intended meaning:

well-advised	well-favored	well-read
well-bred	well-founded	well-versed
well-disposed	well-mannered	well-worn

Most other compound adjectives containing participles are hyphenated both before nouns and in the predicate position.

an interest-bearing account	This is time-consuming.
a government-owned utility	Your statement is thought-provoking.
an awe-inspiring sight	
long-playing records	We were panic-stricken.
ready-made covers	You were ill-advised.
	She has always been soft-spoken.

Be careful to distinguish between compound adjectives that are hyphenated and compound nouns that are not.

an air-conditioning system	Air conditioning is expensive.
a profit-sharing plan	The company began profit sharing.

Do not place a hyphen between an *ly* adverb and a participle.

> a widely known fact
>
> a beautifully arranged bouquet

Do place a hyphen between an *ly* adjective and a participle.

> a neighborly-seeming person
>
> a friendly-looking young woman

Hyphenate the following expressions only when they are used as adjectives before nouns.

down-payment plan	over-the-counter sales
easy-to-understand directions	part-time work
face-to-face discussion	partial-payment plan
full-rate telegram	past-due account
house-to-house canvass	ready-to-wear department
low-cost housing	up-to-grade materials
out-of-state taxpayers	up-to-standard work

The following expressions are hyphenated in all adjectival positions:

all-purpose	first-rate	out-of-doors
all-around	heavy-duty	uncalled-for
brand-new	high-grade	unheard-of
built-in	long-range	up-to-date
color-blind	middle-class	up-to-the-minute
first-class	out-of-date	worn-out

Compound verbs   Use a hyphen in the following compound verbs:

air-condition the room	court-martial the offender
air-cool the cylinders	dry-clean the draperies
double-space the letter	quick-freeze the produce
air-dry the fibers	spot-check the branch stores
blue-pencil the letter	tape-record the session
water-cool the motor	cross-examine the witness
X-ray the shoulder	cross-question the attorneys

Miscellaneous compounds   Compounds with the word *sales* are not hyphenated. Some are written as one word, and some are written as two words.

salesclerk	salesperson	sales slip
salesgirl	salesroom	sales staff
salesman	saleswoman	sales talk
salespeople	sales representatives	sales tax

Use a hyphen in most compound nouns and adjectives that include a letter of the alphabet.

a T-shirt	on D-day
a T-shaped emblem	X-rated movies

Use a hyphen when two professional capacities or functions are joined in one person.

businessman-author	secretary-treasurer
lawyer-banker	actor-director

Compounds involving numbers   When they are spelled out, numbers from 21 through 99 are hyphenated.

his twenty-first birthday

seventy-five copies

In a compound number used as a proper noun, a lower-case letter follows the hyphen.

on Forty-second Street

A combination of a number and a noun is hyphenated when it precedes the noun that it modifies.

a 75-cent saving

a ten-day trip

NOTE: A hyphen is never used to connect a number to the word *percent*.

a 10 percent deduction

a one-half percent discount

Hyphens in Words with Prefixes and Suffixes

In general, words with prefixes or suffixes are not hyphenated.

anticlimax	leadership	preoccupied	reopen
biannual	nonnegotiable	readjust	reschedule
businesslike	overall	rearrange	semiannual
bylaws	overdue	reengage	semiskilled
coauthor	postwar	reexamine	undercover (adj.)
cooperate	preeminent	reiterate	underestimate
fourfold	preempt	replay	withholding

Occasionally, a hyphen is placed after a prefix to distinguish words of different meaning that would otherwise be spelled alike.

re-collect the votes	recollect what happened
re-cover the couch	recover from surgery
re-create the scene	recreate after work
re-lease the apartment	release the figures
re-count the votes	recount a story

A hyphen is usually placed between a prefix and the base word when the prefix ends with the same vowel as that with which the base word begins and the prefix has four or more letters.

anti-inflationary   semi-independent   ultra-ambitious

This pattern is not followed when the prefixes are short, as are *co-*, *non-*, *pre-*, or *re-*.

cooperative   nonnegotiable   preexisting   reelect

NOTE: Such words as *co-op, co-owner, co-publisher, co-worker,* and *de-emphasize* are hyphenated to prevent momentary misunderstanding.

A hyphen is used between a prefix or a suffix and a proper noun or proper adjective.

mid-January   pre-Elizabethan
post-World War II   Kennedy-like
     BUT
transatlantic   transpacific

Use a hyphen after the prefix *ex-* when it means "former" and before the adjectives *elect* and *designate* when they follow titles.

ex-official   President-elect Hayes
ex-president   the Senator-elect

Use a hyphen after *self-* in all but three words: *selfish, selfless, selfsame.*

self-addressed   self-confident
self-appointed   self-satisfied

End-of-Line Word Division

The following editorial rules should be applied with the aid of a standard dictionary that identifies the syllabification of words.

Do not divide a word at the end of the first line of typing, at the end of a paragraph, or at the end of a page unless the word is unusually long.

No more than two consecutive lines should end with hyphens.

Divide words only between syllables. Consult a dictionary.

Do not divide a word of one syllable.

> length   styles   through

Do not divide a word after an initial one-letter syllable.

> a·bout   about   e·nough   enough

Do not carry over to the next line a one-letter or a two-letter syllable.

> cop·y   copy   ab·so·lute·ly   abso-lutely or ab-solutely

Divide hyphenated words only at the hyphen.

> by-prod·uct   by-product
> self-re·spect   self-respect

Divide words between double consonants only when the consonants are in separate syllables, not when both belong to the root word.

> be·gin-ner   re·mit-tance
>
> **BUT**
>
> kiss-ing   purr-ing

Carry a single vowel syllable over to the next line only when it precedes a final syllable of two letters.

> read·i·ly   read-ily
> rem·e·dy   rem-edy
>
> **BUT**
>
> com·pet·i·tor   com-petitor or competi-tor
> hol·i·day   holi-day

Divide a word between two single vowel syllables unless doing so would cause confusion to the reader.

> per·pet·u·a·tor   per-petuator or perpetu-ator
>
> **BUT**
>
> mim·e·o·graph   mimeo-graph

Keep the suffixes *able*, *ible*, and *uble* intact.

> ad·vis·a·ble   ad-visable or advis-able
> re·vers·i·ble   re-versible or revers-ible
> vol·u·ble   vol-uble

Avoid a final syllable in which only a liquid *l*-sound is heard.

au·di·ble	au-dible
ici·cle	icicle
waf·fle	waffle

Compound words are divided into their separate elements.

busi·ness·man	business-man
ev·er·y·where	every-where

Acceptable Divisions in Special Cases

The following rules provide for special cases of end-of-line divisions that are acceptable to avoid conspicuous indentation of the right margin.

Dividing persons' names and titles   If a person's name or title must be divided, observe the following guidelines:

1. Keep a person's first name or initials on the same line with the person's courtesy title.

> . . . for the purpose of welcoming the director, Ms. J. C.
> Martinson, the committee . . .

2. A long title of respect or position may be separated from the name.

> . . . received a cordial invitation from the Honorable
> Jonathan B. Woodbridge of . . .

Dividing addresses   If an address must be divided, observe the following guidelines:

If the name of a street has two or more words, a separation may be made between the words.

> She moved last month to 15 Pelham / Manor Road.

Such words as *Street*, *Avenue*, and *Road* may be separated from the rest of the street address in the body of a letter.

> He said that they preferred the office at Nine Center
> Street.

Place names may be divided between the city and the state or between the state and the ZIP Code.

> Chicago / Illinois   Brooklyn, New York / 11209

If the name of a city, a state, or a country has two or more words, the division may occur between the words.

> San / Francisco   New / Jersey   West / Germany

Long state names may also be divided when necessary.

> Cali / fornia   Califor / nia

Dividing dates If it is necessary to do so, a year may be separated from the month and day. Do not use a hyphen.

> The last check you sent us was dated April 8,
> 1982.

In formal writing in which the day of the month is spelled out, separation may be made between the month and the day. Do not use a hyphen.

> They will have their fiftieth anniversary dinner on January
> twenty-seventh at the Glenn Arbor Inn.

Dividing numbers Try not to divide figures between lines. If a number of five or more figures must be divided, use a hyphen and divide only after a comma.

45,365,820   45,-   OR   45,365,-
          365,820   820

Dividing telephone numbers When it is necessary to write a telephone number on two lines, write the Area Code on one line and the rest of the number on the next line. Use a hyphen after the third digit in the number.

> Area Code 212
> 555-7780

NOTE: Abbreviations and short numbers should not be divided or separated from the elements with which they belong (*c.o.d.*, *No. 43*, *Style 998*, *4 P.M.*). Academic degree letters and the designations *Jr.*, *Sr.*, and *Esq.* should not be separated from the names to which they belong.

PARENTHESES

Parentheses ( ) usually enclose material that is related to the sentence thought, not to the sentence structure. Such material provides supplementary information or directions to the reader.

With supplementary information Use parentheses to enclose supplementary information that is related to the sentence thought but is independent of the main sentence structure.

> Mr. Roberts's company (Kenneco is the name it recently adopted) is
> showing continued strong operating performance.

Use parentheses to enclose abbreviations, dates, and explanations that provide supplementary information.

> The American Booksellers Association (ABA) will hold its seminar on
> Thursday.

> The Bicentennial (1976) was a year-long celebration.

> Their source of information (Data Retrieval System) was their most
> important communications link.

Use parentheses to enclose editorial cross-references. References that appear at the end of a sentence may be considered part of the main sentence or as a separate sentence.

> Costs rose in 1982 (Figure 10).

> Remember, verbals are not verbs. (See page 62.)

>> OR

> Remember, verbals are not verbs (see page 62).

With enumerations   Use parentheses to enclose numbers or letters in a run-on enumeration.

> Our company has two objectives: (1) It hopes to serve the public interest by making superior television available, and (2) it hopes to create a greater knowledge of our capabilities, products, and services.

> The following are the tenant's responsibilities: (a) to pay all rent due on the first of the month, (b) to keep the premises in a clean and sanitary condition, and (c) to make all utility payments on time.

With other marks   In using parentheses with other marks of punctuation, observe the following rules:

Within a sentence the first word of the enclosed material is capitalized only if it is a proper noun, a proper adjective, or the pronoun *I*.

> We understand that its overseas growth (I have just learned of its new plant in Milan) has been remarkable.

When a question or an exclamation is enclosed in parentheses, a question mark or an exclamation point is placed before the closing parenthesis. No punctuation follows the closing parenthesis.

> The landscaping of Bloomfield Hills Park (you were the designer of the gardens, were you not?) is receiving national acclaim.

A question mark enclosed in parentheses expresses doubt about the word, figure, or statement preceding it.

> The two companies merged in 1965 (?) and moved to New Jersey.

When material enclosed in parentheses is not part of another sentence, the first word begins with a capital letter, and the appropriate end punctuation is placed before the closing parenthesis.

> The annual meeting was held in Memphis. (A copy of the program is enclosed.)

Within a sentence never place a punctuation mark before the opening parenthesis. Place any punctuation required at that point after the closing parenthesis.

> If we should decide to send an exhibit (our plan to do so is quite uncertain), we will telephone you.

PERIODS

The period (.) is the most frequently used mark of end punctuation.

To end a sentence Use a period at the end of a sentence that states a fact or an indirect question, gives a command, or requests an action.

>The director agreed with your assessment. (fact)
>
>She asked which memo contained the relevant information. (indirect question)
>
>Put your requests in my box before noon on Friday. (command)
>
>Will you please return the enclosed form before January 15. (request)

With abbreviations Despite the trend toward expressing abbreviations without periods, certain types of abbreviations, such as courtesy titles, academic degrees, and professional designations, retain the use of periods.

>Mr. John Adams   Diane Namm, M.A.   Ann Martin, M.D.

With initials Use a period after each initial in a person's name.

>Mr. A. L. Collins   E. F. Hutton

In lists and topical outlines Use a period after numbers and letters in a tabulation or topical outline except those enclosed in whole or half parentheses.

>I. Educational facilities
>>A. Expansion
>>>1. Public schools
>>>>a. Centralization
>>>>b. Departmentalization
>>>>>(1) Central school
>>>>>(2) Annexes
>>>>>>(a) Rehabilitation
>>>>>>(b) New buildings
>>>>>>>1) New equipment
>>>>>>>2) Repairs to old equipment
>>>2. Private schools
>>B. Students
>II. Recommendations

Use a period after each independent clause in a tabulation or topical outline.

>A good training program is designed to serve a number of purposes:
>>1. It supplements academic training with technical skills.
>>2. It introduces the trainee to company policies and procedures.

The use of a period after the last item in a tabulation or topical outline of words, phrases, or dependent clauses is optional. Be consistent within a given text.

>These topics will be discussed on March 16:
>>1. Our fiscal policy
>>2. The role of taxes
>>3. Anticipated expenditures. (period optional)

QUESTION MARKS

Question marks (?) follow interrogative sentences or expressions.

After direct questions Use a question mark after direct requests for information.

> Will you be able to attend next month's meeting?

Use a question mark after each question in a series of short interrogations, even if they are elliptical.

> We might ask these questions: Is the product appealing? Is it convincing? Is it reasonably priced?
>
> OR
>
> We might ask these questions: Is the product appealing? Convincing? Reasonably priced?

Questions within sentences Use a question mark after independent questions that appear within a larger sentence. Capitalize the first word of the question.

> The question Why do homework? sparked a lively discussion.

NOTE: Do not use a question mark after an indirect question.

> She asked whether you had finished the report.

Use a question mark after a question enclosed in parentheses within a longer sentence.

> His latest book (did you see the review in last Sunday's *Times*?) is selling very well.

Use a question mark after a question quoted within a longer sentence. The question mark is placed inside the quotation marks because it is part of the quoted material.

> Whenever he asks, "Has anyone seen my keys?" we all groan.

Use a question mark at the end of sentences that contain an added or inserted direct question.

> You were present for her talk, weren't you?

To express doubt Use a question mark enclosed in parentheses to express doubt about a preceding word, figure, or statement.

> The two companies merged in 1965 (?) and moved to New Jersey.

With polite requests A *polite request* refers to a question to which no direct answer is expected. The phrasing of the request as a question is intended to suggest an action. Such requests often begin with *May we, Will you, Won't you.* The use of a question mark instead of a period is often preferred. When a direct answer to the question is expected, a question mark must be used.

Polite request with either a period or a question mark:

> Will you please let us have your decision immediately.

Question requiring an answer; question mark required:

> May we have our salesman call?

QUOTATION MARKS

Quotation marks (" ") are used to indicate the actual words of a speaker or writer.

Direct quotations   Use quotation marks to enclose the exact words of a speaker or writer. Use a comma or a pair of commas to set off the source of a direct quotation. Notice that the concluding period in each example falls within the quotation.

> Mr. Decker said, "The board will meet tomorrow at 10 A.M."
>
> "The educational value of the film," he continued, "is remarkable."

Use a colon after a formal introduction to a quotation or after the introduction to a quotation of more than one sentence. *Spoke thus, said in part, as follows, the following,* and *stated* are examples of formal introductions to quotations.

> The President continued as follows: "Much will depend on you, the citizens of our nation, who . . ."
>
> Our architect, Mr. Wells, wrote: "When one specifies such quality products, an $80,000 house will rise in cost by $10,000. The additional cost will result in increased monthly mortgage payments."

If a direct quotation at the beginning of a sentence is a question or an exclamation, a question mark or an exclamation point instead of a comma follows the quotation.

> "Will the board meet tomorrow at ten?" Mr. Decker asked.

Indirect quotations   Do not use quotation marks for indirect quotations.

> He said that he would attend.

Long quotations   When a quotation consists of four or more lines, it should be presented as a separate paragraph with quotation marks at the beginning and at the end of the paragraph.

Consecutive paragraphs of quoted material may be presented in either of two ways:

1. With quotation marks at the beginning of each paragraph and with closing quotation marks placed only at the end of the quotation or
2. Without quotation marks but indented from the left and right margins and centered a double space below the paragraph above.

Titles   Use quotation marks to indicate the title of a chapter, short story, or poem. Use underscoring for the titles of a book, magazine, or other large work.

> "Punctuation," Chapter IV of this book, is one you will refer to often.

"The Cask of Amontillado" is anthologized in A Treasury of Short Stories.

Quotations within quotations   Use single quotation marks (' ') for a quotation appearing within another quotation.

> "Then I heard her ask, 'Is this the way to Portland?' "

Special expressions   Use quotation marks to enclose the following:

Coined words, slang, or words used out of context

> The government may soon "lower the boom" on that industry.
>
> We refer to him as our "Monday-morning quarterback."

Technical terms used in nontechnical writing

> My course in word processing included "hands-on" training.

Definitions

> The word *nice* should be reserved to mean "delicate, precise, characterized by discrimination."

Slogans, mottoes, or other familiar quotations

> "All's well that ends well" was his only comment.
>
> My first thought was "There goes the ball game."

Notations quoted from signs, packages, and papers of various kinds. Such notations are enclosed in quotation marks but are not set off by commas. Each word in the notation begins with a capital letter.

> The letter was returned with "Address Unknown" stamped on it.
>
> Please write "Paid" on these bills.

Omissions in quoted material   Part of a quotation may be omitted if the omission is indicated by a mark of ellipsis (. . .). Three periods plus the closing punctuation mark indicate that an omission occurs at the end of the quoted sentence.

> Mr. Hart said in his letter: "The staff is well-qualified to make an analysis of . . . prevailing wage rates. . . ."
>
> He concluded: "What more could we hope for . . . ?"

With other marks   A period and a comma are always placed inside the closing quotation marks.

> "Your terms are acceptable," he wrote.
>
> The check was marked "Account Closed."

A colon and a semicolon are always placed outside the closing quotation marks.

> The check is marked "Account Closed"; however, I am sure that an error has been made.

A question mark and an exclamation point are placed inside the closing quotation marks if they refer to just the quoted material or if they refer to the quoted material and to the sentence as a whole. Never use one of these marks and a period at the end of a sentence.

> Mr. Barnes asked, "Can you ship the copper tubing this week?"

> How pleased we were to hear you say, "A remarkable achievement!"

A question mark and an exclamation point are placed outside the quotation marks if they refer to the sentence as a whole but not to the quoted material.

> Did he say, "We consider its styling to be the reason for its success"?

SEMICOLONS

A semicolon (;) is used to indicate a stronger break in thought than a comma would indicate.

Between independent clauses without a coordinate conjunction Use a semicolon to separate two closely related independent clauses when a coordinate conjunction does not join them.

> The radios were shipped today; the television sets will be shipped tomorrow.

> The State Senate has two members on the committee; the State Assembly, four.

> This morning the personnel manager interviewed three applicants; this afternoon, two.

> These campers are easy to tow; furthermore, they are comfortable.

Between punctuated independent clauses When either or both clauses contain punctuation and a comma before the coordinate conjunction does not seem to be a strong enough break or could cause misreading, use a semicolon before the coordinate conjunction.

> The State Senate has two members on the committee; and the State Assembly, four.

> I will arrive in Kalamazoo on Wednesday, October 16; and on Thursday, October 17, I will call you to discuss your proposal.

In a series When the items in a series already contain commas, use semicolons to separate the items from each other. Place the last semicolon before the conjunction.

> Invitations have come from Houston, Texas; Omaha, Nebraska; Lynchburg, Virginia; and several Eastern cities.

> Monday, January 2; Tuesday, January 3; and Wednesday, January 4, have been set for the hearings.

> The officers we elected were Mr. John M. Scott, president; Mr. James Barry, vice-president; and Mr. Roger Ashe, secretary-treasurer.

CHAPTER V
EFFECTIVE BUSINESS WRITING

A few years ago interviewers from *Fortune* magazine asked successful business executives the following question: "What kind of training best prepares business school students to succeed in their careers?" The answer? "Teach them to write better."

Business writing that is wordy and confusing is damaging to the image of the sender and expensive in terms of time and materials. Even the cost of a well-written business letter constantly increases as salaries rise and postage and stationery go up in price. Despite the cost, however, business letters are often the best means of communication. Several facts support the usefulness of letters and other written communications in business.

- A written communication provides a permanent record of the facts it contains.

- A written communication can be duplicated and sent to any number of people.

- Because it can be planned, revised, and edited, a written communication is often clearer, more forceful, and therefore more effective than oral communication.

This chapter discusses the principles and techniques essential to writing an effective business communication.

Every written business communication should be . . .

Clear Business writing should be easy to read and should ensure effortless understanding of the message that it contains.

Correct Business writing should contain accurate information and should follow accepted standards of grammar, spelling, punctuation, and sentence construction.

Complete Business writing should include all essential information and should be sufficiently detailed to be clear.

Concise Business writing should be free of nonessential detail, containing only what is necessary for completeness, clarity, and courtesy.

Courteous Business writing should be friendly in tone without being informal, should show good will and an understanding of the reader's viewpoint, and should reflect a sincere wish to be helpful.

The following "Five Steps" will help the business writer to produce communications that are clear, correct, complete, concise, and courteous.

FIVE STEPS IN WRITING A BUSINESS COMMUNICATION

1. Plan the communication by thinking about the topic and gathering the pertinent facts. Before beginning to write, answer these questions.

   Topic: What is the topic of your communication?
   Message: What do you want to say about the topic?
   Reader: To whom is your message directed?
   Purpose: Why are you writing this communication?
   Essential details: How? When? Where? How much?

2. Organize the facts by numbering them (1, 2, 3, and so forth) according to the order of their importance. The topic of a communication will always be first in importance.

3. Write the first draft, expressing the facts in sentences and paragraphs. Follow the order determined in step 2. Write quickly and naturally.

4. Rewrite according to the principles of effective writing discussed in the remainder of this chapter. Edit for tone, transition, sense, and vocabulary. If possible, leave some time between writing the first draft and rewriting. Read the work aloud so that you can hear what you have written.

5. Type the communication and proofread for the following:

   > completeness and accuracy of information
   > spelling
   > punctuation
   > style points
   > spacing
   > general appearance

You may wish to have a second reader proofread the finished communication as a final check.

The five steps outlined above describe the process that business writers use to produce effective letters. However, to use this five-step process most effectively, it is important to understand the principles of organization that underlie any well-constructed piece of writing—namely, organize the whole, write effective sentences, build unified paragraphs, choose the right words, and set the appropriate tone.

ORGANIZE THE WHOLE

Be aware of the structure of the whole communication. Have a beginning, middle, and end to the presentation. Determine the main point. State the main point in the beginning, and sustain it throughout the communication. Develop the subject in the middle. Summarize it in the end, or recommend a course of action. Be specific and clear. Include transitions. Subordinate less important material to more important. Eliminate anything that does not belong in the communication.

The beginning, middle, and conclusion of the communication may correspond to the following example:

- **Beginning:** What is the message?
- **Middle:** What do I want to say about that message?
- **Conclusion:** What will I do about that message?

OR

What am I asking the reader to do about that message?

Beginning Section

The opening paragraph is the most important paragraph in a communication. It should tell the reader clearly and concisely what the communication is about.

The opening sentence of the first paragraph should be a strong and positive one. This "headline" position should never be given to an introductory participial or prepositional phrase, such as *Answering your inquiry, Acknowledging your letter, In reference to (In response to, Regarding) your letter.* Similarly, the phrases *We have received your letter* and *Your letter has been received* should not occupy the important first-sentence position, since the fact that the letter is being answered is evidence that it was received.

A necessary reference to the date of a letter being answered should be placed in a dependent clause or in a phrase.

> Your Sylvania Early American console, about which you asked in your letter of April 16, will be sent to you early next week.

When the date is unimportant, it should be omitted.

> Your Sylvania Early American console will be sent to you early next week.

Middle Section

The middle section of a communication develops the message by providing explanatory or supporting facts. This middle section may consist of more than one paragraph. In a lengthy report, for example, there may be a number of paragraphs in the middle section, and these paragraphs may have an order within the larger whole. For instance, chronological order or order of importance might be appropriate to the middle section of a communication.

Conclusion

The concluding paragraph of a communication should perform one or more of the following functions:

Express a forward-looking conclusion.

> If I have not heard from you by June 25, I will call your office to inquire about the status of my application.

Express good will.

> You have our best wishes for success with your seminar.

Briefly summarize the action you expect the reader to take.

> Your evaluation of Plan B, which we would like to receive before May 17, will assist the Program Committee in completing its preparations for the annual board meeting. Mrs. Kelley and I will be very grateful for this help.

WRITE EFFECTIVE SENTENCES

Effective sentences use the basic techniques of good writing. These techniques, as explained and illustrated below, will result in sentences that are unified, concise, and logical. In addition, such sentences will be clearly and correctly punctuated and will provide a variety of patterns from which the writer can choose.

Write Unified Sentences

Unified sentences express one complete thought or use coordination to connect closely related and equally important thoughts.

> Yesterday I interviewed Carla Benson, a former employee of your organization.
>
> **OR**
>
> Yesterday I interviewed Carla Benson, a former employee of your organization, and I was impressed by her attitude and her skills.

Simplify Clauses and Phrases

To achieve conciseness in writing, reduce clauses and phrases to simpler constructions.

Change compound sentences to simple sentences.

> COMPOUND: We will accept the returned motor, and we will credit your account.
>
> SIMPLE: We will accept the returned motor and credit your account.

Change dependent clauses to phrases.

> DEPENDENT CLAUSE: Mail the card today so that you will not miss the first issue of *Keynotes*.
>
> PHRASE: Mail the card today to avoid missing the first issue of *Keynotes*.

Change dependent clauses to appositives.

> DEPENDENT CLAUSE: The No. 5, which is our best grade, is $3 a yard.
>
> APPOSITIVE: The No. 5, our best grade, is $3 a yard.

Change dependent clauses or phrases to one-word adjectives or adverbial modifiers.

> DEPENDENT CLAUSE: We appreciate the suggestions that you sent us.
>
> ADJECTIVE: We appreciate your suggestions.
>
> PHRASE: She spoke with confidence about her plans for the revision.
>
> ADVERB: She spoke confidently about her plans for the revision.

Vary Sentence Structure

> SIMPLE: Because of its excellent reputation, their school attracts many students.
>
> COMPOUND: Their school has an excellent reputation, and therefore it attracts many students.
>
> COMPLEX: Their school, which has an excellent reputation, attracts many students.

To emphasize an important thought, use a simple sentence.

> Puerto Rico is a pleasant vacation spot.

To emphasize that two or more thoughts are closely related and equally important, use a compound sentence.

> Puerto Rico is a pleasant vacation spot, and it attracts many visitors.

Use Transitional Words and Expressions

Transitional words and expressions link two thoughts by clearly pointing to the relationship between them.

> TRANSITIONAL WORDS: She is alert and intelligent; she claims, *however*, that the ability to concentrate is the key to her success.

It is not necessary or desirable to use a transitional word in every sentence. Pronouns, synonyms, and summary words and phrases also connect sentences and lend variety to a communication.

> TRANSITIONAL PRONOUNS: *Bermuda* is a pleasant spot, and *it* attracts many visitors.
>
> SYNONYMS: We hope you will enjoy using your new *IBM typewriter*. *This machine* has . . .
>
> This course will introduce you to the *authors* of the Lost Generation. You will meet such *writers* as Ernest Hemingway and F. Scott Fitzgerald.
>
> SUMMARY WORDS AND PHRASES: We suggest that you consider opening schools on the West Coast. *This expansion* . . .

Begin Sentences With a Phrase or Clause

> DEGREE-RESULT CLAUSES: The sooner you make your reservation, the more certain of comfortable accommodations you will be.
>
> INTRODUCTORY ADVERBIAL CLAUSE: *When you are making your flight reservation*, please specify first-class or tourist.

PREPOSITIONAL-GERUND PHRASE: *By making your reservations now,* you will be assured first-class accommodations.

INTRODUCTORY INFINITIVE PHRASE: *To be assured of a flight reservation,* reconfirm it before noon on Monday.

PARTICIPIAL ABSOLUTE PHRASE: *Flight reservations being in demand,* we suggest that you make your arrangements early in the fall.

INTRODUCTORY ADVERB: *Finally,* we agreed to meet with the reporter.

Avoid Overburdened Sentences

INCORRECT: Yesterday I interviewed Carla Benson, a former employee of your organization, and was impressed by her attitude and skills, and I am considering hiring her because I need a pleasant and efficient person as secretary-receptionist in our main office.

CORRECT: Miss Carla Benson, a former employee of your organization, has applied for the position of secretary-receptionist in our main office. [*one main thought*] I interviewed Miss Benson yesterday, and I was impressed by her attitude and her skills. [*two closely related thoughts*]

Subordinate Less Important Material

To emphasize that one thought is more important than a related thought, express the more important one in an independent clause and the less important one in a dependent clause, a phrase, or an appositive.

DEPENDENT CLAUSE: *Because Puerto Rico is a pleasant vacation spot,* it attracts many visitors.

INFINITIVE PHRASE: *To attract visitors,* Puerto Rico offers excellent package plans.

APPOSITIVE: Puerto Rico, *a pleasant vacation spot,* attracts many visitors.

Punctuate Correctly

Avoid sentence fragments, groups of words that do not express complete thoughts.

FRAGMENT: Because I need a pleasant and efficient person.

SENTENCE: I need a pleasant and efficient person.

Avoid run-on sentences, sentences that run into each other because of missing or incorrect punctuation.

RUN-ON: Yesterday I interviewed Carla Benson, I was impressed by her attitude and by her skills.

NOTE: When a run-on sentence is the result of the misuse of a comma to connect independent clauses (see the example above), the error involved is frequently referred to as "comma fault" or "comma splice."

Correct run-on sentences in the following ways:

> Yesterday I interviewed Carla Benson, and I . . . (comma with coordinate conjunction)
>
> Yesterday I interviewed Carla Benson; I . . . (semicolon)
>
> Yesterday I interviewed Carla Benson. I . . . (two sentences)

Use Parallelism

Parallelism in writing means that similar ideas are expressed in similar grammatical constructions. The effective use of parallelism in sentences enables the reader to grasp quickly the relationship between similar facts or ideas.

Parallelism of structure

> INCORRECT: The antiques on display are neither appealing nor of value.

(The conjunction is joining an adjective to a prepositional phrase.)

> CORRECT: The antiques on display are neither appealing nor valuable.

(The conjunctions are joining similar constructions—adjectives.)

> INCORRECT: She told me *to request a cash advance and that I should call her when I receive it.*

(The conjunction is connecting an infinitive phrase to a noun clause.)

> CORRECT: She told me *to request a cash advance and to call her when I receive it.*

(The conjunction is joining similar constructions—infinitive phrases.)

> INCORRECT: You can both use your telephone credit card when you are at home and when you travel.

(One part of the correlative conjunction precedes a verb, and the other part precedes an adverbial clause.)

> CORRECT: You can use your telephone credit card both when you are at home and when you travel.

(Each part of the correlative conjunction precedes an adverbial clause.)

Parallelism of ideas

> INCORRECT: He changed the reel on the machine and changed his mind about retiring early.

(The conjunction *and* is connecting the same constructions, but these constructions express ideas that have no logical relationship to each other.)

> CORRECT: He changed the reel on the machine and lowered the volume.

(The conjunction *and* connects the same constructions, and these constructions express logically related ideas.)

> INCORRECT: Not only is she a good stenographer, but also her typing is excellent.

(Don't connect a fact about a person to a fact about her typing.)

> CORRECT: She is not only a good stenographer but also an excellent typist.

(Each part of the conjunction precedes the same structure and logically related ideas, facts about a person.)

> OR
> CORRECT: Not only are her shorthand skills good, but her typing is excellent.

(Each part of the conjunction precedes logically related ideas, facts about a person's skills.)

Avoid Misplaced and Dangling Constructions

Phrases and clauses should be placed as close as possible to the word or words they modify.

> DANGLING PHRASE: To complete the questionnaire, a great deal of research will be necessary.

(The infinitive phrase dangles: There is no logical doer of the action.)

> CORRECT: To complete the questionnaire, we will have to do a great deal of research.

(The infinitive phrase precedes the word *we,* the logical doer.)

> MISPLACED PHRASE: Winston Churchill celebrated his birthday by eating a 30-pound birthday cake along with his grandchildren.

(This sentence attributes cannibalistic tendencies to Churchill.)

> CORRECT: Winston Churchill, along with his grandchildren, celebrated his birthday by eating a 30-pound cake.

BUILD UNIFIED PARAGRAPHS

A paragraph is unified when it relates to one aspect of a message and when every sentence in the paragraph develops that one aspect.

Because long paragraphs look formidable to the reader, the paragraphs in business writing should be short (three to five sentences). Keeping a paragraph short means that it may sometimes be necessary to treat one aspect of a message in two separate paragraphs. Be sure, however, to divide paragraphs at a logical point.

CHOOSE THE RIGHT WORDS

Choose precise, natural-sounding words. Avoid jargon and clichés. Be concise. Use strong verbs and clear pronoun references. Be consistent in number, tense, and voice.

Omit unnecessary words and phrases, such as those enclosed in parentheses in the following list.

at (the hour of) six	the (matter of) cost
because (of the fact that)	proved (to be) accurate
came (at a time) when	revert (back)
consensus (of opinion)	small (in size)
during (the course of) the discussion	smaller than we expected (it to be)
	(temporarily) suspended
five (in number) were	throughout (the year of) 1979
for (the purpose of)	(true) fact
(in order) to	until (such time as) we can
neat (in appearance)	warn (beforehand)
postpone (until later)	

Use short, natural-sounding words instead of long, indirect expressions.

Instead of	Say
a check in the amount of	a check for
at all times	always
at the present time, at the time of writing	now
due to the fact that	because of
during the time that	while
give consideration to	consider
inasmuch as	as
in the event that	if
in view of the fact that	because
I wish to bring to your attention	Please note
previous to, prior to	before
put in an appearance	came
under separate cover	separately

Choose the better known of two words, and use more one-syllable words than words of two or three syllables.

Instead of	Say
ostensibly	apparently
cognizant	aware
initiate	begin
discrepancy	difference
expiration	end
terminated	ended

sufficient	enough
equivalent	equal
commensurate with	equal to
equitable	fair
finalize	finish
initial	first
procure	get
render	give
preclude	prevent
transmit	send
minimal, nominal	small
recapitulate	summarize
endeavor	try
utilize	use
communicate	write, telephone

Use specific instead of general words.

Instead of	Say
furniture	chairs
	desks
	tables
office equipment	desk
	file
	typewriter
employee	secretary
	salesperson
merchandise	boots
	shoes
	belts
color	aqua
	burgundy
contact	write
	telephone
feel	think
	believe
	am confident
get	receive
	obtain
	acquire
do	write
	type
	research

Use modern English instead of so-called business jargon.

Instead of	Say
per (*as in* $4 per dozen)	a *or* an ($4 a dozen; 23 patients an hour)
concerning in reference to in regard to regarding relative to with respect to	about
in compliance with your request pursuant to your request	as you requested
line	business trade profession
per (as in a letter signature)	by (United Aircraft, Incorporated, By James A. Allen)
under separate cover	separately by airmail, by messenger
are (not) in a position to	can cannot
enclosed please find attached hereto enclosed herewith	enclosed is, I have enclosed, the enclosed pamphlet
acknowledge receipt of are in receipt of	have received
encounter difficulty	have trouble
the undersigned the writer	I
same	it they them
communication	letter telegram
proposition	plan proposal
kindly	please
do not hesitate	please
our Mr. Baldwin	Mr. Baldwin our attorney our representative
said plan said person	this *or* that plan this *or* that person

at an early date	soon,
by return mail	today,
in due course	tomorrow
in due time	
at your convenience	
in the near future	
we regret to say	we are sorry

Avoid sexual bias in the use of language. Whenever possible, choose words that do not contain *man* and *woman* as elements.

Instead of	Say
businessman, businesswoman	business executive, manager
chairman, chairwoman	chairperson, moderator
clergyman	member of the clergy priest minister rabbi
delivery boy	messenger courier
fireman	firefighter
foreman	supervisor manager
gentleman's agreement	unwritten agreement
girl Friday	secretary assistant
the girls (for females over age eighteen)	the women
ladylike	well-mannered
lady of the house	head of the household
housewife	homemaker
mailman	mail carrier
man-hours	total hours, staff hours, working hours
mankind	humanity human race
man-made	synthetic, manufactured
manpower	human resources human energy workers
policeman	police officer

repairman	maintenance person
handyman	carpenter
	electrician
salesman	salesperson
	sales clerk
stewardess, steward	flight attendant
workman	laborer
	worker

Use Pronouns Correctly

Use clear antecedents for pronouns   The antecedent to which a pronoun refers should be immediately clear to the reader.

> INCORRECT: The benefits are excellent. They said that I would have six days' vacation every six months.

(*They* has no clear antecedent. Either give *they* an antecedent, or replace it with a noun.)

> CORRECT: Mr. Bronson assured me that the benefits are excellent. *He* said . . .

(*He* clearly refers to the antecedent *Mr. Bronson.*)

> OR

> CORRECT: The benefits are excellent. *Mr. Bronson* said that . . .

(The use of the noun *Mr. Bronson* eliminates the need for an antecedent.)

Use correct pronoun references   A pronoun takes the place of a noun or of another pronoun, not of an idea.

> INCORRECT: The train was delayed, which caused our late arrival.

> CORRECT: The train delay caused our late arrival.

> OR

> CORRECT: The train was delayed. This delay caused our late arrival.

> INCORRECT: I arrived home at 3 A.M. This infuriated my father.

> CORRECT: My arriving home at 3 A.M. infuriated my father.

> OR

> CORRECT: My father was furious because I arrived home at 3 A.M.

Avoid incorrect shifts in person and number

This example illustrates an incorrect shift in number.

> INCORRECT: Yesterday I interviewed Carla Benson, a former employee of your organization, and we were impressed by her attitude and skills.

> CORRECT: Yesterday I interviewed Carla Benson, a former employee of your organization, and I was impressed by her attitude and skills.

This example illustrates an incorrect shift in person and in number.

INCORRECT: If one really wants to succeed, you can often do so.

CORRECT: If you really want to succeed, you can often do so.

Avoid Incorrect Shifts in Verb Tense

This example illustrates an incorrect shift in tense.

INCORRECT: Only a single window opened onto the street; the back has generous windows and doors.

CORRECT: Only a single window opens onto the street; the back has generous windows and doors.

OR

CORRECT: Only a single window opened onto the street; the back had generous windows and doors.

Avoid Incorrect Shifts in Voice

This example illustrates an incorrect shift to the passive voice.

INCORRECT: We shipped the dishes today, and glasses will be sent to you next week.

CORRECT: We shipped the dishes today, and we will send you the glasses next week.

OR

CORRECT: The dishes were shipped today, and the glasses will be sent to you next week.

Use Strong Verbs to Make Sentences Emphatic and Direct

Instead of	Say
made an adjustment	adjusted
made an announcement	announced
came to the conclusion	concluded
gave consideration to	considered
made him a loan	lent
held a meeting	met
raised an objection	objected
made an offer of (to)	offered
placed an order	ordered
gave some thought to	thought about

Avoid Indirect Expressions

May I suggest that . . . You do not need permission to make a statement. Express your requests and suggestions in a polite, direct manner.

Please send me . . .

I suggest that you . . .

I (We) wonder whether . . . Be direct.

> INSTEAD OF: We wonder whether you will take the chairmanship.
>
> SAY: Will you take the chairmanship? Are you willing to take the chairmanship? Can you take the chairmanship?

Express Appreciation Appropriately

Thank you again . . . Once is enough. Don't repeat what you have already clearly stated.

Thank you in advance for . . . Express appreciation in the present tense after a request has been granted. Before a request has been granted, express appreciation in the conditional (use *should* or *would*): Your being grateful is based on the condition that the request be granted.

Before the request has been granted, say

> I would appreciate your sending me an autographed copy of your latest book.

After the request has been granted, say

> I appreciate your sending me an autographed copy of your latest book.

Before the request has been granted, say

> I would be grateful for the opportunity to discuss this matter in person.

After the request has been granted, say

> I am grateful to you for giving me the opportunity to discuss this matter in person.

Use Clear Connections

Clear, precise connections between sentence parts tie ideas together smoothly and logically.

> INCORRECT: We looked forward to meeting him, and he canceled at the last minute.

(The conjunction *and* does not express the contrast that the sentence was intended to convey.)

> CORRECT: We looked forward to meeting him, but he canceled at the last minute.

(The conjunction *but* properly expresses the contrast between the two facts it connects.)

> INCORRECT: She enjoys using her shorthand, while I prefer typing.

(The conjunction *while* is incorrectly used to express the contrast between the two facts. *While* is correctly used when it expresses simultaneous time.)

> CORRECT: She enjoys using her shorthand, whereas I prefer typing.

(The conjunction *whereas* correctly expresses the intended contrast between the two facts.)

SET THE APPROPRIATE TONE

Tone reflects the writer's attitude toward the reader. Acknowledge the dignity of the reader by making the tone of the communication reader-centered. Write in a manner that is courteous and natural. Prefer the active to the passive voice to achieve directness. If a negative statement is necessary, subordinate it to a positive thought. Include personal comments only when they are appropriate.

Keep the Reader in Mind

Whenever it is possible to do so without writing awkward sentences, use the pronouns *you* and *your* instead of *I, my, we,* and *our.* Following this guideline, especially in your first paragraph, will produce writing that is reader-centered.

> INSTEAD OF: I was attracted by your advertisement in Sunday's *Boston Globe* for the book *Aunt Pasta's Italian Specialties.*
>
> SAY: Your advertisement in Sunday's *Boston Globe* for the book *Aunt Pasta's Italian Specialties* attracted my attention.
>
> INSTEAD OF: I want you to know that your talk on the opportunities available to today's secretaries was both enjoyable and informative.
>
> SAY: Your talk on the opportunities available to today's secretaries was both enjoyable and informative.

Be careful to avoid a forced, unnatural opening sentence. Do not start a letter with *you, your,* or the topic if such a beginning results in a stiff, heavy, passive construction. Do start with *I, my, we,* or *our* when doing so produces a more natural and effective sentence.

> We have decided that it is time to give our letterhead a new look and would like you to design it for us.

Keep the Tone Positive

Stress what is and what can be.

Negative	Positive
Unless you take reasonable care, these playsuits cannot be washed without fading.	With reasonable care you can wash these playsuits dozens of times, and their colors will stay as bright as ever.
These jeans are not the kind that sag or stretch out of shape.	These jeans will retain their shape and fit.

The Negative Letter

Business letters should have a positive tone whenever possible, but they cannot always avoid negative statements. Denying a request, refusing an invitation, or pointing out defects in workmanship or dissatisfaction with service may actually be the purpose of a letter. In handling such material, keep the following points in mind:

1. Every letter has an important underlying purpose: to create or sustain good will and to make a favorable impression on the reader.

   Keeping that purpose in mind might lead, for example, to a brief expression of previous satisfaction with products and service. In addition, the closing paragraph might include an expression of confidence that the present difficulty will be settled satisfactorily.

2. Reserve the opening and closing paragraph positions for positive statements. In refusing an invitation to be a guest speaker, for instance, use the first paragraph to express appreciation to the reader for having extended the invitation to you.

3. When using a negative-sounding word, such as *unfortunately*, place it within the sentence.

   AVOID: Unfortunately, Miss Grayson will not be available.

   PREFERRED: Miss Grayson will, unfortunately, not be available at the time of your meeting.

The Editorial *We*

When a letter is written on behalf of a company or organization, the use of the editorial *we (our, us)* is appropriate, although not necessary. The use of *we* indicates to the reader that the contents of the letter have the support and approval of the company and are not just the thoughts and opinions of the individual.

Use the Active Voice

To write sentences that are direct and concise, use the active voice. When a verb is in the active voice, the subject performs the action. Using the active voice makes writing more vivid and more interesting. In addition, the active voice automatically makes writing more concise: It always takes more words to express an idea in the passive voice than it takes to express that same idea in the active voice.

   PASSIVE: Thirty-five minutes can be saved when you fly to Mapleton.

   ACTIVE: You can save 35 minutes by flying to Mapleton.

The passive voice is not incorrect but should be used carefully and deliberately. It is wordier, less direct, and less vivid than the active voice. However, it is correct and appropriate when the emphasis is on the receiver of an action.

If, for example, a customer has inquired about the delay in the delivery of a set of dishes and a set of glasses, a response might read as follows:

   Your dishes were shipped today, and your glasses will be shipped on Thursday.

CHAPTER VI

MODEL LETTERS:

EXAMPLES OF WRITTEN COMMUNICATION FOR BUSINESS PURPOSES

Audience, purpose, and amount of subject matter determine the form of a communication, which may be a memorandum, a letter, or a report. The memorandum is the preferred form of informal written communication within an organization. When the writer's purpose is more formal or the communication is directed to someone outside the organization, a letter is the appropriate form. A lengthy presentation of a subject involving research is usually written in the form of a report. This chapter provides examples of letters and memorandums.

Social Invitation

Topic, background of request, and reader involvement

The members of the Social Committee at Katharine Gibbs School in Norwalk invite you to attend a farewell dinner for Carol Lane on Friday, December 6. Carol has decided to make Los Angeles her permanent home and will leave for the West Coast sometime next month.

Essential facts amplifying the topic

The December 6 activities will take place at the Silvermine Tavern in Norwalk (see enclosed map) and will begin with a cocktail hour at 5:30. For dinner you will be able to choose any item on the regular menu. After dinner we will give Carol a gift from all of us to thank her for making our work so much easier and to wish her success in her new job.

A forward-looking conclusion and an expression of good will

If you plan to join us, please send a check for $15, payable to Katharine Gibbs School, to Mrs. Ann Mason, treasurer of the Social Committee, by Friday, November 27. I know that Carol would be happy to see you, and I hope that you will be with us on December 6.

Request for an Adjustment
(in the form of a claim letter)

Topic, background of request, and reader involvement

The copy of *Technology in the Office of the 21st Century*, which I ordered from you on August 15, has not yet arrived. However, I did receive a bill for it on September 4. Can you explain the delay in my receipt of the book?

Essential facts amplifying the topic	The invoice number on the bill you sent me was 763248. The bill was dated September 1 and included the price of the book ($18.95) plus a postage charge of one dollar ($1). I planned to pay the bill as soon as I received the book.
A forward-looking conclusion and an expression of good will	Because your company has an excellent reputation, I am confident that you will trace this order at once and that I will receive a copy of *Technology in the Office of the 21st Century* within the next few weeks.

The preceding letter, frequently called a claim letter, points out the importance of the following:

- Including all specific details relevant to the topic
- Avoiding a negative tone
- Expressing confidence that the matter will be handled promptly and satisfactorily.

Request for an Appointment
(in the form of a job application letter)

Topic, background, and reader involvement	Your advertisement in last Sunday's *Times* for an administrative assistant to the president of Alamo Paper Products describes the type of job I have been looking for. I will be in Houston on vacation during the week of March 12. Would you be able to give me an interview appointment sometime that week?
Essential facts amplifying the topic	The enclosed résumé will give you the highlights of my education and experience. In addition, _____ _____.
A forward-looking conclusion and expression of appreciation should the request be granted	Please feel free to write to me at the above address or to call me at _____. If I have not heard from you by March 9, I will call your office on Monday, the 12th. I would sincerely appreciate having the opportunity to visit your company and to discuss the job of administrative assistant and my qualifications for it.

Request for Information

Topic, background, and reader involvement	Your excellent reputation as chairperson of the Business English Department at Mannix College has prompted me to request your help. Would you please recommend to me an up-to-date book on business English?
Essential facts amplifying the topic	I work in the Word Processing Center here at Chipps-Foley, where I do a great deal of proofreading. A reference book that covers punctuation, capitalization, number expression, and usage would help me do my work more quickly and more efficiently.

A forward-looking conclusion

Please write to me at the above address with any suggestions you may have. I would sincerely appreciate your help.

It is not appropriate to assume a response or, therefore, to thank someone in advance. Use the conditional *I would appreciate* since the request has not yet been granted.

Request for Reservations

Topic, background, and reader involvement

Our president, Mr. Carl Haas, would like to reserve accommodations at your hotel for the three nights of his stay in Atlanta: Monday, April 4; Tuesday, April 5; and Wednesday, April 6.

Essential facts amplifying the topic

Mr. Haas will arrive at the Carlton on April 4 before 6 P.M. and will depart on April 7 at noon. While at the Carlton, he will require a living room and bedroom suite. In addition, he will need the use of a small conference room (15–20 people) on Wednesday, April 6, from 2 P.M. until 5 P.M.

A forward-looking conclusion and expression of appreciation should the reader respond promptly

Please send me as soon as possible the following information:

Confirmation of this reservation

Cost of the requested accommodations

Amount of an advance deposit if necessary.

I would sincerely appreciate receiving a prompt response to this request.

This letter highlights the need for specific facts: dates, times, number of people involved, and exact information needed in the response.

Positive Response

Topic, background, reader involvement

Every year I note with respect and appreciation the efforts of the United Way to assist service organizations. Your inviting me to speak at the October 5 dinner for the chairpersons of this organization is an honor I am happy to accept.

Essential facts amplifying the topic

A forward-looking conclusion and expression of good will

Since I believe that a long speech is often a "lost" speech, I plan to limit my talk to 10 minutes. To help me prepare a relevant message, would you please send the following information by September 10:

A list of the organizations in the tri-state area that the United Way supports.

The approximate number of people served each year by these organizations.

I look forward to seeing you at 7 P.M. on October 5 at the Claremont Inn.

Negative Response

Topic, background, and reader involvement

Thank you for inviting me to attend the farewell dinner for Carol Lane on December 6. An excellent worker and a fine person, Carol certainly deserves this expression of gratitude.

Essential facts amplifying the topic

My present position, which involves a great deal of travel, requires that I be at a conference in Houston, Texas on December 6; however, I am enclosing a check for Carol's gift.

Expression of good will

Please express to my former colleagues my disappointment at not being able to join them and give all of them my best wishes.

The positive aspects of this response "surround" the negative response to the invitation. (*See p. 134.*)

Telephone Follow-up

Topic, background, and reader involvement

As I explained to you in our phone conversation of Tuesday, January 15, a landlord must resort to the legal process in order to evict a tenant. Failure to follow legal procedures is now considered a misdemeanor in the state of Connecticut.

Essential facts amplifying the topic

If you wish to evict Mr. and Mrs. Jones, you must institute a summary process action in the Superior Court. If you are successful in this court proceeding, the tenants may leave voluntarily, or you may ask the sheriff to evict them.

Forward-looking conclusion

Should you decide to institute a summary process action, please call me, and I will prepare the necessary papers for you.

The follow-up letter does not merely repeat information already communicated by telephone; it provides a permanent record of the fact that such information was communicated to a particular individual.

Sales Letter

Topic and reader involvement

Have you ever wished that the carpeting in your home or office could have a new look? At Aladdin's Magic Carpet Company, we guarantee that we can make that wish come true.

Essential facts amplifying the topic

Aladdin's carpet cleaning experts have perfected the art of removing dirt and stains from any type of carpet. Our prices are reasonable and are based on the size of the area to be cleaned, not on the time it takes us to complete the work. If you decide to use our service, you will receive a written guarantee that you will not be charged unless you are completely satisfied.

Courteous, forward-looking conclusion

May Mr. Alan Cox, our salesman in your area, have the opportunity to give you further details either on the phone or in person? He will call you within the next two weeks for your answer. Please give us a try.

A sales letter, to be successful, must convince the reader of the writer's personal concern and of the fact that the product is one the reader cannot afford to be without. The letter must be courteous and persuasive without being overly aggressive.

Recommendation

Topic, background, and reader involvement

My former secretary, Susan Marino, wrote to me last week telling me that she had applied for the position of your administrative assistant. I am happy to be able to recommend her to you.

Essential facts amplifying the topic

Miss Marino was my private secretary for five years. She has excellent typing and stenographic skills. In addition, she demonstrated initiative, perseverance, and punctuality in carrying out her assignments.

Summary repetition of recommendation

With her intelligence, energy, and pleasant personality, Miss Marino will, I am certain, be an asset to your organization.

Congratulations

Topic, background, and reader involvement

Congratulations on your promotion to the position of Executive Vice-President of the NRA Corporation. Your president and the members of the NRA advisory board have made an excellent choice.

Essential facts amplifying the topic

During the course of our business relationship, I have been impressed by your keen understanding of the market and your ability to analyze today's shifting trends. Conferences with you have always been informative as well as enjoyable.

Supportive expression of good will

Your promotion increases my good feelings about NRA, and I wish you the best of luck in your new position.

Sympathy

Topic, background, and reader involvement

In this morning's paper I read with sadness of the death of your father.

Essential facts amplifying the topic

I consider myself privileged to have been Tom's colleague for the six years I was employed at Hudson's. His warmth and kindness made working with him a pleasure.

Expression of sympathy Please accept my sincere expression of sympathy at your loss.

NOTE: Sympathy letters are usually written in longhand. Occasionally, however, an executive may request that such a letter be typed on letterhead stationery. A typed sympathy letter is usually acceptable only when a business acquaintance or the family of a business acquaintance is not well known to the writer.

Short Memorandum

ALADDIN'S MAGIC CARPET CO.

Interoffice Memorandum

TO: All Employees   FROM: Karla Williams,
                                        Personnel Director

SUBJECT: Vacation Schedules   DATE: April 4, 19__

Would all employees who wish to take vacation time during the months of July and August please submit their requests to Miss Judy Lyons in the Personnel Department before noon on Friday, April 30.

I will attempt to honor all requests. However, where conflicts exist, I will give preference to those who have seniority.

Long Memorandum

ALADDIN'S MAGIC CARPET CO.

Interoffice Memorandum

TO: Employees: SUBJECT: Relocation
        Customer Services

FROM: Roger Arno, President DATE: April 16, 19__

On Monday, April 30, the Customer Services Department will move to the newly renovated offices on the first floor. I hope that this relocation will be effected with a minimum of inconvenience to you and to our clients.

Both the local newspapers and the bulletin board in our lobby will announce the move and the fact that the Customer Services Department will be closed on Monday, April 30. The schedule that follows should allow everyone to provide regular services on the days immediately preceding and following the move.

Schedule for Monday, April 30

A.M.

8:30 – 10	All papers and personal belongings packed and locked in files and desk drawers.
10 – 12	1. Movers transfer furniture to new offices.
	2. Employees meet with Tom White, Sales Director, in the 2nd floor conference room.

P.M.

12 – 2	Employees' Lunch
2 – 4:30	Set up personal belongings in new offices. Prepare appointments for Tuesday. Make any necessary phone calls as soon as the lines are connected.

If you foresee any problem with the preceding schedule, please bring it to the attention of Ann Klein, your department head. I know that I can count on your cooperation, and I hope that the bright, spacious new offices will compensate for the inconvenience involved in this relocation.

CHAPTER VII
PARTS OF A BUSINESS LETTER

A business letter has four principal parts: heading, opening, body, and closing. This chapter explains the smaller elements of information each principal part must or may contain and shows how to position these elements and principal parts to aid the reader in understanding the letter quickly and clearly.

The body of a business letter follows the rules of punctuation explained in Chapter IV. The punctuation styles below apply to the heading, opening, and closing of a business letter.

Mixed (or standard) punctuation   The salutation is followed by a colon, and the complimentary close is followed by a comma.

Open punctuation   No line outside the body of the letter ends with punctuation unless the line ends with an abbreviation.

FORMAT
The punctuation styles in the following illustrations are interchangeable. For example, a letter done in the block format may have mixed rather than open punctuation.

Block
(open punctuation)

LETTERHEAD

DATE

NAME AND TITLE
FIRM NAME
STREET ADDRESS
CITY, STATE ABBREVIATION   ZIP CODE

SALUTATION

BODY OF LETTER

COMPLIMENTARY CLOSING

WRITER'S TYPED SIGNATURE
WRITER'S TITLE

INITIALS

Modified Block With Block Paragraphs
(open punctuation)

```
                        LETTERHEAD
                    _____
                    _____

                             DATE
        CONFIDENTIAL

        NAME AND TITLE
        FIRM NAME
        STREET ADDRESS
        CITY, STATE ABBREVIATION   ZIP CODE

        ATTENTION LINE

        SALUTATION

                    SUBJECT LINE OR FILE REFERENCE
        BODY OF LETTER    _____
        _____
        _____

        _____
        _____
        _____
        _____


                        COMPLIMENTARY CLOSING

                        COMPANY NAME


                        WRITER'S TYPED SIGNATURE
                        WRITER'S TITLE

        INITIALS

        ENCLOSURE

        MAILING INSTRUCTIONS
        COPY NOTATION

        P.S.
                    _____
                    _____
```

The date line, complimentary close, and signature block lines usually start at the center of the page. When the company name or any other line of the closing extends more than two strokes into the right margin, the closing is moved the necessary number of spaces left of the center.

Modified Block With Indented Paragraphs
(mixed punctuation)

LETTERHEAD
_____
_____

DATE

CONFIDENTIAL

NAME AND TITLE
FIRM NAME
STREET ADDRESS
CITY, STATE ABBREVIATION   ZIP CODE

ATTENTION LINE

SALUTATION:

SUBJECT LINE OR FILE REFERENCE

BODY OF LETTER
_____
_____
_____

_____
_____
_____
_____

COMPLIMENTARY CLOSING,

COMPANY NAME

WRITER'S TYPED SIGNATURE
WRITER'S TITLE

INITIALS

ENCLOSURE

MAILING INSTRUCTIONS
COPY NOTATION

P.S.
_____
_____

The standard paragraph indentation is five spaces from the left margin.

Simplified (AMS) Style
(open punctuation)

```
┌────────────────────────────────────────────────────────────────┐
│                                                                │
│                          LETTERHEAD                            │
│                    ─────────────────                           │
│                    ─────────────────                           │
│                                                                │
│       INSIDE ADDRESS                                           │
│       ──────────────────                                      │
│       ──────────────────                                      │
│       ──────────────────                                      │
│                                                                │
│       SUBJECT LINE                                            │
│                                                                │
│       BODY OF LETTER  ─────────────────────────              │
│                    ─────────────────────────                 │
│                    ─────────────────────────                 │
│                    ──────────────────                        │
│                                                                │
│                    ─────────────────────────                 │
│                    ─────────────────────────                 │
│                    ─────────────────────────                 │
│                    ──────────                                 │
│                                                                │
│                    ─────────────────────────                 │
│                    ─────────────────────────                 │
│                    ─────────────────────────                 │
│                    ──────────                                 │
│                                                                │
│                                                                │
│       NAME, TITLE                                            │
│       REF. INITIALS                                          │
│                                                                │
│                                                                │
└────────────────────────────────────────────────────────────────┘
```

This letter style was introduced by the Administrative Management Society (AMS). An AMS letter is characterized by the following: (1) every line begins at the left margin; (2) a subject line, typed in full capitals, replaces the salutation; (3) no complimentary close is used; (4) the signature is typed in full capitals on the fourth or fifth line below the last line of the message.

Executive Style
(mixed punctuation)

LETTERHEAD

DATE

SALUTATION:

BODY OF LETTER

COMPLIMENTARY CLOSING,

WRITER'S TITLE

NAME
STREET ADDRESS
CITY, STATE ABBREVIATION   ZIP CODE

ENCLOSURE

(Reference initials on CARBON COPY *only)*

The Executive style is appropriate for personal and semisocial business letters, such as letters of appreciation, congratulations, condolence, informal business invitations, and responses to typewritten business invitations. Executive-size (Monarch) stationery, 7¼ by 10½ inches, is usually chosen for a letter of this nature.

The inside address is typed below the signature block and flush with the left margin. The executive style, like the modified block style, allows a choice between block and indented paragraphs.

HEADING

Letterhead

The printed letterhead of a company consists of the firm name and the mailing address: the street address, the city, the state, and the ZIP Code number. It may also include the telephone number, the names of the executives, and a company symbol or trademark.

When a printed letterhead is not used, the complete mailing address is typed with single spacing. The first line begins on the seventh line from the top of the page to provide a one-inch margin. Each line of the address is centered on the page.

Bradley Chemical Company
568 East 50th Street
New York, New York   10022
(212) 286-6901

Date Line

The date of a letter should be the date on which the letter was dictated, not transcribed. The placement of the date varies. Although the 15th line down from the top of the paper is often called the date line, the date may be typed between lines 12 and 18, depending on the length of the letter.

In block style the date is typed flush with the left margin. In modified block style the date usually begins at the center of the page.

Special Notations

Special notations, such as PERSONAL and CONFIDENTIAL, are typed in capital letters or with initial capitals and underscores. Such notations are typed at the left margin on the second or third line below the date line.

OPENING

Inside Address Placement

The inside address is single-spaced and blocked at the left margin. It begins four, six, or eight lines below the date line, depending on the length of the letter and the style of typewriter type used.

The inside address consists of the name of the person or company addressed and the mailing address. Names of newspapers or magazines are not underscored. An apartment, floor, or suite number is placed after the street address. The city, state abbreviation, and ZIP Code number are typed on the last line. Two spaces are left between the state abbreviation and the ZIP Code number.

The American Review
987 Holland Avenue
Jackson, MI   49201

Mrs. Jane Parker
611 Palmer Road, Apt. 2E
Yonkers, NY   10701

A letter should be addressed to a specific person within a company whenever it is possible to do so. Type the person's name and title (or just a title if the name cannot be learned) on the first line of the inside address; type the name of the company on the second line.

Copy Editor
The American Review
987 Holland Avenue
Jackson, MI   49201

Titles   Unless a specific title, such as Professor, Senator, or Judge, is more appropriate, a courtesy title should be placed before a person's name. (*See Forms of Address, page 235.*)

In choosing a courtesy title for a woman, always respect an individual's preference. If the preference is unknown, use the title *Ms.*

Ms. Marion E. Blake

Dear Ms. Blake:

If it is not possible to determine the gender of the addressee, omit a courtesy title in the inside address and in the salutation.

Meredith T. Riker

Dear Meredith Riker:

Uniformity of line length determines whether a business or executive title is placed after the name of the person addressed, alone on the second line, or before the company name.

After the name:

Mr. Elbert Dempsey, President
Atlas Pharmaceutical Company
1890 Pennsylvania Avenue
Oakland, CA   95361

On the second line:

Miss Harriet Jorgenson
Personnel Interviewer
United States Silver Company
186 Washington Avenue, N.E.
Washington, DC   20013

Before the company name:

Mr. Alan F. Riley
Manager, Taft Hotel
P.O. Box 630
Boca Raton, FL   33432

With department:

> Mr. Wallace W. Edwards
> Manager, Circulation Dept.
> The Hays Tribune
> Hays, KS   67601

Attention Line

An attention line is used to direct a letter (addressed to a company) to a particular department, to a person with whom the writer has had previous correspondence, or to someone well-qualified to deal with the subject matter of the letter.

Since the letter is addressed to a company, using an attention line ensures that the letter will be opened and the contents handled if the person to whom the letter is directed is not available. The correct salutation in a letter with an attention line is *Gentlemen* or *Ladies* or both.

The attention line is typed with or without a colon, flush with the left margin, a double space below the last line of the inside address and a double space above the salutation. The attention line may be typed in initial capital letters with underscore or in full capitals without underscore.

> Englewood Lumber Company
> 11 East Englewood Avenue
> Englewood, NJ   07631
>
> Attention: Mr. David O. Rice

> Englewood Lumber Company
> 11 East Englewood Avenue
> Englewood, NJ   07631
>
> ATTENTION PURCHASING AGENT

Salutation

The salutation of a letter is typed flush with the left margin a double space below the inside address or attention line.

Capitalize the first word, the name, and the title (if used) in the salutation. A colon follows the salutation unless open punctuation is used. In the simplified (AMS) letter style, a subject line replaces the salutation.

INDIVIDUAL(S) (MASC.)   Dear Mr. Clay:

Dear Sir: (formal and impersonal)

Dear Mr. Clay and Mr. Osborne:

Gentlemen:

Dear Messrs. Clay and Osborne: (formal)

INDIVIDUAL (FEM.)	Dear Mrs. Hill:
	Dear Miss Hill:
	Dear Ms. Hill:
	Dear Madam: (formal and impersonal)
COURTESY TITLE UNKNOWN (FEM.)	Dear Ms. Hill:
	OR
	Simplified (AMS) style—omit the salutation; use a subject line
TWO OR MORE WOMEN, SAME SURNAME	Dear Misses Hill:
	Dear Mses. (or Mss.) Hill:
	Dear Misses Ann and Jane Hill:
	Dear Miss Ann and Miss Jane Hill:
TWO OR MORE WOMEN, DIFFERENT SURNAME	Dear Miss Hill and Mrs. Adams:
	Dear Misses Hill and Adams:
	Dear Mses. (or Mss.) Hill and Adams:
	Dear Mesdames Hill and Adams: (formal)
A MAN AND A WOMAN	Dear Miss Hill and Mr. Clay:
	Dear Mr. Clay and Miss Hill:
	Dear Mr. and Mrs. Clay:
PROFESSIONAL TITLE	Dear Professor Adams:
	Dear Dr. Pelegano:
	Dear Dr. and Mrs. Marsh:
	Dear Drs. Marsh:
	Dear Drs. John and Alice Marsh:
	Dear Dr. Alice and Mr. Frank Marsh:
ORGANIZATION ALL MEN	Gentlemen:
ALL WOMEN	Ladies:
	Mesdames: (formal)
MEN AND WOMEN	Gentlemen:
	Dear Sir or Madam:
	Gentlemen and Ladies:
	Ladies and Gentlemen:
	Simplified (AMS) style—omit the salutation; use a subject line
PERSONS UNKNOWN (OFTEN ON A LETTER OF RECOMMENDATION)	To Whom It May Concern:

NOTE: The salutation must agree with the first line of the address, not with the attention line.

> Englewood Lumber Company
> 11 East Englewood Avenue
> Englewood, NJ   07631
>
> Attention: Mr. David O. Rice
>
> Gentlemen:

Subject Line

A subject line summarizes the content of a letter for the convenience of the reader and is a reference to related correspondence on the same subject. Moreover, a subject line eliminates an introduction to the subject in the opening paragraph of the letter and assists the secretary in filing the letter by subject.

In the simplified (AMS) style, the subject line is typed flush with the left margin in full capitals or initial capitals with underscore and begins on the third line below the inside address.

In other styles the subject line may be centered or blocked a double space below the salutation. If five-space indented paragraphs are used, the subject line may also be indented five spaces.

The terms *Subject:*, *In re:*, or *Re:* may precede the subject but are not necessary. The current trend is to omit these terms except in legal correspondence, where *In re:* and *Re:* are still frequently used.

The subject may be typed in full capitals or with initial capitals on the first and all important words. If initial capitals are used, the subject should be underscored.

> Subject: Estate Tax Rates and Exemptions
>
> OR
>
> Estate Tax Rates and Exemptions
>
> OR
>
> ESTATE TAX RATES AND EXEMPTIONS

BODY

A letter should be so situated on the page that the effect is that of a well-framed picture. The width of the margins is determined by the number of words in the letter, the size of the stationery, the number of paragraphs, and the style of the typewriter type.

Letter Placement Table

Letter Length	Words in Body	Side Margins	Lines Below Date Line
Short	Up to 100 words	2 inches	8–10
Medium	100–150	1½ inches	8
	150–175		6
	175–200		4
Long	Over 200 words (or more than one page)	1 inch	4–6

Centering point (when paper guide is set at zero on line scale):

8½- by 11-inch paper	Executive (Monarch) paper (7¼ by 10½ inches)
Elite—51	Elite—43
Pica—43	Pica—36

The first or second line of the letter should be typed to the right margin and should establish a guideline for the rest of the letter. The longest line should not extend more than a space or two beyond the established margin.

The approximate number of words in a letter can be gauged by multiplying the number of lines of shorthand notes by the average number of words on a line.

The body of the letter usually begins on the second line below the salutation or on the second line below the subject line. In the simplified (AMS) letter, the body of the letter begins on the third line below the subject line. If the body of the letter is double-spaced, indent the first word of each paragraph.

In an average letter paragraphs from four to six lines in length are preferable. No paragraph should be over eight lines. A very short paragraph is sometimes used for emphasis but loses its emphatic value if used more than once in a given letter.

Spacing and Indention

Material to Be Typed	Spacing	Indention
All but very short letters	Single	Block or 5 spaces
Very short letters	Double	5 spaces
Legal papers	Double	10 spaces
Reports, manuscripts, specifications, editorials	Double or triple	5 spaces

Two-page letters   In a two-page letter page 1 ends with a bottom margin of approximately the same width as the side margins. The last paragraph of page 1 must have at least two lines of typing. Do not hyphenate the last word on the page.

Type page 2 on plain paper of the same quality, color, and size as the letterhead paper. Leave a top margin of one inch; begin typing on the seventh line. The side margins are the same as those on page 1. The second page must have at least two lines on it.

The heading on page 2 and on succeeding pages must be the same as the first line of the inside address. The heading may be set up as follows:

American Trucking Company
page 2
January 13, 19___

OR

American Trucking Company   2   January 13, 19___

When a letter addressed to a company has an attention line, the name of the heading is that of the company, not the name in the attention line. Leave two blank lines between the heading and the first line of the continued letter.

CLOSING

Complimentary Closing

Type the complimentary closing two spaces below the last line of the body of the letter. In block style the complimentary closing begins at the left margin. In the simplified (AMS) style, the complimentary closing is omitted. In other styles it begins at the center of the page.

If a closing is not indicated, use one of the following:

CONSERVATIVE BUSINESS LETTERS	Very truly yours, Yours very truly,
SEMIPERSONAL AND CONSERVATIVELY FRIENDLY	Sincerely yours, Yours sincerely, Very sincerely yours, Yours very sincerely, Yours truly,
PERSONAL, INFORMAL	Sincerely, Cordially, Cordially yours, Yours cordially,

VERY FORMAL (Used in official letters and in transmitting reports or other communications to superior authority to indicate special respect)	Respectfully yours, Yours respectfully, Very respectfully yours, Yours very respectfully, Respectfully submitted,

Signature

Company signature When a correspondent writes as a representative of a firm, the company name is typed in full capitals a double space below the complimentary closing. Four spaces are left for the handwritten signature between the company name and the typed signature of the writer.

Very truly yours,

TOLEDO LOCKS, INCORPORATED

Henry L. Benton

Henry L. Benton, President

OR

Henry L. Benton
President

When the letterhead is considered sufficient identification or when the letter is being sent from an executive office, the company signature is often omitted.

Yours very truly,

Mary B. Wilken

Mrs. Mary B. Wilken
Vice-President

Typed and pen-and-ink signatures The writer's typed signature ensures legibility and identifies the writer on the carbon copy. The official title of the writer is placed on the same line or on the next line.

When a person wishes to be addressed by a special title, place the appropriate abbreviation or title after the surname in the typed signature. (Exception: titles that always precede the name)

James F. Pelegano, M.S.

Robert E. McHugh, Ph.D.

Ann R. Blake
Dean of Secretarial Studies

BUT

Reverend Richard A. McCarthy

Honorable Ellen G. Cole

If an individual has a name that both men and women use, the appropriate courtesy title should be included in the typed signature.

Sincerely yours,   Sincerely yours,

Meredith Ryan   *Meredith Green*

Mr. Meredith Ryan   Miss Meredith Green

If a woman does not use a special title, such as *M.D.* or *Dean of Students*, she should include her courtesy title in the typed signature.

If a woman does not want to indicate her marital status, she should use the title *Ms.*

Sincerely yours,

Ann L. Riley

Ms. Ann L. Riley

If a woman wishes to indicate that she is single, she should use *Miss.*

Sincerely yours,

Ann L. Riley

Miss Ann L. Riley

If a married woman uses her maiden name for professional purposes, she may use either *Miss* or *Ms.*

A woman who wishes to use *Mrs.* may choose any one of the four styles of signature given below for a woman whose maiden name is Clare A. Conti and whose husband's name is Roger D. Durkin.

Sincerely yours,   Sincerely yours,

Clare A. Durkin   *Clare C. Durkin*

Mrs. Clare A. Durkin   Mrs. Clare C. Durkin

Sincerely yours,   Sincerely yours,

Clare Conti Durkin   *Clare A. Conti-Durkin*

Mrs. Clare Conti Durkin   Mrs. Clare A. Conti-Durkin

Including a husband's given name in the typed signature is considered an acceptable option in social correspondence but is inappropriate in business correspondence. It is always inappropriate for a divorced woman to use her former husband's given name in the typed signature.

Secretary's signature   When a secretary signs a letter that she has written for her employer, the following forms are correct:

> Very truly yours,
>
> *Marjorie M. Nelson*
>
> Marjorie M. Nelson
> Secretary to Mr. White
>
> Very truly yours,
>
> *Barbara Nolan*
>
> Miss Barbara Nolan
> Secretary to Mrs. Norton
>
> Very truly yours,
>
> *Marion Edwards*
>
> Ms. Marion Edwards
> Secretary to Mr. John Doane

When a secretary signs for her employer, the following forms are correct:

> Yours very truly,   Yours very truly,
>
> *Lester J. Knowles*   *Janet S. Merry*
>   J.S.N.
>
> Lester J. Knowles   For Lester J. Knowles

When a letter is written and signed by a secretary and the name of the person who authorized the letter also appears in the signature group, the following form is correct.

> Yours very truly,
>
>
> MURCHISON FARMS, INC.
> F. S. Crawford, Manager
>
> *Frances Holbrooke*
>
> By Miss Frances Holbrooke
> Secretary to Mr. Crawford

The writer who responds to the preceding letter uses this form in the inside address:

> Mr. F. S. Crawford, Manager
> Murchison Farms, Inc.
> Benzonia, MI   49431
>
> ATTENTION: MISS FRANCES HOLBROOKE
>
> Dear Mr. Crawford:

Reference Initials

The initials of the typist (or of the writer and the typist) are typed at the left margin, usually two spaces below the last line of the typed signature. They identify the person who dictated the letter (or the person responsible for its contents) and the person who transcribed the letter.

The first initials are those of the person who dictated the letter or who is responsible for its contents. The second initials, usually two, are those of the transcriber. Initials may be typed in several ways.

LRB:AK   LRB/AK   LRB   LRB/ak   AK
ak

Enclosure Notation

When one or more items are to be sent with a letter, an enclosure notation is typed at the left margin a double space below the identifying initials. If more than one item is enclosed, specify the number. If an enclosure or enclosures are important ones, specifying the items enclosed is acceptable.

Enclosure

Enclosures (2)

Enclosures 2

Enc. 2

Enclosures: 1. Check for $80
2. December Statement

Enclosures
Check for $80
December Statement

Mailing Instructions

When a letter is to be sent by a method other than regular mail, such information is usually typed in full capitals at the left margin a double space below the date line. An additional mailing notation, if any, is typed on the next line.

REGISTERED MAIL
RETURN RECEIPT REQUESTED

Special mailing instructions are sometimes typed below the enclosure notation or below the reference initials if no enclosure notation is used.

KM/jrb

Enclosure

SPECIAL DELIVERY
RETURN RECEIPT REQUESTED

Carbon Copy Notation

A carbon copy notation (cc) indicates that a copy of the letter is being sent to someone other than the person to whom it is addressed. It is typed a double space below the reference initials or the enclosure notation.

LRB:AK   LRB: AK

cc   Mrs. Henry Dale   Enclosure

                                cc   Mr. Wallace Edwards
                                     Dr. John E. Smith

Blind carbon copy notation   If the writer does not wish the original letter (the one sent to the addressee) to show that a copy is being sent to someone else, a blind carbon copy notation (bcc) is placed in the upper left-hand corner of the carbon copy. This position is a reminder that the notation did not appear on the original letter.

bcc   Miss S. R. Brown

Postscript

A well-planned letter does not usually require a postscript. Occasionally, however, a postscript is deliberately used to give a point special emphasis or to include an important afterthought or information not available before the transcription of the letter.

The postscript may be preceded by *P.S., PS.,* or *PS:,* but the trend is to omit the abbreviation.

The postscript is typed as a regular paragraph of the letter with the same margins. It is indented or blocked to agree with the letter style. If space permits, it is typed four spaces below the last line of typing; otherwise, it is double-spaced after the last line of typing. At the end of the postscript, either on the same line or two spaces below, the secretary types the dictator's initials. The dictator may choose to add pen-written initials.

PS: This is an illustration of how the postscript may appear on a letter. L.R.B.

This is another illustration of how the postscript may appear on a letter.

L.R.B.

THE MEMORANDUM

Many businesses have full- and half-size printed forms that are used for interoffice communications. The guidelines that follow apply to printed forms as well as to memorandums typed on plain paper.

- Personal titles are usually omitted from memo headings, but professional titles are included.

- Triple space between the last line of the heading and the message.
- Use block style for the body, lining up the paragraphs with the heading items.
- Single space within paragraphs; double space between paragraphs.
- Type the reference initials at the left margin on the second line below the last line of the message.
- Block and double space any additional notations such as enclosures, carbon copy, and so on.

If a memorandum is to be typed on plain paper, follow these additional guidelines.

- Leave side margins of 1 inch and a top margin of 1½ inches.
- Double space between headings.
- Headings may be typed down or across the page. Except for *To:*, which is always typed first, the order of the headings may vary.

Horizontal Headings

MEMORANDUM
Katharine Gibbs School

To:_____   Subject:_____
From:_____   Date:_____

Vertical Headings

MEMORANDUM
KATHARINE GIBBS SCHOOL

To:
From:
Date:
Subject:

The address on an envelope containing an interoffice memorandum includes the name and personal title as well as the business title or department name (or both) of the addressee. If an organization does not provide special envelopes for memorandums, type COMPANY MAIL in capital letters in the postage location.

```
                                    COMPANY MAIL




            Mrs. Eve Rouke
            Director of Education
            Executive Office
```

If the memorandum is personal or confidential, type the appropriate notation in full capital letters above the name of the addressee.

```
                                    COMPANY MAIL




        PERSONAL
        Mrs. Eve Rouke
        Director of Education
        Executive Office
```

If the memorandum is addressed to several persons, list the names on the envelope, and check the first name. Readers will cross out their names, write the date, check the next name on the list, and pass the memorandum to that person.

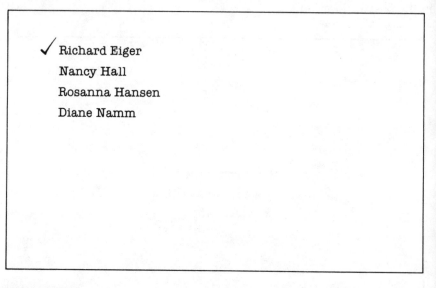

ENVELOPES

An envelope should be of the same quality and color as the letterhead paper. The size of the envelope for a particular letter depends upon the size of the stationery, the number of pages to be inserted, and the number of enclosures.

General Guidelines

The United States Postal Service (U.S.P.S.) now uses optical character recognition equipment to process mail more efficiently. To ensure the highest degree of address readability by this equipment, the U.S.P.S. has developed the following guidelines:

- Use rectangular envelopes that provide a good color contrast with the address. Black type on white paper is best. The envelope must be no smaller than 3½ by 5 inches and no larger than 6⅛ by 11½ inches.
- Capitalize everything in the address.*
- Eliminate all punctuation.*
- Use only those abbreviations listed in the "Address Abbreviations" section of the *National ZIP Code Directory*.*

The traditional address style (upper- and lower-case letters with punctuation) is still commonly used for the inside address.

*Recommended for best possible service.

- Single space the address block. Space twice between the two-letter state abbreviation and the ZIP Code. (*See page 28 for state abbreviations and page 174 for ZIP + 4 information.*)

- The destination address and a return address should each be put in block style and located as illustrated on this page. The destination address block must be more than 1 inch from both the left and right edges and at least ⅝ inch, but not more than 3 inches, from the bottom of the envelope.

- Mailing notations, such as REGISTERED MAIL and SPECIAL DELIVERY, are typed below the stamp position. AIRMAIL is no longer a special service for domestic mail weighing 12 ounces or less, but the AIRMAIL notation should be included on international mail.

- If a letter has an attention line, the envelope must also have one. Type the attention line on the envelope on the line directly above the street name or box number.

- No typing may appear in the destination address block except the destination address itself.

- Always use an appropriate personal title before the name (or the appropriate academic or professional degree abbreviation after the name) when the letter is addressed to an individual.

- Type the return address in block style in the upper left corner. Start three spaces from the left edge on line 2, and use single spacing.

- Type such address notations as PERSONAL, CONFIDENTIAL, and PLEASE FORWARD a triple space below the return address and three spaces from the left edge of the envelope.

RETURN ADDRESS

ADDRESS NOTATION

MAILING NOTATION

DESTINATION ADDRESS BLOCK

Special Mailing Information

The following examples show the correct envelope placement of an address with an IN CARE OF notation and addresses that require apartment, post-office box, room, and rural-delivery numbers.

Traditional Style	U.S.P.S. Style
Mrs. Ross Prescott % Mrs. James Phelps 189 Beacon Street Boston, MA 02109	MRS ROSS PRESCOTT C/O MRS JAMES PHELPS 189 BEACON STREET BOSTON MA 02109
Mr. James R. Newhall 202 East Main Street, Apt. 4G Providence, RI 02904	MR JAMES R NEWHALL 202 EAST MAIN STREET APT 4G PROVIDENCE RI 02904
Messrs. Tower and Wade Post Office Box 145 Montclair, NJ 07042	MESSRS TOWER AND WADE POST OFFICE BOX 145 MONTCLAIR NJ 07042
Miss Rosemary Markwick Tyler Arcade 990 East 181st Street, Room 17 Bronx, NY 10460	MISS ROSEMARY MARKWICK TYLER ARCADE 990 EAST 181ST STREET ROOM 17 BRONX NY 10460
Mr. Donald J. Sargent R.F.D. 1 Lakewood, OH 44107	MR DONALD J SARGENT RFD 1 LAKEWOOD OH 44107

A post office box number and a street address may both be included, but the address where the mail is to be delivered must appear on the line immediately above the bottom line.

Mail will be delivered here ⟶	GRAND PRODUCTS INC 100 MAJOR ST PO BOX 200 PORTLAND OR 97214

OR

Mail will be delivered here ⟶	GRAND PRODUCTS INC PO BOX 200 100 MAJOR ST PORTLAND OR 97293

Foreign Mail

Type the name of a foreign country in full capital letters as the last line of the address. In the inside address the name of the country is typed with an initial capital.

Traditional Style	U.S.P.S. Style
Mr. Edward J. Cousins 15 Roxbury Street London, E.C. 1 ENGLAND	MR EDWARD J COUSINS 15 ROXBURY STREET LONDON EC 1 ENGLAND

Dr. Alfredo Perales	DR ALFREDO PERALES
Obregon Sur 108	OBREGON SUR 108
Saltillo, Coahuila	SALTILLO COAHUILA
MEXICO	MEXICO

Envelope Placement Chart

Envelope Size	First Line Position from Top of Envelope	Spacing from Left Edge of Envelope
No. 6¾ (3⅝ by 6½)	12	2½ inches (elite, 30) (pica, 25)
No. 10 (4⅛ by 9½)	15	4 inches (elite, 48) (pica, 40)
Monarch (3⅞ by 7½)	13	3 inches (elite, 36) (pica, 30)
Baronial* (4⅛ by 5⅛) (4½ by 5¾)	14 15	2 inches (elite, 24) (pica, 20)

* Baronial refers to a style, not a size. It is a formal envelope with a pointed flap. Baronial envelopes are used in business, but in most instances the envelopes are handwritten because they are primarily used for invitations and announcements.

Folding and Inserting Letters in Envelopes

For the small business envelope (No. 6¾), 8½ by 11 paper:

- Place the letter face up on the desk.
- Fold the sheet up from the bottom slightly less than one half of its length to within approximately one-half inch of the top. With the edges even at the sides, crease the fold.
- Fold from right to left slightly less than one third of the width of the sheet.
- Fold from left to right, leaving a margin of about one-half inch at the right.
- Place the last folded edge into the envelope so that the one-half-inch margin shows at the top just under the flap.

For the large business envelope (No. 10), 8½ by 11 paper, and for the Monarch envelope, executive-size paper:

- Fold the sheet up from the bottom slightly less than one third of its length. With the edges even at the sides, crease the fold.
- Fold the top downward not quite one third of the sheet to within approximately one-half inch of the first crease. With the edges even at the sides, crease the second fold.

- Place the second folded edge into the envelope so that the one-half-inch margin shows at the top just under the flap.

For a window envelope:

- Fold the sheet up from the bottom one third of the length of the sheet.
- Fold the top third of the sheet backward from the first fold so that the address will be on the outside.
- Insert the letter into the envelope so that the address shows through the window.

ZIP + 4

The United States Postal Service has begun converting to nine-digit ZIP Codes, adding a hyphen and four additional numbers to the present five-digit ZIP Code.

Large firms, which have their own five-digit ZIP Codes, will have the option of assigning nine-digit ZIP Codes within the firm to various departments, offices, floors, or individual executives.

A number of programs are available to assist customers in converting their current mailing lists: a national system for nine-digit ZIP Code information, computer record tapes to aid in converting large mailing lists, programming assistance for qualified mailers, and a national program for exchanging ZIP Code information.

The Postal Service encourages businesses and households to convert to the nine-digit ZIP Code as soon as they are notified of their new numbers.

CHAPTER VIII
GLOSSARY OF USAGE

The entry words in this glossary are listed alphabetically; they are also cross-referenced in the Index.

a	deem	may
about	disburse	meantime
above	disinterested	media
accept	double negatives	more important
adapt	due to	most
adverse	each other	one another
advice	eager	opposite
affect	effect	party
alike	emigrate	personal
all of	eminent	precede
all ready	ensure	principal
all right	equally as	prior to
all together	etc.	proved
all ways	every day	provided
almost	everyone	raise
although	except	Re:
among	farther	real
amount	fewer	reason is that
anyone	first	respectfully
anyplace	formally	retroactive
any time	former	said
any way	go	scarcely
anywhere	good	set
anxious	hardly	shall
apt to	healthful	so
as	if	some time
bad	immanent	somewhere
balance	immigrate	someone
because of	imply	stationary
being as	in	sure
beside	into	take
between	in regard to	than
biannual	inform	that
bring	insure	their
but . . . however	irregardless	therein
can	it	uninterested
cannot	its	well
can't hardly	kind of	whereas
can't help but	last	whether
capital	latter	while
come	lay	who
complement	leave	who's
consensus	lend	whose
continually	less	will
council	like	would
data	*ly* adverbs	you're

Standard English usage is based on the language of educated speakers and writers, but such usage varies in its degree of formality according to the individual situation. Formal English is characterized by longer sentences, more difficult vocabulary, and fewer contractions than are found in the more conversational style of informal English. The term *colloquial,* included in some of the following entries, describes usage that is standard and "generally characteristic of conversation and informal writing" *(Webster's New World Dictionary of the American Language,* Second College Edition).

In written business English the current trend is to avoid both the stiffness of very formal English and the casualness of very informal usage. Written business English should be clear and concise, reflecting care and precision in word choice. As a general rule, avoid the use of colloquialisms in business writing; using them in conversation is a matter of individual taste and judgment.

The following list of words and phrases should clarify the most common usage problems.

a, an   The indefinite articles *a* and *an* denote one among other persons or things. The choice between them is determined by the *sound* of the following word.

A is placed before a word beginning with a consonant sound and before a long *u,* a sounded *h,* or an *o* pronounced like a *w:* a broker, a wonderful invention, a unique experience, a handful, a one-way street.

An is placed before a vowel sound: an appointment, an F.O.B. shipment, an heir, an honor, an understanding.

about   Distinguish between *at* (precise) and *about* (approximate). Do not use *at about.*

> INCORRECT: I will meet you *at about* 6:30.
>
> APPROXIMATE: I will meet you *about* 6:30.
>
> PRECISE: I will meet you *at* 6:30.

above The use of *above* as an adjective meaning "placed, found, or mentioned earlier" is acceptable. The use of *above* as an adverb to express that same meaning is preferred.

> ACCEPTABLE: the above description
>
> PREFERRED: the description given above
>> OR
>> the preceding description

accept, except *Accept* means "to receive willingly or formally; to approve."

> I cannot *accept* any excuse for that behavior.

Except, as a verb, means "to omit; to exclude." *Except* as a preposition means "with the exception of."

> She *excepted* that essay from the contest.
>
> I will be able to finish everything *except* the filing.

adapt, adopt *Adapt* means "to change so as to make suitable."

> We *adapted* the building to our current needs.
>
> Miss Barnes *adapts* very well to new situations.

Adopt means "to take as one's own."

> The board *adopted* the committee's suggestions.

adverse, averse *Adverse* means "opposed; unfavorable; harmful."

> It is difficult to write under such *adverse* conditions.

Averse means "not willing; reluctant."

> I am *averse* to continuing this discussion.

advice, advise, inform *Advice* is a noun meaning "opinion given as to what to do or how to handle a situation; counsel."

> I would appreciate your *advice* in this matter.

Advise is a verb meaning "to give advice or an opinion; to recommend."

> He *advised* me to reconsider my decision.

Inform means "to give knowledge of something; to tell; to acquaint with a fact."

> My lawyer *informed* me that several sections of our contract are unclear.

affect, effect *Affect* is a verb meaning "to influence or to make a pretense of."

> The weather *affects* his mood.
>
> She *affected* a sophisticated air.

Noun use: *Affect* is a technical term in psychology referring to emotion or emotional response.

> Her *affect* was clearly inappropriate.

As a verb, *effect* means "to bring about; to produce."

> The board is *effecting* changes in its bonus plan.

> His closer attention to detail has *effected* an improvement in his work.

Effect is also a noun meaning "consequence or result."

> We discussed the *effect* of the recent strike on company morale.

alike   *Alike* is correctly used as an adjective to mean "like one another; similar; showing resemblance" or as an adverb to mean "in the same manner; similarly." Do not use the expression *both alike*.

> INCORRECT: They *both* think *alike* about politics.

> CORRECT: They think *alike* about politics.

all of   Do not use "of" unless a pronoun follows.

> *All* the committee members will be present.

> Be sure to invite *all of* them.

all ready, already   *All ready* means "completely prepared to act or be used immediately."

> This material is *all ready* for mailing.

> We were *all ready* to offer our assistance.

Already is an adverb meaning "previously; before a specified time."

> I have *already* completed the survey you requested.

all right   Do not use *alright,* an incorrect spelling of *all right.*

all together, altogether   Do not confuse *altogether,* meaning "entirely; completely," with *all together,* meaning "collectively; everyone in one group or place."

> It was an *altogether* satisfactory experience.

> I would like to meet with you and your staff *all together.*

all ways, always   Do not confuse *always,* meaning "at all times; forever; with no exception," with *all ways,* meaning "every manner or method."

> She is *always* the first to arrive.

> I have examined *all ways* of approaching that problem.

almost, most   Use *almost* rather than *most* to modify *all, any,* and the indefinite pronouns *anybody, anyone, anything, everybody, everyone, everything, nobody, no one,* and *nothing. (See most, page 192.)*

> We have called *almost* all the board members.

> *Almost* everyone was present at last night's meeting.

although, whereas, while   *Although,* meaning "in spite of the fact that," should be used when the adverbial clause it introduces expresses concession: an idea that is opposed but not contradictory to the idea in the main clause.

> *Although* we have a sufficient supply of paper on hand, we shall accept this shipment.

Use *whereas* when the adverbial clause it introduces is one of contrast.

> Iron rusts, *whereas* steel resists corrosion.

While introduces an adverbial clause that relates to time.

> Mr. Croft will supervise the department *while* Mr. Harris is away.

among, between In general, use *among* when referring to more than two and *between* when referring to two.

> A heated discussion went on *between* the director and his assistant.

> The five of us discussed his offer *among* ourselves before the meeting.

Between is used for more than two when each member of the group is relating *individually* to each of the others.

> The negotiations resulted in an arms agreement *between* the three nations.

Avoid using *amongst.*

amount, number Use *amount* when referring to a singular word. Use *number* when referring to a plural word.

> I was surprised at the *amount* of paperwork.

> The *number* of papers he has to review is overwhelming.

anyone, everyone, someone Write as one word:

Anyone when *anybody* could be substituted.

Everyone when *everybody* could be substituted.

Someone when *somebody* could be substituted.

(*See also Pronouns, page 51, for use as two words.*)

anyplace Colloquial for the word *anywhere,* which means "in, at, or to any place."

> COLLOQUIAL: He is willing to travel *anyplace* the job requires.

> WRITTEN BUSINESS ENGLISH: He is willing to travel *anywhere* the job requires.

any time Always write as two words.

any way, anyway *Any way,* consisting of the adjective *any* and the noun *way,* means "no matter what means or method."

> I will help you in *any way* I can.

Use *anyway* as an adverb to mean "nevertheless."

> He is extremely busy but will attend the convention *anyway.*

anywhere Always write as one word.

anxious, eager To be *anxious* is to look forward to something with uneasiness and worry.

> She is *anxious* to receive the results of the examination.

To be *eager* is to look forward to something with enthusiasm.

> We are *eager* to hear the details of your promotion.

apt to, liable to, likely to *Apt to* expresses habitual tendency.

> Miss Fisher is *apt to* leave the use of punctuation up to her secretary.

Liable to expresses risk.

> The pavement is icy, and the car is *liable to* skid.

Likely to expresses probability.

> Their report is *likely to* be true.

as Do not confuse with *that* or *whether*.

> INCORRECT: I do not know *as* you are invited.

> CORRECT: I do not know *whether* you are invited.

as . . . as, so . . . as The connectives *as . . . as* in adverbial clauses of comparison are used in both affirmative and negative statements.

> This letter is *as* long *as* that one.

> This letter is not *as* long *as* that one.

So . . . as is used only in negative statements.

> This letter is not *so* long *as* that one.

as, like *As* is correctly used as a conjunction meaning "in the same manner that; at the same time that; because."

> She writes *as* she talks—bluntly.

As is also used as a preposition meaning "in the function, role, or sense of."

> *As* a supervisor she is demanding but fair.

Like is a preposition meaning "similar to; in a manner characteristic of."

> It will be hard to find someone *like* Peter for that job.

> She sounds just *like* you on the telephone.

The use of *like* as a conjunction is restricted to colloquial English.

> COLLOQUIAL: Nobody works *like* she does.

> WRITTEN BUSINESS ENGLISH: Nobody works *as* she does.

Never use *like* as a substitute for *as if* or *as though*.

> INCORRECT: She acted *like* she hadn't heard the news.

> CORRECT: She acted *as if* (or *as though*) she hadn't heard the news.

bad, badly *Bad* is correctly used as an adjective after a linking verb to describe the subject.

> I *feel bad* (sad) about what happened.

Badly is correctly used as an adverb after an action verb.

> She *reacted badly* to the announcement.

Do not use *badly* to mean *urgently, very much, greatly,* or *extremely* or to modify words denoting "to want" and "to need."

> The office *urgently needs* reorganization.
>
> Sally *wants very much* to take a December vacation.

balance   The word *balance*, in the sense in which it is often misused, is a financial term referring to the amount remaining on the credit or debit side of an account. Do not use *balance* when you mean *rest* or *remainder*.

> He has a large *balance* in his checking account.
>
> The *rest* of the books are still in the storeroom.
>
> She left the *remainder* of her meal untouched.

because of, due to   To introduce an adverbial prepositional phrase, use *because of*.

> *Because of* the hazardous weather conditions, he canceled his trip.

Used most frequently after a form of the verb *be*, *due to* means "caused by; resulting from."

> The accident was *due to* hazardous weather conditions.

The use of *due to* as a synonym for *because of* is colloquial.

being as, being that   Do not use either of these incorrect expressions as substitutes for *because*.

> INCORRECT: Being as he will be in Chicago, he will be unable to attend.
>
> CORRECT: Because he will be in Chicago, he will be unable to attend.

beside, besides   Do not confuse *beside*, meaning "at the side of; next to," with *besides*, meaning "in addition to."

> She sat *beside* me at yesterday's conference.
>
> *Besides* the budget we have the election to consider.

between   See *among, between*.

between you and me   Never use the pronoun *I* after the preposition *between*.

biannual   This adjective means "occurring twice a year at no particular time intervals."

Biennial means "occurring every two years."

Semiannual means "occurring twice a year at six-month intervals."

Bimonthly means "occurring every two months."

Semimonthly means "occurring twice a month."

bring, take   Use *bring* when the action is directed toward the speaker or toward the place where the speaker is.

> *Bring* it *here* this afternoon.
>
> He *brought* this machine *to me* at my office yesterday.

Use *take* when the action is directed away from the speaker.

>Please *take* these to Chicago with you.

>She *took* that book back to the library yesterday.

(See also *come, go.*)

but . . . however   Use one or the other but not both.

>INCORRECT: The atmosphere was depressing, *but* the food was good, *however*.

>CORRECT: The atmosphere was depressing, *but* the food was good.

>The atmosphere was depressing; *however*, the food was good.

can, could, may, might   *Can* and *could* express ability or freedom to act or be acted upon and possibility of existence. *Could* also expresses conditional or past ability.

>ABILITY TO ACT: *Can* you meet that deadline?

>ABILITY TO BE ACTED UPON: The papers *can be sent* to the office.

>POSSIBILITY: The caller *could* be he.

>CONDITIONAL ABILITY: If you have the time, he *could install* the equipment today.

>PAST ABILITY: When Mr. Carle was younger, he *could* speak several foreign languages.

May expresses permission and possibility.

Might expresses possibility but implies doubt or a remote possibility.

>PERMISSION: *May* I use your name as a reference?

>POSSIBILITY: We *may* be able to increase our use of noncommercial timber.

>POSSIBILITY WITH DOUBT: You *might* be able to reach him at home this evening.

The substitution of *can* for *may* is colloquial English.

>COLLOQUIAL: *Can* I tell him to request an advance?

>WRITTEN BUSINESS ENGLISH: *May* I tell him to request an advance?

cannot   Always write as one word.

>She *cannot* attend tomorrow's luncheon.

can't hardly, can't scarcely   See *double negatives.*

can't (cannot) help but   After *can't* (*cannot*) use either *help* or *but,* but not both.

>INCORRECT: I *can't help but* wonder why he called.

>CORRECT: I *can't help* wondering why he called.

>I *cannot but* wonder why he called.

capital, capitol   The word *Capitol* refers to the building in Washington, D.C., in which the United States Congress meets. Without a capital letter, *capitol* refers to the building in which a state legislature meets.

The adjective *capital* usually means "involving or punishable by death" or "of or having to do with wealth." It also indicates "the form of an alphabetical letter used to begin a sentence or a proper noun."

> He doesn't believe in *capital* punishment.
>
> They made a *capital* investment of $85,000.
>
> Every sentence begins with a *capital* letter.

The noun *capital* usually refers to one of the following:

A city that is the official seat of government of a state or nation or the hub of an industry

> Madison is the *capital* of Wisconsin.
>
> New York City is the financial *capital* of the United States.

Wealth—money or property.

> If I had sufficient *capital,* I would invest in that business.

come and In written business communications use *come to.*

> COLLOQUIAL: *Come and* meet the president.
>
> WRITTEN BUSINESS ENGLISH: *Come to* meet the president.

come, go *Come* indicates motion toward the speaker; *go* indicates motion away from the speaker.

> If you *come* to my office at 6 P.M., I will *go* out to dinner with you.

(See also *bring, take.*)

complement, compliment *Complement,* used as a noun or a verb, denotes a balance or harmonious completion.

> Bold headings will be a good *complement* to the fine print of the text.
>
> Those designs will certainly *complement* our layout.

Compliment, used as a noun or a verb, means "to praise; something said in praise."

> I want to *compliment* you on the fine job you did for us.

Compliments means "courteous greetings; respects."

> Please accept the enclosed material with our *compliments.*

consensus The word *consensus* means "an opinion held by all or most." It is therefore redundant to write "consensus of opinion."

continually, continuously Do not confuse *continually* ("occurring at frequent intervals") with *continuously* ("occurring without interruption").

> She is *continually* inventing excuses for her absences.
>
> He talked *continuously* for over an hour.

could of After *could, ought to, might,* use the verb *have.* The use of the preposition *of* after these words is incorrect.

> They *ought to have* finished the repairs by now.

council, counsel   *Council* refers to "a group of people called together for consultation, discussion, or advice."

>The City *Council* will meet at 8 P.M.

Counsel means "advice; to advise."

>I am going to seek *counsel* from my lawyer before I proceed.

data   The word *data* is plural.

>These *data* are surprising, and I would like to discuss them with you.

The use of a singular verb with *data* is now acceptable in standard English. The singular form, *datum*, is rarely used today.

deem   Use a less stilted word, such as *think, consider,* or *believe.*

disburse, disperse   *Disburse* means "to pay out; to expend."

>They are willing to *disburse* every cent they have to make this project succeed.

Disperse means "to scatter in all directions; to spread about, to distribute widely."

>After the meeting the crowd *dispersed* quickly and quietly.

disinterested, uninterested   Do not confuse *disinterested* ("impartial, unbiased") with *uninterested* ("not interested; indifferent").

>We need a *disinterested* person as mediator.

>She seemed *uninterested* in the results of the survey.

double negatives   Only one negative word should be used to express a single negative idea. With such negative words as *barely, hardly, scarcely,* and *but* (meaning *only*), the use of *not* is incorrect.

>We *can hardly* refuse to hear his point of view.

>As Mr. Colby told you, we *can take but* one more carload of coal.

due to   See *because of, due to.*

each other, one another   Use *each other* when referring to two persons or things. Use *one another* when referring to more than two.

>Mr. Harris and Mr. Jones are helping *each other* with their budgets.

>If all six of us help *one another,* we should finish before 5 P.M.

eager   See *anxious, eager.*

effect   See *affect, effect.*

emigrate, immigrate   *Emigrate* means "to go out of one country or region to settle in another."

>When they *emigrated* from Russia, they left everything behind but the clothes they were wearing.

Immigrate means "to come into a new country or region, usually to settle there."

>This country was founded by people who *immigrated* here to escape religious persecution.

eminent, immanent, imminent *Eminent* means "high; lofty; renowned; distinguished."

>He is an *eminent* author and lecturer.

Immanent means "living, remaining, or operating within; inherent."

>Humor is an *immanent* part of his writing.

Imminent means "likely to happen without delay."

>They said that a severe snowstorm is *imminent*.

ensure, insure *Ensure* means "to make sure or certain; to make safe; to protect." (*Insure* may be used in this context as well.)

>Careful proofreading *ensures* accuracy.

Insure means "to contract to be paid or to pay money in the case of loss or damage."

>We will *insure* all the new equipment.

equally as Do not use together.

>INCORRECT: She plays *equally as well*.

>CORRECT: She plays *as well as he*.
>She plays *just as well as he*.
>They play *equally well*.

etc. (abbreviation of the Latin *et cetera,* meaning "and the rest") The expressions *and others, and so forth,* or *and so on* are preferable in writing to the abbreviation *etc.* Use a comma before and after these expressions unless end punctuation eliminates the need for the second comma.

Never use *etc.* or one of its equivalents after examples introduced by *such as,* which indicates the selection of a few out of many, or in any context where the reader cannot easily fill in what is omitted.

>He named every state in alphabetical order: Alabama, Alaska, *and so forth.*

every day, everyday Use *everyday* as an adjective.

>an *everyday* occurrence

>one's *everyday* clothes

Otherwise, write as two words.

>I eat an apple *every day* of my life.

everyone See *anyone, everyone, someone.*

except See *accept, except.*

farther, further *Farther* and *farthest* refer to measurable distance.

>Electric cars run even *farther* without battery recharging.

>His office is the *farthest* from the hospital.

Further and *furthest* denote figurative distance in degree, quality, or time.

>That report requires *further* study.

>Public recognition was the *furthest* thing from his mind.

fewer, less, lesser *Fewer* answers the question How many? and modifies a plural noun.

> *Fewer* persons attended the meeting than we expected.

Less answers the question How much? and refers to quantity in mass or bulk. It modifies a singular noun.

> Last year we expended *less* money for repairs than we did the year before.

Lesser is used in reference to value or importance.

> The *lesser* sum is the correct one.

first When the word *first* introduces the first item of a run-on enumeration, use *second* and *third*, not *secondly* and *thirdly*, to introduce subsequent items.

> *First*, outline the problem. *Second*, list the possible solutions.

formally, formerly *Formally* means "in a formal manner."

> We were asked to dress *formally* for dinner.

Formerly means "at an earlier time; in the past."

> She was *formerly* the director of personnel with a large marine insurance company.

former, latter *Former* and *latter*, respectively, refer to the first and the second of two persons or things mentioned.

> Carol Smith and John Noble have decided to join us. The *former* will arrive on May 1; the *latter* will arrive on May 8.

go See *come, go*.

good, well *Good* is an adjective and is correctly used after a linking verb. *Good* is never used to modify a verb.

> The repertory plays this year were quite *good*.

> The benefits seem *good*, and the salary is excellent.

> I feel *good* about our investment.

Well is correctly used . . .

As an adverb meaning satisfactorily or skillfully

> The repairs are proceeding very *well*.

> I was amazed at how *well* she typed.

As an adjective meaning in good health or suitable.

> She has looked and felt *well* for the past three months.

> It is just as *well* that we didn't schedule our meeting until next month.

hardly See *double negatives*.

healthful, healthy *Healthful* means "beneficial to one's health"; *healthy* means "enjoying good health."

> Her diet is a *healthful* one.

> You're looking *healthy*.

if, whether *If* is correctly used to introduce an adverbial clause of condition.

> He will attend the meeting *if* it is held in Miami.

Use *whether* to introduce a noun clause; do not use *if*.

> Mr. Beck will tell us today *whether* he can attend the meeting.

In colloquial usage *if* and *whether* are often used interchangeably.

> COLLOQUIAL: Ask him *if* he knows her.

> WRITTEN BUSINESS ENGLISH: Ask him *whether* he knows her.

immanent, imminent See *eminent, immanent, imminent.*

immigrate See *emigrate, immigrate.*

imply, infer *Imply* means "to suggest something without specifically stating it." A speaker or writer implies.

> He *implied* by what he said that the cost was prohibitive.

Infer means "to come to a conclusion; to interpret; to judge from evidence." A listener or reader *infers.*

> From what he said, we *infer* that an announcement is imminent.

in, in to, into *In* describes the location of a thing or person within a certain space.

> Mr. Bates is *in* his office.

> The group will spend two weeks traveling *in* Italy.

In to is composed of the adverb *in* and the infinitive *to.*

> He stopped *in to* tell us about his promotion.

Into denotes motion from outside to within or a change in form.

> Mr. Wells has gone *into* Mr. Ellis's office.

> The proposal will be divided *into* three parts.

in regard to Use *in regard to, with regard to,* or *as regards.* Do not use *in regards to.*

inform See *advice, advise, inform.*

insure See *ensure, insure.*

irregardless Do not use. The correct word is *regardless.*

it *It* is correctly used in reference to time and weather.

> *It* is almost nine o'clock.

> I wonder whether *it* is raining.

It is sometimes used as an expletive, a word that occupies the position of the subject but has no meaning of its own.

> *It* is a pleasure to serve on your committee.

Because the use of the expletive delays the meaningful part of the sentence, expletives are used sparingly in business writing.

> *To serve on your committee* is a pleasure.

its, it's *Its* is a possessive pronoun.

> The cat is licking *its* dish clean.

It's is a contraction of *it is* or *it has*.

> *It's* time to reconsider our decision.
>
> *It's* been several weeks since her call.

kind of, sort of, type of *Kind, sort,* and *type* are singular nouns and are correctly modified by *this* or *that*.

> That *kind* of policy is favored by young executives.

Kinds, sorts, and *types* are plural nouns and are correctly modified by *these* or *those*.

> We no longer manufacture those *kinds*.

Do not use *kind of* and *sort of* to replace such adverbs as *somewhat* and *rather*.

> Mr. Wells's schedule is *rather* crowded this week.
>
> We are *somewhat* late in mailing our new price lists.

Do not use the articles *a* or *an* after *kind of* and *sort of*.

> INCORRECT: That *kind of* a paint is not practical.
>
> CORRECT: That *kind of* paint is not practical.

last, late, latest *Late,* adjective or adverb, refers to time.

> We didn't finish these figures until *late* last night.

Last and *latest* are superlative forms of *late*. *Last* refers to the final item in a series. *Latest* means "the most recent."

> *Country Squire* is the author's *latest* novel, and it is also the *last* one he intends to write.

latter See *former, latter*.

lay, lie *Lay (lay, laid, laid, laying)* is a transitive verb meaning "to put or place." It always has a receiver.

> Mr. Baldwin *lays* great stress on accuracy.
>
> They are *laying* the foundation today.
>
> The cornerstone was *laid* in 1980.
>
> The pipeline will have been *laid* by November 1.

Lie (lie, lay, lain, lying) is an intransitive verb meaning "to rest or recline."

> Responsibility for promotion will *lie* with Mr. Burns's office.
>
> The mail is *lying* on your desk.
>
> Yesterday the catalog *lay* on Mr. Ryan's desk.
>
> The manuscript *had lain* unnoticed on top of the files.

leave, let   *Leave* means "to depart; to abandon"; *let* means "to allow."

> Will you *let* me go if I *leave* these documents with you?

lend, loan   *Lend*, not *loan*, is the preferred verb form; use *loan* as a noun.

> If you *will lend* me the money, I will repay the *loan* with interest in six months.

less, lesser   See *fewer, less, lesser*.

like   See *as, like*.

ly **adverbs**   Separate two or more adverbs ending in *ly*.

> AVOID: We are *usually particularly* rushed during December.

> CORRECT: *Usually* we are *particularly* rushed during December.

may, might   See *can, could, may, might*.

meantime   Use *meanwhile* or *in the meantime*.

media   *Media* is the plural form of *medium* and therefore requires a plural verb.

> Other *media* are being considered for the ad campaign.

more important, more importantly   Use *more important* (a short form of "what is more important is that"), not *more importantly*, to introduce a thought.

> *More important*, the deadline has been moved back from June 1 to March 1.

most   *Most*, the superlative form of *more*, is correctly used before an adjective or adverb to mean "to the highest degree" when more than two items are compared.

> Miss Welch was the *most* cordial of all the receptionists.

> The actors are seen *most* clearly from these seats.

Most is also correctly used as an adjective or as an indefinite pronoun.

> *Most* letterheads are conservative in appearance.

> *Most* of the mail has been sorted.

Do not use *most* to modify an adjective when no comparison is intended. Instead, use an adverb such as *greatly, very*, or *exceedingly*.

> INCORRECT: Miss Welch was *most* cordial.

> CORRECT: Miss Welch was *very* cordial.

most   See *almost, most*.

one another   See *each other, one another*.

opposite   As a noun *opposite* is followed by *of*. Otherwise, it is followed by *from* or *to* or is not used with a preposition.

> Mr. Poole's temperament is the *opposite of* hers.

> Mr. Poole's temperament is *opposite to* hers.

> Your desk will be *opposite* the window.

party   In general, except in legal usage, avoid using *party* as a substitute for *person*.

personal, personnel   *Personal* means "private; individual; belonging to oneself."

> I requested a *personal* interview with the president.

Personnel refers to employees.

> Please direct that memorandum to all company *personnel*.

precede, proceed   *Precede* means "to be, come, or go before in time, place, order, or importance."

> He spoke last but gave us more information than any of the speakers who *preceded* him.

Proceed means "to advance or go on, especially after stopping."

> Turn right; then *proceed* down the hall until you reach my office.

principal, principle   As a noun, *principal* means "chief; head; presiding officer, specifically of a school; main performer."

> We have discussed the schedule change with the *principal*.

Used in a financial sense, it refers to the amount of a debt or investment minus the interest.

> Mrs. Bently was able to use her interest as income without touching her *principal*.

As an adjective *principal* means "first in rank, authority, or importance."

> Miss Kantor was the *principal* speaker at this morning's meeting.

Principle means "the source or origin of something; a fundamental truth, law, doctrine, or motivating force."

> The *principle* behind his actions is a simple one: You must spend money to make money.

prior to   Use *before*, which is less stilted than *prior to*.

proved, proven   Use *proved* as a verb; use *proven* as an adjective.

> We *proved* that success was possible.

> We have a *proven* formula for success.

provided, providing   *Provided* or *provided that*, equivalent to *if*, introduces an adverbial clause of condition.

> You can make a substantial saving *provided that* you pay your bills within the discount period.

Providing is a participle and means "giving or offering."

> Redwood enclosures, *providing* privacy and attractive fencing, are widely used in the suburbs.

raise, rise   *Raise* (*raising, raised*) is a transitive verb meaning "to lift; to cause to rise in level or amount; to bring up for consideration; to collect; to rear or grow."

Manufacturers are *raising* the price of automotive parts.

The issue of an employment freeze was *raised* by the committee.

We must *raise* $10,000 to pay the mortgage.

Raising corn may be especially lucrative this year.

Rise (rising, rose, risen) is an intransitive verb meaning "to move or to extend upward."

Prices often *rise* at this time of year.

The price of the stock *rose* twelve points.

Re:, In re: Avoid these Latin terms meaning *regarding, concerning,* or *about* in written business English.

real, sure, really, surely   *Real* and *sure* are adjectives. *Really* and *surely* are adverbs. If *certainly* or *very* can be inserted correctly, use *really* or *surely*.

INCORRECT: Your exhibit at the show was *real* impressive.

CORRECT: Your exhibit at the show was *really* impressive.

reason is that   Use *that,* not *because,* to introduce a noun clause after *the reason is*.

INCORRECT: *The reason* I suggested Sheila Blake *is because* she has had more experience in that field.

CORRECT: *The reason* I suggested Sheila Blake *is that* she has had more experience in that field.

respectfully, respectively   *Respectfully* means "in a respectful manner; with deference."

He treats his employees fairly and *respectfully*.

Respectively means "in regard to each (of two or more) in the order named."

Ann and Tom were elected president and vice-president, *respectively*.

retroactive   Use *retroactive to,* not *retroactive from*.

The new increases will be *retroactive to* July 1.

said   Except in legal usage do not use expressions such as *"said* client" when you mean *"this* client" or "the client *mentioned above*."

scarcely   See *double negatives*.

set, sit   *Set* is usually a transitive verb meaning "to put or place something in position; to establish."

She *sets* her marginal stops before she begins to type.

Last week she *set* a new record for speed and accuracy.

Set is used intransitively in sentences like these:

The sun is *setting*.

We can't begin until the cement has *set*.

Sit is an intransitive verb meaning "to rest; to assume a sitting position." A person *sits* or *seats* himself voluntarily; a thing *sits* where it has been placed.

> The caller is *sitting* in the reception room.

> Your package has *sat* on the table ever since you placed it there.

shall, should, will, would   *Shall* and *should* were once considered the only correct verb forms to express the future and conditional tenses, respectively, when *I* or *we* was the subject. Today, except in very formal speech and writing, *will* and *would* are used to express the future and conditional tenses, respectively, with all three persons.

> VERY FORMAL: I *shall* (*should*) be glad to review the final copy.

> LESS FORMAL: I *will* (*would*) be glad to review the final copy.

Shall in all three persons signifies control by some authority.

> The bylaws state that he as chairman *shall* preside.

> Mr. Barnes is determined that his son *shall* assume more of the management responsibilities.

Would and *should* also imply a conditional circumstance or uncertainty.

> I *would* provide office space for you if you *should* decide to take the job.

Would expresses past action as well.

> When we were students, we *would* take advantage of the reduced rates on buses, planes, and trains during the holidays.

> Mr. Johnson *would* always take the shuttle when he went to Washington, D.C.

Will and *would* denote willingness, promise, and intention.

> We *will* gladly accommodate you.

Should can also express moral obligation.

> Everyone *should* comply with the terms of the agreement.

so   In writing, avoid the use of *so* to connect clauses.

> AVOID: We will complete the budget, so we should be able to submit it by Thursday morning.

> CORRECT: We will complete the budget today and should, therefore, be able to submit it by Thursday morning.

> CORRECT: Since we will complete the budget today, we should be able to submit it by Thursday.

some time, sometime, sometimes   *Some time*, written as two words, consists of an adjective and a noun, and means "an amount of time."

> He spent *some time* working on the plan.

> For *some time* we have been considering major renovations.

> *Some time* ago we quoted them a price on our steel files.

Sometime is an adverb and means "at an unspecified time."

> Please come to see the demonstration *sometime*.

Sometimes is an adverb and means "occasionally; now and then."

> *Sometimes* another salesman takes an order.

somewhere *Somewhere* is preferable to *someplace*.

someone See *anyone, everyone, someone*.

stationary, stationery *Stationary* means "fixed in position; unchanging in condition or value."

> The interest rate has remained *stationary* for the last six weeks.

Stationery refers to writing materials, especially paper and envelopes used for letters.

> Office *stationery* should be plain but of good quality.

sure, surely See *real, sure, really, surely*.

take See *bring, take*.

than, then *Than* is a conjunction used to introduce the second element in a comparison.

> Our profits were higher *than* we had expected them to be.

Then is an adverb meaning "at that time; soon afterward; next in order; in that case."

> We will complete a rough estimate of costs involved and *then* meet with our clients.

that, which, who In general, *that* is used as a connective when the adjective clause following is essential, providing information necessary to the meaning or identification of the noun or the pronoun that it modifies.

> We need a duplicator *that* is small but *that* will produce legible copies.
>
> The duplicator *that* produces legible copies is the one we want.

That usually refers to things, although it is sometimes used in an impersonal reference to people.

> Is the dictionary *that* you selected thumb-indexed?
>
> The candidate *that* wins this election will need the full support of the party.

Which is used when the adjective clause is nonessential, unnecessary to the identification of the noun or pronoun that it modifies.

> Duplicator 236, *which* is small and *which* produces legible copies, is our choice.

EXCEPTION: When a sentence contains a noun clause or an adverbial clause beginning with *that*, an essential adjective clause should begin with *which*.

> We said *that* the duplicator *which* we need must be small.
>
> We are glad *that* the duplicator *which* Mr. Branton ordered is portable.

Which usually refers to things but may also refer to a collective noun, a group of persons acting as a unit.

> The Harcourt Building, *which* is on Maple Street, has been sold.

> The Maxwell Company, *which* has an office in this building, is a brokerage firm.

Who refers to persons.

> Mr. Bell is the man *who* founded our company.

their, there, they're   *Their* is a possessive adjective indicating "of, belonging to, made, or done by them."

> They gave us *their* statistics this afternoon.

There is an adverb meaning "at or in that place."

> I will try to be *there* by 3 P.M.

There may also be used as an expletive, a word that occupies the position of the subject but has no meaning of its own. Because the true subject is delayed and appears after the verb in such a sentence, avoid the use of expletives (*it* and *there*) in written business English.

> AVOID: *There* are several letters on your desk. (*Letters* is the true subject.)

> CORRECT: Several letters are on your desk.

They're is the contraction of *they are.*

> *They're* sending us their revised figures tomorrow.

therein, thereon   Avoid such overly formal words in ordinary business communications.

uninterested   See *disinterested, uninterested.*

well   See *good, well.*

whereas   See *although, whereas, while.*

whether   See *if, whether.*

while   See *although, whereas, while.*

who, whom   Use *who* as the subject of a verb or as the complement of a linking verb.

> *Who* answered the telephone?

> She is the secretary *who answered* the telephone.

> I don't know *who* she is.

Use *whom* . . .

As the direct object of a verb

> Miss Granger is the secretary *whom* we employed. (We employed *her.*)

> *Whom* did you call? (You did call *her.*)

As the object of a preposition

> She is the secretary to *whom* I gave the letter. (I gave the letter *to her*.)
>
> To *whom* did you give the letter? (You did give the letter *to her*.)

As the subject of an infinitive

> She is a person *whom* we believe to be very capable. (We believe *her to be* very capable.)
>
> *Whom* did you ask to do that job? (You did ask *her to do* that job.)

As the complement of an infinitive.

> He is the one *whom* we wish to interview. (We wish *to interview him*.)
>
> *Whom* do you wish to interview? (You do wish to interview *him*.)

NOTE: In choosing between *who* or *whom*, put the sentence or clause to which *who* or *whom* belongs in subject-verb-complement order. Substitute *he* or *him* (*she* or *her*) for *who* or *whom*. If *he* (*she*) is correct, use *who*. If *him* (*her*) is correct, use *whom*.

who's, whose   *Who's* is the contraction for *who is* and *who has*.

> We don't know *who's* been recommended for that position.

Whose is the possessive form of *who*.

> *Whose* are these?
>
> She is the applicant *whose* résumé I discussed with you yesterday.

Whose may be used as a substitute for *of which the* to avoid awkwardness.

> We rented an office *whose* windows overlooked Park Avenue.

will, would   See *shall, should, will, would*.

you're, your   *You're* is the contraction for *you are*.

> Please call me by Friday to let me know whether *you're* willing to undertake this project.

Your is a possessive adjective.

> I would appreciate knowing *your* opinion of the enclosed material.

CHAPTER IX
PLURALS

Knowing and following the rules for writing the plural forms of words is essential to correct spelling. When in doubt about writing a plural form, consult a dictionary.

Most nouns   Form the plural of most nouns by adding *s* to the singular.

      machine, machines   friend, friends

Nouns ending with *s, x, z, ch,* **or** *sh*   Form the plural of most nouns ending with *s, x, z, ch,* or *sh* by adding *es* to the singular.

bus, buses	fox, foxes	topaz, topazes
business, businesses	wish, wishes	church, churches

Nouns ending with *y*   For nouns ending with a vowel before *y*, form the plural by adding *s*.

      boy, boys   alloy, alloys

      key, keys   monkey, monkeys

For nouns ending with a consonant before *y*, form the plural by changing the *y* to *i* and adding *es*.

      lady, ladies   reply, replies

      berry, berries   flurry, flurries

Nouns ending with *o*   For nouns ending with a consonant before *o*, form the plural by adding *es*.

      hero, heroes   tomato, tomatoes

      veto, vetoes   potato, potatoes

For nouns ending with a vowel before *o* and for musical terms ending in *o*, form the plural by adding *s*.

      radio, radios   alto, altos

      piano, pianos   stereo, stereos

Some nouns ending in *o* have two acceptable plural forms.

      mottos, mottoes   zeros, zeroes

Nouns ending with *f* **or** *fe*   For most nouns ending in *f* or *fe*, form the plural by adding *s*.

      proof, proofs   chief, chiefs

      safe, safes   gulf, gulfs

To form the plural of other nouns ending in *f* or *fe,* change the *f* or *fe* to *v* and add *es.*

knife, knives	life, lives
leaf, leaves	half, halves

Nouns that change spelling   Certain irregular nouns form their plurals by changing their internal spellings.

foot, feet	woman, women
mouse, mice	goose, geese
tooth, teeth	

Some irregular nouns add *ren* or *en* to the singular.

child, children   ox, oxen

Some irregular nouns are spelled the same in both their singular and plural forms.

sheep	fish	species
salmon	deer	series

Compound nouns   When a compound noun is written as one word, form the plural by adding *s.*

cupful, cupfuls	drugstore, drugstores
railroad, railroads	daytime, daytimes

NOTE: The plural of *passerby* is *passersby.*

When a compound noun contains two or three separate words written with or without hyphens, add *s* to the most important word. Generally, if the compound noun contains a prepositional phrase beginning with *of* or *in,* the most important word is the noun before the preposition.

attorney at law	attorneys at law
chamber of commerce	chambers of commerce
editor in chief	editors in chief
runner-up	runners-up
lieutenant general	lieutenant generals
stock exchange	stock exchanges

Proper nouns   Form the plurals of proper nouns by adding *s* or *es* to the singular. To any proper noun ending in *y,* add *s* in order to retain the original spelling.

Adams, Adamses	Hoffman, Hoffmans
Bell, Bells	Lacey, Laceys
Barnes, Barneses	Macy, Macys
Hendrix, Hendrixes	Russo, Russos

Plurals of Nouns Ending in *s*

Singular and plural nouns   Some nouns ending in *s* are singular and are made plural by adding *es*.

> lens, lenses   summons, summonses

Some nouns ending in *s* are always singular and have no plural forms.

> news   happiness

Some nouns ending in *s* are always plural and have no singular forms.

> assets   riches   belongings   earnings
>
> thanks   savings   winnings   proceeds
>
> remains   grounds   goods

A few nouns ending in *s* are either singular or plural, depending on the intended meanings. The number of the noun must be determined from the context in which it is used.

> *One means* of transportation *is* . . .
>
> *Several means* of transportation *are* . . .
>
> *A series* of plays *is* . . .

Nouns ending in *ics*   Nouns ending in *ics* are singular when they name a science, a branch of learning, or a course of study.

> *Physics is* an exact science.
>
> *Economics is* a large field of study.
>
> *Statistics is* a difficult course.

Nouns ending in *ics* are plural when they name an activity or quality or when they are used in a nonacademic sense.

> The *statistics were* overwhelming.
>
> *Athletics are* performed in the gym.
>
> The *acoustics* of the hall *were* poor.
>
> The *economics* of his proposal *were* not feasible.

Nouns ending in *sis*   Most *sis* nouns end in *ses* as in (basis, bases).

Other Plurals

Plurals of foreign nouns and proper nouns with titles follow different rules from ordinary English nouns. In addition, the plurals of letters, numbers, words used as words, and abbreviations follow special rules.

Foreign nouns   In some cases, foreign nouns retain the plural form of the original language.

> alumna, alumnae   alumnus, alumni
>
> madam, mesdames   stimulus, stimuli
>
> datum, data

NOTE: In current English usage *data* is often used with a singular verb.

Other foreign nouns have both an original and an English plural, of which the English plural is usually preferred.

Noun	Original	English
appendix	appendices	appendixes
curriculum	curricula	curriculums
formula	formulae	formulas
index	indices	indexes
memorandum	memoranda	memorandums
criterion	criteria	criterions

Proper nouns with courtesy titles   Forming plurals with courtesy titles includes options. Because the English language does not provide a plural form for *Mr.* or *Mrs.*, the title is usually repeated before each proper name. *Dr.* and *Miss*, however, do have English plural forms. In very formal writing, the French plural forms of *Mr.* and *Mrs.* can be used.

Dr. Holmes and Dr. Mallory   OR   Drs. Holmes and Mallory

the Miss Mallorys   OR   the Misses Mallory

Mrs. Jane Holland and Mrs. Carol Holland   OR   the Mrs. Hollands

Mr. A. Herrold and Mr. J. Herrold   OR   the Mr. Herrolds

FORMAL: the Mesdames Holland

the Messrs. Herrold

the Mesdames Green and Finch

the Messrs. Green and Finch

Letters used as nouns   To form the plurals of capital letters referred to as nouns, add *s*. If this addition causes misreading, add *'s*.

has two *Bs*   has several *A's*

To form the plurals of lower-case letters, add *'s*.

cross your *t's*   dot your *i's*

Words used as words   To form the plurals of words used as words, add *s*. Words used as words are underscored in typed manuscript, italicized in printed material.

no *ifs* about it   too many *ands*

Numbers   To form the plurals of numbers expressed in figures, add *s*. Although *'s* is occasionally used, it is not required.

during the 1960s   temperature in the 50s

after the 1800s

Numbers expressed in words follow the normal rules.

ones   twos   threes   sixes   thirties   forty-eights

Plurals of abbreviations   Use an 's to form the plural of lower-case abbreviations with internal periods.

> c.o.d.'s   f.o.b.'s

Add s to the singular of lower-case abbreviations that do not have internal periods.

> vol., vols.   dept., depts.

Add s to the singular of abbreviations ending with capital letters.

> M.D.s   Ph.D.s   CPAs

A lower-case s is used to form the plurals of the abbreviations for doctor (Drs.), esquire (Esqs.), and number (Nos.).

The abbreviations of most weights and measures remain the same in the singular and plural.

ounce(s)	oz.	kilometer	km
foot(feet)	ft.	dekameter(s)	dam
inch(es)	in.	centigram(s)	cg
mile(s)	mi.	milliliter(s)	ml
degree(s)	deg.		

For a few single-letter abbreviations, the plural is the letter doubled.

> p., pp.   (page, pages)   p. 42, pp. 42–48
> f., ff.   (following page, lines, and so forth)
> pp. 247 f., pp. 247 ff.

REFERENCE SECTIONS

ABBREVIATIONS AND ACRONYMS

FORMS OF ADDRESS

WEIGHTS AND MEASURES

GLOSSARY OF WORD-PROCESSING TERMS

PROOFREADING

BIBLIOGRAPHY

ABBREVIATIONS AND ACRONYMS

A

AA	Alcoholics Anonymous; American Airlines, Inc.
A.A.	Associate in Arts
AAA	American Automobile Association; American Accounting Association
AAU	Amateur Athletic Union
A.B., B.A.	Bachelor of Arts
ABA	American Bankers Association; American Bar Association
ABC	American Broadcasting Company
abr.	abridged; abridgment
abs.	absent
ac, a.c.	alternating current
a/c, A/C, acct.	account
A.C.	Air Corps
ACE	AMEX Commodities Exchange
ACLD	Association for Children with Learning Disabilities
ACLU	American Civil Liberties Union
ACS	American Cancer Society
actg.	acting
ad	(pl. **ads**) advertisement
A.D.	(L. *anno Domini*) in the year of the Lord
ADC	Aid to Dependent Children; Air Defense Command
add.	addition
addl.	additional
adj.	adjective; adjustment
Adj. Gen., A.G.	Adjutant General
Adm.	Admiral; Admiralty
adm.	administration; administrative
ADP	Automatic Data Processing
adv.	ad valorem; adverb; (L. *adversus*) against
ad val., a/v adv.	(L. *ad valorem*) according to the value
adv. chgs.	advance charges
advg., advtg.	advertising
advt.	(pl. **advts.**) advertisement
AEC	Atomic Energy Commission
AF	Air Force; Air France
Af., Afr.	African; Africa
a.f., AF	audio-frequency
AFA	Armed Forces Act; Air Force Academy
AFB	Air Force Base
AFDC	Aid to Families with Dependent Children
AFL	American Federation of Labor
AFL-CIO	American Federation of Labor and Congress of Industrial Organizations
AFT	American Federation of Teachers
agcy.	agency
agt.	agent; against; agreement
AK	Alaska (ZIP Code abbrev.)
aka, a.k.a.	also known as
AICPA	American Institute of Certified Public Accountants

AL	Alabama (ZIP Code abbrev.)	**A.R.**	Accounts Receivable; (Fr. *Ans de reception*) return receipt
Ala.	Alabama		
ALGOL	algorithmic language used in programming computers	**Arch. E.**	Architectural Engineer
		Ariz.	Arizona
		Ark.	Arkansas
alt.	alternate; alternating; altitude; alto	**arr.**	arrangements; arrival
Am.	America; American; Associate Member	**A.S.**	Associate of Science
		asap, ASAP	as soon as possible
A.M., M.A.	Master of Arts	**ASCAP**	American Society of Composers, Authors, and Publishers
a.m., A.M.	(L. *ante meridiem*) before noon; amplitude modulation (radio)		
		ASCE	American Society of Civil Engineers
AMA	American Management Association; American Medical Association	**ASME**	American Society of Mechanical Engineers
amb.	ambassador	**assn.**	(pl. **assns.**) association
AMEX	American Stock Exchange	**asso., assoc.**	associate; associated
amt.	amount	**asst.**	assistant
A.N.	arrival notice (shipping)	**AST**	Atlantic Standard Time
anal.	analogous; analogy; analysis; analytic	**AT&T**	American Telephone and Telegraph Company
anon.	anonymous	**Atl.**	Atlantic
ans.	answer	**atm.**	atmosphere; atmospheric
A-1	first quality or first-class	**att., atch., attm.**	attach; attached; attachment
AP	Associated Press	**attn.**	attention
A.P.	Accounts Payable	**atty.**	(pl. **attys.**) attorney
APO	Army Post Office	**Atty. Gen.**	Attorney General
app.	appendix; appointed; approved; applied	**at. wt.**	atomic weight
		au.	author
approx., ap.	approximate	**AUS**	Army of the United States
appt.	appointed; appointment	**Aust.**	Australia; Austria
apt.	(pl. **apts.**) apartment	**aux.**	auxiliary
AR	Arkansas (ZIP Code abbrev.); Army Regulation	**AV**	audiovisual
		Ave., ave.	(pl. **Aves.**) Avenue
ar.	arrives; arrival	**avg.**	average

AWOL	absent without leave (military term)
AZ	Arizona (ZIP Code abbrev.)

B

B.A., A.B.	Bachelor of Arts
bal.	balance
bar.	barometer; barometric
BASIC	Beginner's All-purpose Symbolic Code (computer programming language)
B.B.A.	Bachelor of Business Administration
BBC	British Broadcasting Corporation
bbl.	(pl. bbl. or bbls.) barrel
B.C.	before Christ; British Columbia, Canada
B.C.E.	Bachelor of Civil Engineering; before the Common Era
bch.	(pl. bchs.) bunch
B.C.S.	Bachelor of Commercial Service
bd.	board; bond
B.D.	Bachelor of Divinity
b.d.	bank draft; bills discounted
B/E., b.e.	bill of exchange
B.E.	Bachelor of Education (also B. Ed.); Bachelor of Engineering
bet.	between
B/F	brought forward
bk.	(pl. bks.) bank; book
bkg.	banking
B/L	(pl. BS/L) bill of lading
B.L.	Bachelor of Laws

bldg.	building
B.L.S.	Bachelor of Library Science; Bureau of Labor Statistics
Blvd., Bv.	boulevard
b.o.	back order; bad order; branch office; broker's order; buyer's option
bor.	borough
bot.	(pl. bots.) bottle
B.O.T.	Board of Trade
BP	blood pressure
B.P.	bills payable
b.p., bp	boiling point
Br.	British; Branch; Brother
B.R., b. rec.	bills receivable
Brig. Gen.	Brigadier General
Brit.	British; Britain
bro.	(pl. bros.) brother
B.S.	Bachelor of Science; balance sheet; Bureau of Standards
b.s., B/S	bill of sale
B.t.u	British thermal unit
bu.	bushel(s)
bull.	(pl. bulls.) bulletin
bur.	bureau
bus.	business
b.v.	book value
BWI	British West Indies
bx	(pl. bxs.) box
BX	base exchange(s) (Air Force)

C

C, C.	Centigrade or Celsius; (L. centum) 100; Congress
c, c.	carat (metric); coupon; cent; copyright; cost

c., ca.	(L. *circa*) about	**CEEB**	College Entrance Examination Board
CA	California (ZIP Code abbrev.)	**cen.**	central; century
C.A.	chartered accountant; chief accountant; Central America; capital account; credit account; current account	**cert., ct., ctf.**	certificate; certification; certified
		CETA	Comprehensive Employment Training Act
CAA	Civil Aeronautics Administration	**c. & f.**	cost and freight
		c/f	carried forward
CAB	Civil Aeronautics Board	**cfm**	cubic feet per minute
cal.	small calorie; calendar; caliber	**CFR**	Code of Federal Regulations
Calif.	California	**cfs**	cubic feet per second
Can.	Canada; Canadian	**cg, cg., cgm.**	centigram(s)
canc.	cancel; canceled; cancellation		
		c.g.	center of gravity
CAP, C.A.P.	Civil Air Patrol	**Ch.**	China; Chinese; Chaplain; Church
cap.	capital; capitalize; capacity	**C.H., c.h.**	clearing house; courthouse, customhouse
Capt.	Captain	**chap., ch.**	(pl. **chaps.** or **chs.**) chapter
car.	carat		
cat.	catalog	**Ch. E., Chem. E.**	Chemical Engineer
CATV	community antenna television	**chem., ch.**	chemical; chemist; chemistry
CBD, c.b.d.	cash before delivery	**Chin.**	China; Chinese
CBS	Columbia Broadcasting System	**chron.**	chronological; chronology
cc, c.c.	carbon copy; cubic centimeter	**CIA**	Central Intelligence Agency
		Cia.	(Sp. *Compañía*) company
CD, C/D	(pl. **CDs**) Congressional District; Certificate of Deposit; Civil Defense	**Cie**	(Fr. *Compagnie*) company
		CIO	Congress of Industrial Organizations
Cdr., Cmdr., Comdr.	Commander	**cir.**	circa; circular; circumference
C.E.	Chemical Engineer; Chief Engineer; Civil Engineer	**cit.**	citation; cited; citizen
		civ.	civil; civilian
c.e.	(L. *caveat emptor*) at buyer's risk	**ck.**	(pl. **cks.**) check
		cm	centimeter

CO	Colorado (ZIP Code abbrev.)
C/O	certificate of origin
c/o, c.o.	care of; carried over
Co., co.	(pl. **cos.**) company; county
C.O., CO	Commanding Officer; cash order
COBOL	common business-oriented language (computer programming language)
C.O.D., c.o.d.	cash on delivery
Col.	Colonel; Colombia
col.	column; colony
coll.	collection; collateral; college
colloq.	colloquial
Colo.	Colorado
com., comm.	commerce; commission; committee; communication; commonwealth
Comdr., Cdr., Cmdr.	Commander
Comdt.	Commandant
Cong., C.	Congress; Congressional
Conn.	Connecticut
contd., cont.	continued
cor.	corner; correct; corrected
Corp.	Corporal
corp., corpn.	corporation
corr.	corrected; corresponding; correspondence
cor. sec.	corresponding secretary
CPA, C.P.A.	Certified Public Accountant
CPFF	cost plus fixed fee

CPI	consumer price index
Cpl.	Corporal
cpm	cycles per minute
CPO	Chief Petty Officer
CPS	Certified Professional Secretary
cps	cycles per second
CSC	Civil Service Commission
CST	Central Standard Time
CT	Connecticut (ZIP Code abbrev.)
ct.	(pl. **cts.**) cent; county; court
ctn.	carton
ctr.	center
cu.	cubic
cu. ft.	cubic foot or feet
cu. in.	cubic inch or inches
cum.	cumulative
cur.	currency; current
cu. yd.	cubic yard or yards
CWO	chief warrant officer
c.w.o., C.W.O.	cash with order
cwt.	hundredweight
cyl.	cylinder; cylindrical

D

D.	Democrat; Democratic
d.	date; day
D.A.	District Attorney
db	decibel (unit of sound)
d.b.a.	doing business as (name of firm)
DC	District of Columbia (ZIP Code abbrev.)
D.C.	District of Columbia
d.c., dc	direct current

D.C.L.	Doctor of Civil Law	**dkg.**	decagram
dd.	delivered	**dkl.**	decaliter
D.D.	Doctor of Divinity	**dkm.**	decameter
D.D.S.	Doctor of Dental Surgery	**dl**	deciliter
DE	Delaware (ZIP Code abbrev.)	**D/L**	demand loan
		D.Lit(t).	Doctor of Letters
D.E., **D. Eng.**	Doctor of Engineering	**D.L.S.**	Doctor of Library Science
		dlvy., dly.	delivery
Dec.	December	**dm**	decimeter (metric)
dec.	deceased; decrease	**D.O.**	Doctor of Osteopathy
def.	defendant; defense; defined; definition; deferred	**d.o., DO**	delivery order; defense order
deg.	degree; degrees	**DOA**	dead on arrival
Del.	Delaware	**doc.**	document
del.	delegate; delete	**DOD**	Department of Defense
Dem.	Democrat; Democratic	**DOE**	Department of Energy
Den.	Denmark	**dol., dl.**	(pl. **dols.**) dollar
dep.	department; departure; deposit; depot; deputy	**dom.**	domestic; dominion
		doz.	dozen; dozens
dept.	(pl. **depts.**) department; deponent	**DP**	(pl. **DPs**) displaced person; data processing
der.	derivation; derived	**dp**	depart
det.	detachment; detail	**D.P.H.**	Doctor of Public Health
D.F.A.	Doctor of Fine Arts	**dpt.**	department
dg	decigram	**Dr.**	(pl. **Drs.**) Doctor; Drive
DHQ	Division Headquarters	**D.S., D.Sc.**	Doctor of Science
di., dia., **diam.**	diameter	**D.S.C.**	Distinguished Service Cross
diag.	diagonal; diagram	**D.S.M.**	Distinguished Service Medal
dict.	dictator; dictionary		
dir.	director	**DST**	daylight saving time
dis.	discount; distance	**dstn.**	destination
dist.	distance; district; distribution	**dtd.**	dated
div.	(pl. **divs.**) dividend; division	**D.T.s,** **DTs**	delirium tremens
D.J., DJ	Dow Jones; district judge; disc jockey	**Du.**	Dutch
DJI	Dow-Jones Index	**D.V.M.**	Doctor of Veterinary Medicine

E

E., e.	east; eastern
ea.	each
EB	eastbound
econ.	economic; economics; economy
ed.	(pl. **eds.**) edited; editor; edition; education
Ed.B.	Bachelor of Education
Ed.D.	Doctor of Education
Ed.M.	Master of Education
EDP	electronic data processing
EDT	Eastern Daylight Time
educ.	education; educational
E.E.	Electrical Engineer
e.g.	(L. *exempli gratia*) for example
elec.	electric; electrical; electricity
elem.	element(s); elementary
elev.	elevation
e.m.p.	end of month payment
enc., encl.	enclosure(s)
ency., encyl.	encyclopedia
end.	endorsed; endorsement
Eng.	England; English
eng., engr.	engineer; engineering; engraved
Ens.	Ensign
env.	(pl. **envs.**) envelope
e.o.m.	end of month
eq.	equal; equator; equivalent; equipment; equation
equiv.	equivalent
ERA	Equal Rights Amendment
ESP	extrasensory perception
esp., espec.	especially
Esq.	(pl. **Esqs.**) Esquire
EST	Eastern Standard Time
est.	established; establishment; estimate; estate
ETA, e.t.a.	estimated time of arrival
et al	(L. *et alii*) and others
etc.	(L. *et cetera*) and so forth
et seq.	(L. *et sequens*) and the following
ETV	educational television
Eur.	Europe; European
ex.	(pl. **exs.**) example; exchange; executive; exercise; express; exception; execute
exc., exch.	exchange
exec.	executive
exp.	expenses; express; export; experiment
exr.	executor
ext.	extension; exterior; extract; external; extra

F

F, Fahr.	Fahrenheit
f.	(pl. **ff.**) and the following [page]; female; father
FAA	Federal Aviation Administration
f.a.s.	free alongside ship
FBI	Federal Bureau of Investigation
FCC	Federal Communications Commission
FDA	Food and Drug Administration
FDIC	Federal Deposit Insurance Corporation
Feb.	February

Fed.	Federal; Federated; Federation
fem.	feminine
FET	federal excise tax
ff.	and the following [pages]; folio
FHA	Federal Housing Administration
FICA	Federal Insurance Contributions Act
fig.	(pl. **figs.**) figure
Fin.	Finland; Finnish
fin.	finance; financial, finis; finished
FIT	federal income tax
FITW	Federal Income Tax Withholding
FL	Florida (ZIP Code abbrev.)
fl.	fluid; floor
Fla.	Florida
FM	frequency modulation
fm.	fathom; from
fn.	footnote
F.O.	field officer; Foreign Office
F.O.B., f.o.b.	free on board
fol.	folio; following
for.	foreign; forestry
FOR, f.o.r.	free on rail (or road)
FORTRAN	formula translation (computer programming language)
FOT, f.o.t.	free on truck
f.p., fp	freezing point
FPC	Federal Power Commission
f. pd.	full paid
fpm, f.p.m.	feet per minute

FPO	Fleet Post Office (U.S. Navy)
fps, f.p.s.	feet per second
FR	full rate (cables)
Fr.	France; French; Father; *Frau*
freq.	frequent; frequently; frequency
Fri.	Friday
FRS	Federal Reserve System
frt.	freight
FSLIC	Federal Savings and Loan Insurance Corporation
ft.	foot; feet; fort
FTC	Federal Trade Commission
fth., fthm.	fathom
furn.	furnished; furniture
fut.	future; futures (exchange)
fwd.	forward
FX	foreign exchange
FYI, fyi	for your information

G

g	gram(s)
g.	gravity
GA	General Agent; General Assembly; Georgia (ZIP Code abbrev.)
Ga.	Georgia
G.A., g.a.	general average
gal.	(pl. **gals.**) gallon
GAO	General Accounting Office
G.B.	Great Britain
g-cal.	gram calorie
GCT	Greenwich Civil Time

GD	general delivery
gds.	goods
GDR	German Democratic Republic
Gen.	(pl. **Gens.**) General
gen.	gender; general; generally; generator; genus
geog.	geography; geographic; geographical; geographer
geol.	geology; geologic; geological; geologist
Ger.	Germany; German
GHQ	General Headquarters
GI	(pl. **GIs**) Government Issue
Gk.	Greek
gloss.	glossary
GM	General Motors; general manager; guided missile
GMT	Greenwich Mean Time
G.N.	(pl. **G.N.s**) Graduate Nurse
GNP, **G.N.P.**	gross national product
G.O.P.	Grand Old Party (Republican)
Gov.	(pl. **Govs.**) Governor
govt.	government
G.P.	Graduate in Pharmacy; general practitioner
GPA, **g.p.a.**	grade point average
g.p.m., **gpm**	gallons per mile
GPO	Government Printing Office
Gr.	Greece; Grecian
gr.	gross; grade; gravity; graph
grad.	graduate; graduated; graduation
gr. wt.	gross weight
g.s.	ground speed
GSA	General Services Administration
gtd., gu., **guar.**	guaranteed

H

h.	hours
hdbk.	handbook
hdlg.	handling
hdw.	hardware
hf.	half
h-f., HF	high-frequency (sound waves)
hg	hectogram (metric)
HI	Hawaii (ZIP Code abbrev.)
hist.	history; historical; historian
hm	hectometer (metric)
H.M.S.	His (or Her) Majesty's Ship, or Service
hol.	holiday
Hon.	(pl. **Hons.**) Honorable

I

I.	Island(s); Isle(s)
IA	Iowa (ZIP Code abbrev.)
ib., ibid	(L. *ibidem*) in the same place
IBM	International Business Machines Corporation
ICMB	intercontinental ballistic missile
ICC	Interstate Commerce Commission
ID	Idaho (ZIP Code abbrev.)
id.	(L. *idem*) the same

i.e.	(L. *id est*) that is
IHS	monogram for Greek word for Jesus
IL	Illinois (ZIP Code abbrev.)
ILA	International Longshoremen's Association
ILGWU	International Ladies' Garment Workers' Union
Ill.	Illinois
ill., illus.	illustration; illustrated
ILO	International Labor Organization
imp.	imperative; imperfect; import; importing; imported; importer; imprimatur; imprint
IN	Indiana (ZIP Code abbrev.)
in.	inch(es)
Inc.	Incorporated
inc.	increase; income; incoming
incl.	inclusive; including
incog.	(It. *incognito*) in secret; unknown
Ind.	Indiana
ind.	industry; industrial; independent
Ind. E.	Industrial Engineer
init.	initial
in re	in regard to (L.)
ins.	insurance; inspector
Inst.	Institute; Institution; Institutional
inst.	instant; installment
instr.	instructor; instruction(s); instrument; instrumental
int.	interest; international; interjection; interim; interior; internal; intransitive

Intl., Int.	International
inv.	invoice; investment; inventor; invention; invented
invt.	inventory
i.p.s., ips	inches per second
IQ, I.Q.	intelligence quotient
i.q.	(L. *idem quod*) the same as
Ir.	Irish
Ire.	Ireland
IRS, Int. Rev.	Internal Revenue Service
is., isl., i.	(pl. **is.** or **isls.**) island
iss.	issue
It.	Italian; Italy
ix.	index

J

J.	(pl. **JJ.**) Judge; Justice
J.A.	Judge Advocate
Jan.	January
JD	juvenile delinquency (or delinquent)
J.D.	(L. *Jurum Doctor*) Doctor of Laws
jnt. stk.	joint stock
jour., j.	journal
J.P.	Justice of the Peace
Jpn.	Japan; Japanese
Jr., jr.	(pl. **jrs.**) junior
J.S.D.	Doctor of Juristic (or Juridical) Science
jt.	joint
Ju.	June
Jul.	July

K

K., k.	karat (carat); kilo
k., kn.	knot

Kans.	Kansas
kc	kilocycle (radio)
K.C.	Knights of Columbus
kcal.	kilocalorie(s)
kg.	keg(s); kilogram(s)
kgps, kg/s	kilograms per second
KKK, **K.K.K.**	Ku Klux Klan
kl	kiloliter
km	kilometer
KO	knockout
kph, k/h	kilometers per hour
KS	Kansas (ZIP Code abbrev.)
kt., K	karat
kw	kilowatt(s)
kwh, **kw-hr.,** **kwhr**	kilowatt-hour
KY	Kentucky (ZIP Code abbrev.)
Ky.	Kentucky

L

L.	Latin
l	liter
l.	line (pl. **ll.**) league; left; length; lira; lire; liter(s)
LA	Louisiana (ZIP Code abbrev.)
La.	Louisiana
L.A.	Local Agent; Los Angeles
lab.	laboratory
lang.	language
lat.	latitude
lb.	(L. *libra*; pl. **lbs.**) pound
L/C	(pl. **Ls/C**) letter of credit
lc., l.c.	lower case; left center
LCdr., **Lt. Cmdr.**	Lieutenant Commander
lea.	league; leather

Leg.	Legislature, Legislative, Legislation
leg.	legal
LF, L.F., lf, **l.f.**	low frequency
lg.	large
L.H.D.	Doctor of the Humanities
L.I.	Long Island
lib.	library
Lieut., Lt.	(pl. **Lts.**) Lieutenant
liq.	liquid
lit.	literature; literally
Litt.D.	Doctor of Letters or Literature
ll.	lines
LL.B.	Bachelor of Laws
LL.D.	Doctor of Laws
loc.	location; local
loc. cit.	(L. *loco citato*) in the place cited
long.	longitude
Lt., Lieut.	(pl. **Lts.**) Lieutenant
Lt. Col.	Lieutenant Colonel
Lt. Comdr.	Lieutenant Commander
Ltd., ltd.	limited
Lt. Gen.	Lieutenant General
Lt. Gov.	Lieutenant Governor
ltr.	letter
lv.	leave(s)

M

M	(L. *mille*) 1000
m, m.	meter(s)
m²	square meter
M.	(pl. **MM.** or **Messrs.**) Monsieur; Master; Monday
m.	male; married; masculine; medium; mile(s); mill(s); minute(s); month

MA	Massachusetts (ZIP Code abbrev.)	**meas.**	measure, measurement
M.A.	Master of Arts	**mech.**	mechanic; mechanics; mechanical
mach.	machine; machinery	**med.**	medical; medicine; medium
mag.	magazine; magnitude		
Maj.	Major	**Messrs., MM.**	Messieurs
maj.	majority		
Maj. Gen.	Major General	**met.**	metropolitan; meteorological; metal
Man.	Manhattan; Manitoba (Canada)	**Mex.**	Mexican; Mexico
Mar.	March	**mfd.**	manufactured
mar.	market; marine; maritime; married	**mfg.**	manufacturing
		mfr.	(pl. **mfrs.**) manufacture; manufacturer
masc., mas., m.	masculine		
		mg	milligram
Mass.	Massachusetts	**m/g**	miles per gallon
mat.	maturity; matinee	**Mgm**	(pl. **Mgms**) mailgram
math.	mathematics; mathematician; mathematical	**mgm**	milligram(s)
		Mgr.	Manager; Monseigneur; Monsignor
MATS	Military Air Transport Service		
		mgt., mgmt.	management
max.	maximum		
M.B.A.	Master of Business Administration	**M.H., MH**	Medal of Honor
		MI	Michigan (ZIP Code abbrev.)
MBS	Mutual Broadcasting System	**mi.**	mile(s); mill(s)
mc	megacycle	**Mich.**	Michigan
M.C.	Master of Ceremonies; Member of Congress; Military Cross	**mid.**	middle; midshipman
		mil.	military; mileage; million
		min.	minute(s); minimum; mineral; mining
MD	Maryland (ZIP Code abbrev.)		
		Minn.	Minnesota
Md.	Maryland	**misc.**	miscellaneous
M.D.	Doctor of Medicine	**Miss.**	Mississippi
Mdm.	Madam	**M.I.T.**	Massachusetts Institute of Technology
mdse.	merchandise		
ME	Maine (ZIP Code abbrev.)	**mk.**	(pl. **mks.**) mark
		mkt., mar.	market
M.E.	Mechanical Engineer; Military Engineer; Mining Engineer; Managing Editor	**ml**	milliliter
		Mlle	(pl. **Mlles.**) Mademoiselle (Fr.)

mm	millimeter
MM.	Messieurs (Fr.)
Mme.	Madame (Fr.)
Mmes.	Mesdames (Fr.)
MN	Minnesota (ZIP Code abbrev.)
Mn	House (Fr., *maison*)
mng.	managing
MO	Missouri (ZIP Code abbrev.)
Mo.	Missouri
mo.	(pl. **mos.**) month
m.o.	money order; mail order
mod.	modified; moderate
mol.	molecule
Mon., M., or Mo.	Monday
Mont.	Montana
MP	(pl. **MPs**) Military Police; Member of Parliament; Mounted Police
mp, m.p.	melting point
m.p.g., mpg, m/g	miles per gallon
m.p.h., mph, m/h	miles per hour
Mr.	(pl. **Messrs.**) Mister
Mrs.	(pl. **Mmes.**) Mistress
MS	Mississippi (ZIP Code abbrev.)
m/s	meters per second
Ms.	(pl. **Mss.**) Miss or Mrs.
ms., MS	(pl. **mss., MSS**) manuscript
M.S., M.Sc.	Master of Science
msg.	message
Msgr.	Monsignor
msgr.	messenger
M. Sgt., M/Sgt.	Master Sergeant
MST	Mountain Standard Time
MT	Montana (ZIP Code abbrev.)
mt.	(pl. **mts.**) mount; mountain; material
mtg.	meeting; mortgage
mun.	municipal
mus.	music; musical; musician; museum
Mus.D.	Doctor of Music
m.v.	market value

N

N.	Navy; north; noon
n.	note; net; new; noun; noon; name
n/30	net in 30 days
n.a.	no account (bank); not available (data)
NAACP	National Association for the Advancement of Colored People
NAS	National Academy of Sciences
NASA	National Aeronautics and Space Administration
nat., natl.	national
NATO	North Atlantic Treaty Organization
naut.	nautical
nav.	naval; navigation
NB	northbound; Nebraska (ZIP Code abbrev.)
N.B.	New Brunswick, Canada
n.b., N.B.	(L. *nota bene*) note well
NBC	National Broadcasting Company
NBS	National Bureau of Standards
NC	North Carolina (ZIP Code abbrev.)

N.C.	North Carolina	**non. pros.**	(L., *non prosequitur*) he does not prosecute
n.c.	no charge		
NCO	noncommissioned officer	**non. seq.**	(L., *non sequitur*) it does not follow
ND	North Dakota (ZIP Code abbrev.)	**Nor.**	Norwegian; Norway
n.d.	no date; next day's delivery	**Nov.**	November
		N/P	notes payable
N. Dak.	North Dakota	**N.P.**	Notary Public
NE	northeast	**n.p.**	no place (of publication); net proceeds
NEA	National Education Association; National Editorial Association		
		NPO	Navy Post Office
		NR	no ranking or rating
Nebr.	Nebraska	**NRC**	Nuclear Regulatory Commission
neg.	negative; negatively		
Neth.	Netherlands	**N.S.**	Nova Scotia; not specified
Nev.	Nevada		
N.F.	no funds; Newfoundland	**N.S.F.**	not sufficient funds
N.G., NG	National Guard	**nt.wt., n.wt.**	net weight
n.g.	no good		
NH	New Hampshire (ZIP Code abbrev.)	**n.u.**	name unknown
		nuc.	nuclear
N.H.	New Hampshire	**NV**	no value; no valuation; nonvoting; Nevada (ZIP Code abbrev.)
NJ	New Jersey (ZIP Code abbrev.)		
N.J.	New Jersey	**N.V.D., nvd**	no value declared
NL	night letter	**NW**	northwest
n.l.	(L., *non licet*) it is not permitted; (L., *non liquet*) it is not clear; new line	**NW.T.**	Northwest Territories, Canada
		NY	New York (ZIP Code abbrev.)
N.Lat., NL	north latitude		
NLRB	National Labor Relations Board	**N.Y.**	New York
		NYC, N.Y.C.	New York City
NM	New Mexico (ZIP Code abbrev.)		
		NYSE	New York Stock Exchange
N. Mex.	New Mexico		
No., N.	North; northern	**N.Z.**	New Zealand
no., No.	(pl. **nos.**) number		
n.o.c.	not otherwise classified		**O**
nol. pros.	(L., *nolle prosequi*) to be unwilling to prosecute	**O.**	Ocean
		oa, OA	overall

o/a	on account; on or about	ord.	ordinance; order; ordinary
OAS	Organization of American States	Oreg.	Oregon
ob.	(L., *obiit*) he or she died; obstetrics	Org., Orgn.	Organization
obit.	(pl. **obits.**) obituary	orig.	original; originally
obs.	obsolete; observation; observatory	o/s, OS	out of stock
ob.s.p.	(L., *obiit sine prole*) died without issue	OSHA	Occupational Safety and Health Act
O/C	over-the-counter; overcharge	O/T	overtime
oc.	overcharge; ocean	o.w., OW	one way (fare)
Oct.	October	oz.	ounce(s)

P

o.d.	on demand; overdraft	p.	(pl. **pp.**) page; per; pressure; population
OED	Oxford English Dictionary	PA	Pennsylvania (ZIP Code abbrev.)
OEO	Office of Economic Opportunity	P/A	power of attorney
ofc., off.	office; official; officer	Pa.	Pennsylvania
OH	Ohio (ZIP Code abbrev.)	pa.	paper
OK	Oklahoma (ZIP Code abbrev.)	P.A.	(pl. **P.A.s**) Purchasing Agent; Press Agent; private account; public address system
Okla.	Oklahoma	p.a., per an.	per annum (by the year)
OMB	Office of Management and Budget	Pac.	Pacific
Ont.	Ontario, Canada	pam.	pamphlet
op.	opera; (L., *opus*) work	Pan-Am	Pan-American World Airways, Inc.
o.p., OP	out of print; open policy	par.	(pl. **pars.**) paragraph; parallel; parenthesis
op. cit.	(L., *opere citato*) in the work cited	paren.	(pl. **parens.**) parenthesis
OPEC	Organization of Petroleum Exporting Countries	part.	particular
opp.	opposite	pat.	patent; patented
opr.	operate; operating; operation(s)	Pat. Off.	Patent Office
opt.	optional; optician	payt.	payment
OR	Oregon (ZIP Code abbrev.)	PBX	private branch exchange
Or.	Oriental	PC, P.C.	private corporation
		pc.	(pl. **pcs.**) piece

pc., pct.	percent
pcl.	parcel
pd.	paid
P.E.	Professional Engineer
P.E.G.	prior endorsement guaranteed
perf.	perfect; performer; performance; perforated
perm.	permanent
perp.	perpetual; perpendicular
pet., petr.	petroleum
petn.	petition
pf.	perfect
pf., pfd., pref.	preferred (securities)
Pfc., PFC	Private First Class
Pg.	Portuguese; Portugal
ph., PH	phase
Phar.D.	Doctor of Pharmacy
Ph.C.	Pharmaceutical Chemist
Ph.D.	Doctor of Philosophy
P.I.	Philippine Islands
PJ	presiding judge
pk.	(pl. **pks.**) pack; packing; park
pkg.	(pl. **pkgs.**) package; parking
pky., pkwy.	parkway
PL	price list; public law
Pl.	Place
pl.	plural; place
Plf., Ptf.	(pl. **Plfs., Ptfs.**) plaintiff
PLO	Palestine Liberation Organization
PLS	Professional Legal Secretary
Plz.	Plaza
PM, P.M., p.m.	(L. *post meridiem*) afternoon

pm., prem.	premium
pmt., payt.	payment
p.n., PN	promissory note
P.O.	post office; Petty Officer (Navy)
p.o.d.	pay on delivery; payable on death
p.o.e., POE	port of entry; port of embarkation
Pol.	Polish; Poland
pol.	politics; political
pop.	population
Port.	Portuguese; Portugal
pos.	positive; possessive; position
pot.	potential
PP	Planned Parenthood
pp.	pages; privately printed; prepaid; postpaid
P.P., Per Pro.	(L. *per procurationem*) by authorization; by proxy
p.p.	parcel post
ppd.	postpaid; prepaid
p.p.i.	parcel post insured
P.Q.	Province of Quebec, Canada
PR	payroll; Public Relations
Pr.	Professor
pr.	price; present; province; printed; printing; preferred (stock)
PRC	People's Republic of China (mainland China)
pref., pf.	preferred; preference; preface
prem., pm.	premium
prep.	preparatory; preposition
Pres.	President
prim.	primacy
prin.	principal

prob.	problem
prod.	product; produce; produced
Prof.	(pl. **Profs.**) Professor
pron.	pronunciation; pronounced; pronoun
prop.	property; proposition
Prot.	Protestant
pro tem.	(L. *pro tempore*) temporarily
prov.	province; provision; provisional
prs.	pairs
PS	(pl. **PSS**) postscript
Ps.	(pl. **Pss.**) Psalm
p.s.f., psf.	pounds per square foot
psgr., pass.	passenger
p.s.i., psi	pounds per square inch
P.S.T., PST	Pacific Standard Time
pstg.	postage
PT	private terms
pt.	part; payment; pint; point; port
p.t.	pro tempore (L.)
P.T.A., PTA	(pl. **P.T.A.s, PTAs**) Parent-Teacher Association
ptg.	printing
ptr.	printer
PU	pickup
pub.	public; publication; published; publishing; publisher
PUD	pickup and delivery
pur.	purchaser; purchasing
Pvt.	Private (Army and Marines)
pwr., pow.	power
PX	(pl. **PXs**) post exchange (military)

Q

Q.	Quebec; Question
q.	(pl. **qq.**) quart; quarter; quarterly; queer; query; question
Q.E.D.	(L. *quod erat demonstrandum*) which was to be proved
QM., Q.M.	quartermaster
qr.	quarter; quarterly
qt.	(pl. **qts.**) quart
Q.T., q.t.	quiet: usually as **on the Q.T.** (or **q.t.**)
qtr., quar., qu.	quarter, quarterly
qty.	quantity
quad.	quadrant; quadrangle
Que., Q.	Quebec, Canada
que., Q., q., ques.	question

R

R.	Range; Republic; Republican
r.	right; road
R.A.	Rear Admiral; Royal Academy
rad.	radio; radiant; radical
RAF, R.A.F.	Royal Air Force
R & D	Research and Development
RB	Renegotiation Board
R.C.	Red Cross; Roman Catholic
RCA	Radio Corporation of America
rcpt.	(pl. **rcpts.**) receipt
Rd., rd.	Road; road
rd.	rod; round

re	in regard to (L.)	R.I.P.	(L. *requiescat in pace*) may he or may she rest in peace
R.E.	Real Estate		
REA	Railway Express Agency		
Rear Adm., R.Adm.	Rear Admiral	rm.	(pl. **rms.**) room
		R.N.	Registered Nurse; Royal Navy
rec.	record; recorded; recorder; recipe; receipt	R.N.R.	Royal Naval Reserve
recd., rcd.	received	Rom.	Roman; Romance
Rec. Sec.	Recording Secretary	ROTC	Reserve Officers' Training Corps
ref.	reference; referee; refining; refunding	Rp., Rep., R.	Republic, Republican
refr.	refrigerate; refrigerated; refrigerating; refrigerator	R.P.D.	(L. *Rerum Politicarum Doctor*) Doctor of Political Science
reg.	register; registered; regulation; regular	r.p.m., rpm, r/m	revolutions per minute
Rep.	Republic; Republican; Representative	RPO	railway post office
rep.	repeat; report; repair	r.p.s., rps, r/s	revolutions per second
rept., rpt., rep.	report	rpt.	report
req.	requisition; required	RR	(pl. **RRs**) railroad
res.	reserve; residence; resolution; research	R.R.	rural route
		R.S.	Revised Statutes; Recording Secretary
ret.	retired; return		
retd.	returned	r.s.	right side
Rev.	(pl. **Revs.**) Reverend	R.S.V.P.	(Fr. *Répondez s'il vous plaît*) please reply
rev.	review; revenue; reverse; revise; revised; revision; revolve; revolving; revolution	rt.	(pl. **rts.**) right; round trip
		rte., rt.	route
		Rt. Hon.	Right Honorable
Rev. Stat., R.S.	Revised Statutes	Rt. Rev.	Right Reverend
		Rus.	Russian; Russia
rf., rfg.	refunding (bonds); refining (oil)	R/W	right of way
		Ry.	(pl. **Rys.**) Railway
r.f., RF	radio frequency		
R.F.D.	rural free delivery		**S**
rg., reg.	registered	S	Signed (before signature on typed copy of a document, original of which was signed)
RI	Rhode Island (ZIP Code abbrev.)		
R.I.	Republik Indonesia; Rhode Island	S.	south; science; Senate

s.	silver; stock; steamer; second; seconds; section; see
s/a	subject to approval
S.A.	South America; South Africa; Salvation Army
SAE	Society of Automotive Engineers
S. Afr.	South Africa; South African
S. Am.	South America; South American
San.D.	Doctor of Sanitation
S & L	(pl. **S & L's**) Savings and Loan
Sask.	Saskatchewan, Canada
Sat.	Saturday
Sav.	Savings
SB	southbound
S.B.	Bachelor of Science
SBA	Small Business Administration
SC	South Carolina (ZIP Code abbrev.)
sc., sci.	science
S.C.	South Carolina
Sc.D.	Doctor of Science
sch	school; schedule
Scot., Sc.	Scottish; Scotch; Scotland
Script.	Scripture(s)
script.	scriptural
SD	South Dakota (ZIP Code abbrev.)
s.d.	special delivery
S. Dak.	South Dakota
SE	southeast
SEATO	Southeast Asia Treaty Organization
SEC	Securities and Exchange Commission
sec.	section; second(s); security; secretary; sector
secy., sec.	(pl. **secys., secs.**) secretary
sel.	select; selected; selection
Sen.	(pl. **Sens.**) Senate; Senator; Senior
Sep., Sept.	September
sep.	separate
seq.	(L. *sequens,* pl. **seqq.**) the following
ser.	series; serial; service
serv., svc.	service
sess.	session
S.F.	Sinking Fund
SFC	Sergeant First Class
Sgd., S	signed
Sgt.	Sergeant
sh.	(pl. **shs.**) share; sheet
shpg.	shipping
shpt.	shipment
shtg.	shortage
sic	so written; thus
sig., sg.	signature
sim.	similar
sing.	singular
S.J.	Society of Jesus (the Jesuits)
S.J.D.	Doctor of Juridical Science
S.Lat., SL	south latitude
sld.	sailed; sealed; sold
sltx, SLTX	sales tax
sm	small
S.M.	Master of Science
SN	Seaman
So., S.	South; southern
s.o.	shipping order

Soc.	Society; Sociology; Socialist	**S.T.D.**	Doctor of Sacred Theology
sol.	solution; solicitor	**Ste.**	(Fr. *Sainte*) Saint (feminine)
SOP	standard operating procedure	**stge.**	storage
SOR	(pl. **SORs**) stockholder of record	**stk.**	stock
		Stk. Ex., St. Ex.	Stock Exchange
Sp.	Spanish; Spain; Specialist		
sp.	species; special; spelling; specimen; specific	**Stk. Mkt.**	Stock Market
		stmt.	statement
s.p.	(L. *sine prole*) without issue	**stp., st., sta.**	stamped
spec.	(pl. **specs**) specification; specimen	**stud.**	student
s.p.s.	(L. *sine prole superstite*) without surviving issue	**sub.**	substitute; subway; subscriber; subscription; substance; submarine; suburb; suburban
Sq., sq.	square; squadron	**subj., sub.**	subject
sq.	(L. *sequens*, pl. **sqq.**) the following	**Sun.**	Sunday
		sup.	superior; supply
sq. ft.	square foot or feet	**supp., sup.**	(pl. **supps.** or **sups.**) supplement; supplementary
sq. in.	square inch or inches		
Sr.	Senior; Sister; Sir	**Supt.**	Superintendent
S.R.	shipping receipt	**sur.**	surface; surplus
S.R.O., SRO	standing room only	**surg.**	surgeon; surgery; surgical
S.S., SS, S/S	(pl. **SSs.**) steamship; supersonic	**surv.**	survey; surveying; surveyor; surviving
SSA	Social Security Administration	**svc., svce., serv.**	service
S. Sgt., S/Sgt.	Staff Sergeant	**svgs.**	savings
SSR, S.S.R.	Soviet Socialist Republic	**s.v.p.**	(Fr. *s'il vous plaît*) if you please
SSS	Selective Service System	**svy.**	survey
St.	Street; State; Store; (pl. **SS.**) Saint	**SW**	southwest
Sta.	Station	**Sw., Swed.**	Swedish; Sweden
sta.	stamped; stationary	**sw.**	switch
stat.	statistics; statutes	**swbd.**	switchboard
std.	standard; seated	**syl.**	syllable(s)

sym.	symbol; symphony; symptom; symmetrical
synd.	syndicate; syndicated
syst., sys.	system

T

T.	Tablespoon(s); Territory
T., Tp., Twp.	(pl. **Tps., Twps.**) township
t.	temperature; time; teaspoon; ton
tab.	table(s)
T.A.G.	The Adjutant General
t.a.w.	twice a week
TB	tuberculosis
T.B.	trial balance
tbsp., tbs., T.	tablespoon(s)
TC	Tax Court of the United States
T.C., TC	travelers check
TD	touchdown; time deposit; trust deed
tech.	technical; technician
tel.	telephone; telegraph; telegram
temp.	temperature; temporary
Tenn.	Tennessee
ter.	territory; territorial; terrace
Tex.	Texas
tg.	telegraph
tgm.	telegram
thou.	thousand
Thurs., Thur.	Thursday
TM, Tmk.	(pl. **TMs, Tmks.**) trademark
tn., T.	ton; town; train

TN	Tennessee (ZIP Code abbrev.)
tonn.	tonnage
tp	telephone
t.p.	title page
tph	tons per hour
tpm	tons per minute
tr.	trust; trustee; transit; transfer; translated; translation; translator; treasurer
T.R.	tons registered (shipping)
trans., tr.	translated, translation, translator
treas., tr.	treasurer; treasury
T. Sgt., T/Sgt.	Technical Sergeant
tsp., t.	teaspoon(s)
Tues., Tue.	Tuesday
Turk.	Turkish; Turkey
TV	television; terminal velocity
TVA	Tennessee Valley Authority
TWA	Trans-World Airlines, Inc.
twp.	township
TWX	teletypewriter exchange
TX	Texas (ZIP Code abbrev.)
tx.	tax or taxes; text; textbook

U

U., Univ.	University
UA	United Air Lines, Inc.; United Artists
UAW	United Automobile Workers

UFO	(pl. **UFOs**) unidentified flying object
UGT	urgent
UHF	ultrahigh frequency
U.K.	United Kingdom
UL	Underwriters Laboratories
ult.	ultimate, ultimately
UMW	United Mine Workers
UN, U.N.	United Nations
Un.	Union; United
Univ.	University
univ.	universal; university
unl.	unlimited; unlisted
UP	United Press
up	upper
UPI	United Press International
UPS	United Parcel Service
U.S., US	United States
U.S.A., USA	United States of America; United States Army
U.S.A.F., USAF	United States Air Force
U.S.A.R., USAR	United States Army Reserve
U.S.B.S.	United States Bureau of Standards
U.S.C.	University of Southern California; under separate cover
U.S.C.G.	United States Coast Guard
U.S.D.J.	United States District Judge
USIA	United States Information Agency
U.S.M.C., USMC	United States Marine Corps
U.S.N., USN	United States Navy
U.S.N.G., USNG	United States National Guard
U.S.N.R.	United States Naval Reserve
U.S.S.	United States Senate; United States Ship
U.S.S.R., USSR	Union of Soviet Socialist Republics
UT	Utah (ZIP Code abbrev.)
ut.	utilities

V

v	volt
v.	(pl. **vv.**) verse; verb; volume; versus
VA	Virginia (ZIP Code abbrev.)
Va.	Virginia
V.A., VA	Veterans' Administration
vac.	vacuum
val.	value
var.	variety; various
vel.	velocity
Ven.	Venerable
vert.	vertical
v.f., VF	video frequency
V.G.	Vicar General; very good
VHF	very high frequency
V.I.	Virgin Islands; Vancouver Island
Vice Adm., V.A., V.Adm.	Vice Admiral
Vice-Pres., V.P., V. Pres.	Vice-President
VIP	(pl. **VIPs**) very important person
vis.	visibility; visual
viz	(L. *videlicet*) namely

vol.	(pl. **vols.**) volume; volunteer
voy.	voyage
V.P., Vice-Pres.	Vice-President
vs., v.	(L. *versus*) against; verse
V.S.	Veterinary Surgeon
VT	Vermont (ZIP Code abbrev.)
Vt.	Vermont
vv.	verses
v.v.	vice versa

W

W, W., w, w.	watt(s); west; western
W., w.	warehouse; weight; width
WA	Washington state (ZIP Code abbrev.)
WAC	(pl. **WACs**) Women's Army Corps
Wash.	Washington state
WB	westbound
Wed.	Wednesday
whs.	warehouse
whsle.	wholesale
WI	Wisconsin (ZIP Code abbrev.)
W.I.	West Indies
Wis.	Wisconsin
wk.	(pl. **wks.**) work; week
W.O., WO	Warrant Officer; wait order
wpm	words per minute
wps	words per second
W.R.	warehouse receipt
wt.	(pl. **wts.**) weight; warrant

W/Tax	withholding tax
WUX	Western Union exchange
WV	West Virginia (ZIP Code abbrev.)
W. Va.	West Virginia
WY	Wyoming (ZIP Code abbrev.)
Wyo.	Wyoming

X

X	movie rating: persons under 17 not admitted
x	cross, as x-roads, x-ref.; extra, as x-hvy
Xch., X	exchange
Xn.	Christian
Xnty.	Christianity
XP	monogram for Greek word for Christ
XQ	cross-question

Y

yb.	yearbook
yd.	(pl. **yds.**) yard
YMCA	Young Men's Christian Association
YM-YWHA	Young Men's and Young Women's Hebrew Association
YWCA	Young Women's Christian Association
YWHA	Young Women's Hebrew Association

Z

z., Z.	zone; zero
ZIP	Zone Improvement Plan
ZPG	zero population growth

FORMS OF ADDRESS

These tables show the correct forms of address for persons whose rank, office, educational level, or profession requires a special courtesy title and salutation. When the official is a woman, make the appropriate substitution as shown here.

> *Miss, Ms.,* or *Mrs.* replace *Mr.*
>
> *Madam* replaces *Sir.*
>
> *Madam* replaces *Mr.* plus a title. (Madam Mayor)

Title	Address	Salutation	(O) Oral Reference (W) Written Reference
GOVERNMENT: Federal			
President of the United States	The President The White House Washington, DC 20500	Mr. President: OR Dear Mr. President:	(O) Mr. President (W) the President OR President Smith
Former President of the United States	The Honorable Charles B. Smith	Sir: OR Dear Mr. Smith:	(O) Mr. Smith (W) former President Smith OR Mr. Smith
Vice-President of the United States	The Vice-President United States Senate Washington, DC 20510 OR The Honorable Charles B. Smith Vice-President of the United States Washington, DC 20501	Sir: OR Dear Mr. Vice-President:	(O) Mr. Vice-President OR Mr. Smith (W) the Vice-President OR Vice-President Smith
Chief Justice of the United States Supreme Court	The Chief Justice of the United States Washington, DC 20543 OR The Chief Justice The Supreme Court Washington, DC 20543	Sir: OR Dear Mr. Chief Justice:	(O) Mr. Chief Justice (W) the Chief Justice OR Chief Justice Charles B. Smith OR Charles B. Smith, Chief Justice of the U.S. Supreme Court

Associate Justice of the United States Supreme Court	Mr. Justice Smith The Supreme Court of the United States Washington, DC 20543	Sir: OR Dear Mr. Justice: OR Dear Mr. Justice Smith:	**(O)** and **(W)** Mr. Justice Smith OR Justice Smith
Cabinet Member	The Honorable Charles B. Smith Secretary of Defense OR The Secretary of Defense	Sir: OR Dear Mr. Secretary:	**(O)** Mr. Smith OR Secretary Smith OR Mr. Secretary **(W)** the Secretary of Defense, Mr. Smith
United States Senator	The Honorable Charles B. Smith United States Senate Washington, DC 20510 OR The Honorable Charles B. Smith United States Senator (*local address*)	Dear Senator Smith:	**(O)** Senator Smith OR Senator **(W)** Senator Smith OR the Senator from Maine OR Mr. Smith, Senator from Maine
United States Representative	The Honorable Charles B. Smith House of Representatives Washington, DC 20515 OR The Honorable Charles B. Smith Representative in Congress (*local address*)	Sir: OR Dear Mr. Smith:	**(O)** Mr. Smith **(W)** Mr. Smith OR Mr. Smith, Representative (Congressman) from Maine

GOVERNMENT: Diplomats

Ambassador	The Honorable Charles B. Smith American Ambassador (*city and country*)	Sir: OR Dear Mr. Ambassador:	**(O)** Mr. Ambassador OR Mr. Smith **(W)** the American Ambassador

	OR		**OR**
	(*in Central or South America*) The Ambassador of the United States of America (*city and country*)		the United States Ambassador **OR** Mr. Smith, the American Ambassador **OR** the Ambassador
American Minister	The Honorable Charles B. Smith American Minister to (*country*)	Sir: **OR** Dear Mr. Smith:	**(O)** Mr. Minister **OR** Mr. Smith **(W)** the American Minister, Mr. Smith **OR** the Minister **OR** Mr. Smith
Foreign Minister	The Honorable Charles B. Smith Minister of (*country*) **OR** (*for representatives of Great Britain*) British Ambassador **OR** British Minister	Sir: **OR** Dear Mr. Minister: **OR** Dear Mr. Ambassador:	**(O)** Mr. Minister **OR** Mr. Smith **(W)** the Minister of (*country*) **OR** the Minister **OR** Mr. Smith

GOVERNMENT: State and Local

State Governor	The Honorable Charles B. Smith Governor of (*state*) **OR** His Excellency the Governor of (*state*)	Sir: **OR** Dear Governor: **OR** Dear Governor Smith:	**(O)** Governor **OR** Governor Smith **(W)** the Governor **OR** Governor Smith **OR** the Governor of (*state*)
State Senator	The Honorable Charles B. Smith The State Senate (*city and state*)	Dear Senator Smith:	**(O)** Senator **OR** Senator Smith **(W)** Senator Smith **OR** Charles Smith, the State Senator from (*county or district*)

State Representative (Assemblyman or Delegate)	The Honorable Charles B. Smith House of Representatives (State Assembly)	Sir: OR Dear Mr. Smith	(O) Mr. Smith (W) Mr. Smith OR Charles Smith, the State Representative (Assemblyman, Delegate) from (*county or district*)
Mayor	The Honorable Charles B. Smith Mayor of (*city*) OR The Mayor of the City of (*city*)	Sir: OR Dear Mr. Mayor: OR Dear Mayor Smith:	(O) Mayor Smith (W) Mayor Smith OR the Mayor OR Charles Smith, Mayor of (*city*)

RELIGIOUS DIGNITARIES: Roman Catholic

Pope	His Holiness, The Pope OR His Holiness Pope (*name*) Vatican City	Your Holiness: OR Most Holy Father:	(O) Your Holiness (W) the Pope OR His Holiness the Pope OR His Holiness, Pope (*name*)
Cardinal	His Eminence, Charles Cardinal Smith	Your Eminence: OR Dear Cardinal Smith:	(O) Your Eminence OR Cardinal Smith (W) His Eminence Cardinal Smith OR Cardinal Smith
Archbishop and Bishop	The Most Reverend Charles B. Smith Archbishop (or Bishop) of (*diocese*)	Your Excellency: OR Dear Archbishop (or Bishop) Smith:	(O) and (W) Archbishop (or Bishop) Smith
Monsignor	The Right Reverend Monsignor Charles B. Smith	Right Reverend Monsignor Smith: OR Dear Monsignor Smith:	(O) and (W) Monsignor Smith

Priest	Reverend Charles B. Smith OR The Reverend Charles B. Smith OR (*member of a religious order*) Reverend Charles B. Smith, (*appropriate initials*) OR (*with doctoral degree*) Reverend Charles B. Smith, Ph.D.	Reverend Father: OR Dear Father Smith:	**(O)** and **(W)** Father Smith
Mother (or Sister) Superior	The Reverend Mother (or Sister) Superior	Dear Mother (or Sister) Superior:	**(O)** Reverend Mother (or Sister) Superior OR Mother (or Sister) (*name*) **(W)** the Reverend Mother (or Sister) Superior
Sister	Sister (*name, initials of religious community*)	Dear Sister: OR Dear Sister (name):	**(O)** and **(W)** Sister (*name*)

RELIGIOUS DIGNITARIES: Protestant

Episcopal Bishop	The Right Reverend Charles B. Smith Bishop of (*place*)	Right Reverend Sir: OR Dear Bishop Smith:	**(O)** and **(W)** Bishop Smith
Methodist Bishop	The Reverend Charles B. Smith Bishop of (*place*)	Reverend Sir: OR Dear Bishop Smith:	**(O)** and **(W)** Bishop Smith
Clergyman	(with doctoral degree) The Reverend Dr. Charles B. Smith OR The Reverend Charles B. Smith, D.D.	Reverend Sir: OR Dear Dr. Smith:	**(O)** and **(W)** Dr. Smith

	(without doctoral degree) The Reverend Charles B. Smith	Reverend Sir: OR Dear Mr. Smith:	(O) and (W) Mr. Smith

RELIGIOUS DIGNITARIES: Jewish

Rabbi	(with doctoral degree) Rabbi Charles B. Smith, D.D. OR Dr. Charles B. Smith	Dear Rabbi Smith: OR Dear Dr. Smith:	(O) and (W) Rabbi Smith OR Dr. Smith
	(without doctoral degree) Rabbi Charles B. Smith	Dear Rabbi Smith:	(O) and (W) Rabbi Smith

EDUCATION OFFICIALS

President of a college or university	(with doctoral degree) Dr. Charles B. Smith OR Charles B. Smith, Ph.D., President, (*name of college*)	Sir: OR Dear Dr. Smith:	(O) and (W) Dr. Smith
	(without doctoral degree) Mr. Charles B. Smith, President, (*name of college*)	Dear President Smith:	Mr. Smith
University Chancellor	Dr. Charles B. Smith Chancellor, (*name of school*)	Dear Dr. Smith:	(O) and (W) Dr. Smith
Dean or Assistant Dean of a College or Graduate School	Dean Charles B. Smith School of Education (*name of school*) OR (with doctoral degree) Dr. Charles B. Smith	Dear Dean Smith: OR Dear Dr. Smith:	(O) and (W) Dean Smith (W) Dr. Smith, Dean of the School of Education

Professor	Professor Charles B. Smith OR (with doctoral degree) Dr. Charles B. Smith OR Charles B. Smith, Ph.D.	Dear Professor Smith: OR Dear Dr. Smith:	**(O) and (W)** Professor Smith OR Dr. Smith
Superintendent of Schools	Mr. (or Dr.) Charles B. Smith, Superintendent of (*city or town*) Schools	Dear Mr. (or Dr.) Smith:	**(O) and (W)** Mr. Smith OR Dr. Smith
Member of Board of Education	Mr. Charles B. Smith Member, (*city or town*) Board of Education	Dear Mr. Smith:	**(O) and (W)** Mr. Smith
Principal	Mr. (or Dr.) Charles B. Smith, Principal (*name of school*)	Dear Mr. (or Dr.) Smith:	**(O) and (W)** Mr. Smith OR Dr. Smith

PROFESSIONAL

Attorney	Mr. Charles B. Smith Attorney at Law OR Charles B. Smith, Esq.	Dear Mr. Smith:	**(O)** Mr. Smith **(W)** Mr. Smith OR Attorney Smith
Physician	Charles B. Smith, M.D. OR Dr. Charles B. Smith	Dear Dr. Smith:	**(O) and (W)** Dr. Smith
Judge	The Honorable Charles B. Smith	Dear Judge Smith:	**(O)** Your Honor OR Judge Smith **(W)** Judge Smith OR Judge Charles B. Smith

MILITARY

In a military address, rank and full name are followed by a comma and the initials of the service branch: USA (United States Army); USN (United States Navy); USMC (United States Marine Corps); USAF (United States Air Force); USCG (United States Coast Guard).

General, Lieutenant General, Major General, Brigadier General	General (Lieutenant General, Major General, Brigadier General) Charles B. Smith, USA	Dear General Smith: (*not* Dear Lieutenant General Smith:)	**(O)** and **(W)** General Smith
Admiral, Vice Admiral, Rear Admiral	Admiral (Vice Admiral, Rear Admiral) Charles B. Smith, USN	Dear Admiral Smith: (*not* Dear Vice Admiral Smith:)	**(O)** and **(W)** Admiral Smith
Lieutenant, Ensign	Lieutenant (Ensign) Charles B. Smith, USA (USN)	Dear Mr. Smith:	**(O)** Mr. Smith **(W)** Lieutenant (Ensign) Smith OR Mr. Smith
Enlisted Personnel	Airman Charles B. Smith, USAF	Dear Airman Smith:	**(O)** and **(W)** Airman Smith

TABLES OF WEIGHTS AND MEASURES
U.S. Weights and Measures

Linear Measure

1 mil = 0.001 inch = 0.0254 millimeter

1 inch = 1,000 mils = 2.54 centimeters

12 inches = 1 foot = 0.3048 meter

3 feet = 1 yard = 0.9144 meter

5½ yards or 16½ feet = 1 rod = 5.029 meters

40 rods = 1 furlong = 201.168 meters

8 furlongs or 1,760 yards
or 5,280 feet = 1 (statute) mile = 1.6093 kilometers

3 miles = 1 (land) league = 4.83 kilometers

Square Measure

1 square inch = 6.452 square centimeters

144 square inches = 1 square foot = 929.03 square centimeters

9 square feet = 1 square yard = 0.8361 square meter

30¼ square yards = 1 square rod = 25.292 square meters

160 square rods or 4,840 square
yards or 43,560 square feet = 1 acre = 0.4047 hectare

640 acres = 1 square mile = 259.00 hectares or 2,590 square
kilometers

Cubic Measure

1 cubic inch = 16.387 cubic centimeters

1,728 cubic inches = 1 cubic foot = 0.0283 cubic meter

27 cubic feet = 1 cubic yard = 0.7646 cubic meter

Dry Measure

1 pint = 33.60 cubic inches = 0.5506 liter

2 pints = 1 quart = 67.20 cubic inches = 1.2012 liters

8 quarts = 1 peck = 537.61 cubic inches = 8.8098 liters

4 pecks = 1 bushel = 2,150.42 cubic inches = 35.2390 liters

The British dry quart = 1.032 U.S. dry quarts

Liquid Measure

1 gill = 4 fluid ounces = 7.219 cubic inches = 0.1183 liter

4 gills = 1 pint = 28.875 cubic inches = 0.4732 liter

2 pints = 1 quart = 57.75 cubic inches = 0.9464 liter

4 quarts = 1 gallon = 231 cubic inches = 3.7854 liters

The British imperial gallon (4 imperial quarts) = 277.42 cubic inches = 4.546 liters.
The barrel in Great Britain equals 36 imperial gallons, in the United States, usually
31½ gallons.

THE METRIC SYSTEM

Linear Measure

1 millimeter		=	0.03937 inch
10 millimeters	= 1 centimeter	=	0.3937 inch
10 centimeters	= 1 decimeter	=	3.937 inches
10 decimeters	= 1 meter	=	39.37 inches or 3.2808 feet
10 meters	= 1 decameter	=	393.7 inches
10 decameters	= 1 hectometer	=	328.08 feet
10 hectometers	= 1 kilometer	=	0.621 mile or 3,280.8 feet
10 kilometers	= 1 myriameter	=	6.21 miles

Square Measure

1 square millimeter		=	0.00155 square inch
100 square millimeters	= 1 square centimeter	=	0.15499 square inch
100 square centimeters	= 1 square decimeter	=	15.499 square inches
100 square decimeters	= 1 square meter		= 1,549.9 square inches or 1,196 square yards
100 square meters	= 1 square decameter	=	119.6 square yards
100 square decameters	= 1 square hectometer	=	2.471 acres
100 square hectometers	= 1 square kilometer	=	0.386 square mile or 247.1 acres

Land Measure

1 square meter = 1 centiare	=	1,549.9 square inches
100 centiares = 1 are	=	119.6 square yards
100 ares = 1 hectare	=	2.471 acres
100 hectares = 1 square kilometer	=	0.386 square mile or 247.1 acres

Volume Measure

1,000 cubic millimeters = 1 cubic centimeter	=	0.06102 cubic inch
1,000 cubic centimeters = 1 cubic decimeter	=	61.023 cubic inches or 0.0353 cubic foot
1,000 cubic decimeters = 1 cubic meter	=	35.314 cubic feet or 1.308 cubic yards

Capacity Measure

10 milliliters = 1 centiliter = 0.338 fluid ounce

10 centiliters = 1 deciliter = 3.38 fluid ounces or 0.1057 liquid quart

10 deciliters = 1 liter = 1.0567 liquid quarts or 0.9081 dry quart

10 liters = 1 decaliter = 2.64 gallons or 0.284 bushel

10 decaliters = 1 hectoliter = 26.418 gallons or 2.838 bushels

10 hectoliters = 1 kiloliter = 264.18 gallons or 35.315 cubic feet

Weights

10 milligrams = 1 centigram = 0.1543 grain or 0.000353 ounce (avdp.)

10 centigrams = 1 decigram = 1.5432 grains

10 decigrams = 1 gram = 15.432 grains or 0.035274 ounce (avdp.)

10 grams = 1 decagram = 0.3527 ounce

10 decagrams = 1 hectogram = 3.5274 ounces

10 hectograms = 1 kilogram = 2.2046 pounds

10 kilograms = 1 myriagram = 22.046 pounds

10 myriagrams = 1 quintal = 220.46 pounds

10 quintals = 1 metric ton = 2,204.6 pounds

GLOSSARY OF WORD-PROCESSING TERMS

administrative/correspondence support services A system of secretarial support that separates typing and nontyping functions. Some secretaries are designated Administrative Secretaries (AS), whereas others are called Correspondence Secretaries (CS). Administrative Secretaries handle nontyping functions; Correspondence Secretaries handle typing tasks. This organizational approach can serve an entire company from one location or be decentralized to service different departments or floors.

administrative secretary (AS) One who carries out all secretarial functions with the exception of typing. These duties would include processing the mail, handling the phones and making travel arrangements, as well as providing other necessary support services for management.

alphanumeric Containing or using both alphabetical and numerical characters.

automatic carriage return The capability of a typing or word-processing machine to return automatically to the left margin when the end of the line is reached.

automatic centering A feature available on some sophisticated typewriters and most word processors that automatically centers a word, phrase, or line when a designated key is depressed by the operator.

automatic decimal tab A feature that automatically aligns the decimal points in a column of figures regardless of the number of characters to the left or right of the decimal points.

automatic pagination The word-processing machine inserts page numbers automatically when the designated number of lines is reached. If the document is changed or rearranged (paragraphs added or deleted, for instance), the page numbers are changed automatically by the system to reflect the new page endings.

automatic underscore The word processor automatically underlines a word, phrase, or sentence when the appropriate key is depressed.

baud A unit of signaling speed, used to express the transmission speed of a communicating device.

bidirectional printing The capability of a printing unit to print first from left to right and then, when the right margin is reached, from right to left.

bit (binary digit) The smallest unit of information recognized by a computer.

blind text editor A text editor without a visual display screen. The keystrokes are printed directly on a piece of paper, rather than being displayed on a screen.

boilerplate Standard paragraphs or letters that are stored and used repeatedly. Boilerplate material is combined with variable information, such as names and addresses, to form what appear to be individually typed letters or memos.

buffer Temporary storage for material being keyed in and edited before it is transferred to the magnetic medium or memory.

byte A basic unit of computer information (usually eight bits).

cartridge A container holding magnetic tape on which spoken words or typewritten characters are recorded.

cassette A container of magnetic tape that is used to record typewritten characters or spoken words.

cathode ray tube (CRT) A screen, similar to a television screen, on which characters and numbers are displayed as they are keyed into the system or called up from storage.

central dictation system A system in which a number of authors have access to a centrally located dictation system.

central processing unit (CPU) The control unit or "brain" of a computer or computer-based word-processing system. The CPU interprets and executes the instructions entered into the system by the operator.

character Any letter, number, or symbol.

characters per second (cps) Refers to the number of characters that can be printed in a second. Most word processors are available with a 55-cps printer.

character string A consecutive group of characters.

charge-back system The process of billing each user or department for the services performed by the word-processing center.

clear To delete material that is stored in the memory of the word processor or computer.

code Symbols used to represent information. Some codes represent instructions to the word processor such as store, print, delete, and so forth.

command An instruction to the processing unit.

communicating typewriter A typewriter or word processor that can send and receive information electronically with other compatible units through a telephone hookup.

computer An electronic device that is programmed to accept information, perform high-speed calculations, and

provide the results of those calculations. It consists of a central processing unit (CPU), a storage device, and peripherals or attachments such as terminals and printers.

continuous-forms paper Paper designed for continuous printout of items such as form letters, envelopes, and labels. Only the initial sheet is inserted into the printing device. The rest are fed into the printer automatically, one sheet at a time.

correspondence secretary (CS) One who performs the typing, transcribing, and editing tasks of a secretary.

cursor The pointer on a visual display screen that can be moved to the point in the document where the typist wants to make a change.

daisy wheel A printing element, shaped somewhat like a daisy, that is available in a variety of interchangeable type styles.

data base A collection of information stored in a computerized system.

data processing The preparation, input, processing, and storage of data by a computer system.

delete An instruction to a word processor to remove a character, word, line, paragraph, or page from the storage medium.

discrete media Magnetic media that can be physically removed from the word processor for storage. These include diskettes, cartridges, and cassettes.

disk (disc) Also called a diskette or a floppy disk. A magnetic recording medium, about the size and shape of a 45 rpm record, used to store information for word processors and computers.

display text editor A word-processing device that includes a screen on which text is displayed.

distribution The act of sending, transmitting, routing, or delivering oral or written communications.

document Any piece of written or typed information about a specific subject. It may consist of one or more pages. Examples are letters, memos, and reports.

downtime Amount of time lost when equipment is not functioning properly.

draft The unedited version of a document.

dump To transfer the contents of a memory unit onto a storage medium.

duplex The ability of a communications device to send and receive information simultaneously.

duplicate In word processing to copy material electronically from one magnetic medium to another.

edit To change or revise text.

electronic mail A method of sending written messages electronically over telephone or telegraph lines or via a satellite network. Electronic mail systems include facsimile devices, communicating typewriters, and computer-based message systems.

electronic typewriter A typewriter that is totally electronic, rather than electromechanical. It has few moving parts and offers more capabilities than a standard electric typewriter. These include error correction before printout, format storage, and limited memory capability.

element A device in a typewriter or printer that produces characters, numbers, and symbols on a piece of paper.

endless-loop recorder A type of central dictation system that has a loop of magnetic tape as its recording medium. This tape revolves within a

"tank" and provides many hours of continuous recording.

facsimile (fax) A machine that transmits documents over telephone lines from one location to another. It converts alphanumeric or graphic material into electronic signals that are sent over phone wires to a receiving unit that converts the signals into an exact duplicate (facsimile) of the original document.

flow chart A diagram with lines and symbols showing the step-by-step progression of a procedure.

format The way in which a project or document is set up or physically arranged.

form letter A repetitive letter that is recorded and stored for repeated use. The letter becomes more personal when variable data (such as names and addresses) are added.

global search A feature offered on many word processors whereby the system will locate a designated character string (generally a word) wherever it appears in a document. In some instances, the character string can also be replaced throughout the document with a different word or words. This is called "global search and replace."

hard copy Textual material that is typed or printed in readable form on paper.

hard disk A magnetic storage and recording medium used by some large word-processing systems as well as by some computers.

hardware Refers to the physical components of a word-processing or computer system, rather than the programs and instructions (software) that operate the equipment.

highlighting A feature that brightens (or emphasizes in some other fashion) certain sections of text displayed on a screen.

hot zone The area on the right side of the page in which hyphenation decisions are made. When the machine reaches the hot zone, it will either decide to start a new line or will stop in order for the operator to make a hyphenation decision.

ink-jet printer A printing unit that sprays ink onto paper to form characters.

input Information entered into a computer, word-processing, or dictation system.

interface The point of interaction between two machines, or between a person and a machine.

justification A feature ensuring that the right margin, as well as the left one, is perfectly aligned.

K An abbreviation of the suffix *kilo* (meaning one thousand) often used to express the storage capacity of a memory unit. A 20K memory is one in which it is possible to store 20,000 characters.

keyboard The input device for a word-processing system or computer. It contains the typing keys and the function keys, such as "insert," "delete," "move," and so forth.

line To a word-processing unit, a line is a string of words typed in a row, up to and including the carriage return.

load To enter the magnetic medium into the word-processing system.

logging Recording work as it comes in and goes out of a word-processing center.

log sheet The paper on which logging information is recorded.

magnetic card A card coated with a magnetic substance on which approximately one page of typewritten material, or 50 to 100 lines, can be recorded.

Magnetic Card Selectric® Typewriter (MC/ST) A text editing typewriter, manufactured by IBM, that uses magnetic cards as a storage medium.

magnetic media The various storage devices used in word-processing systems. They include cards, cassettes, belts, tapes, and diskettes. Magnetic media are used to store both software programs and input material.

magnetic tape Magnetic-coated tape on which spoken words or keystrokes are recorded.

Magnetic Tape Selectric® Typewriter (MT/ST) The first text editing typewriter, invented by IBM in 1964.

memory An internal device of a word processor or computer in which material may be stored and then recalled upon demand.

microcomputer A small computer that has a microprocessor as its "brain."

micrographics The technology of filming documents at a greatly reduced size so that they can be conveniently and economically stored and retrieved.

microprocessor A tiny silicon chip that gives a computer its processing capability. It is the "intelligence" of a computer or word processor.

minicomputer A small, general purpose computer that offers more capabilities and power than a microcomputer. Many minicomputers have software packages that enable them to be used as word processors.

off-line Equipment that is not directly connected to and controlled by a central processing unit.

on-line Equipment that is directly connected to and controlled by a central processing unit.

optical character recognition (OCR) A technology that involves optically scanning documents. An OCR device reads or scans typed documents and converts them into electronic signals that can be understood by a word processor or computer.

originator The person who composes a document; the author.

output Information that has been printed out by a word processor or computer.

peripherals Equipment that works with the central processing unit but is not an integral part of it. Peripherals include terminals and printers as well as specialized devices such as OCR units.

pitch The number of characters per inch. Most word processors use 10 or 12 pitch. In a 12 pitch unit, 12 characters are typed per inch.

playback The automatic printing of material that has been recorded on a word processor.

prerecord To type material onto some magnetic medium for playback at a later time.

principal The originator or author of a document.

printer The output device that puts text on paper. The most common types of word-processing printers are Selectric® elements, daisy wheels, and ink-jet printers.

priority The order of urgency. Determining the order in which jobs are to be handled so that the most pressing or important ones are completed first.

proportional spacing The spacing of letters so that each character fills a number of units of space. Narrow letters such as *i* use fewer units than wide letters, such as *w*.

random access A feature offered on some magnetic media, such as disks, that makes it possible to locate material that has been filed in a random fashion. The operator does not have to know the location of the information on the medium or the sequence in which it was stored.

record To store typed or spoken material on a magnetic medium for future use.

revision The act of changing, correcting, or editing a typed document.

scrolling The movement (horizontally or vertically) of text on a visual display screen.

search A command given to a word processor to locate a desired word or phrase.

shared logic system A word-processing system in which two or more text editing stations or terminals share the processing power and memory of the central processing unit.

shared resource system A word-processing system in which each of the stations or terminals has its own processing power but shares some resources, such as files and printers, with the other stations in the system.

software The instructions and programs that tell the hardware (equipment) what to do and how to do it.

stand-alone system A self-contained word processor that operates as an independent unit with its own processing power, memory, and storage.

stop code A code entered into the system that causes the equipment to stop during playback.

store To hold a document on a magnetic medium or in memory for future recall and use.

switch code A code entered on the magnetic media that causes the word processor to switch playback from one section of memory to another, or from one medium to another.

terminal A device with a keyboard that is used to input material and, sometimes, to printout recorded material. A terminal can be "dumb" or "intelligent." Dumb terminals cannot operate independently of the processing unit; intelligent terminals have their own processing power.

text editor A typewriter that records keystrokes on magnetic media, providing the ability to change and revise text.

throughput The volume of work produced by a word processor.

time-sharing A system that connects many terminals (generally from different companies) to a large computer system, allowing many users in different locations to share both the processing power and the cost of the computer.

track A specific section of a magnetic medium.

transfer To copy material from one medium onto another.

turnaround time The length of time that elapses between the time a job is given to the word-processing department and the time it is completed and returned to the originator.

unattended printout/playback A feature that permits documents to be printed automatically, without operator intervention.

variables Information that changes from one form letter or document to another; these include names, addresses, amounts, numbers.

PROOFREADING

Proofreading involves finding and noting errors in typing and in format. A careful proofreader contributes to the clarity and accuracy of a text and therefore to the image of the originator and of the company.

There are two methods of proofreading a text: the team method and the individual method.

Team method   One person reads aloud each word and punctuation mark in the text while a second person locates and notes any errors. Because this method involves the expense of two people's time, it is usually reserved for a text containing complex financial or technical information.

Individual method   The secretary or other proofreader works alone and has the responsibility for locating and correcting errors. Before a page leaves the typewriter or before the print button is pressed on word-processing equipment, these steps should be followed:

- Check the material for completeness, accuracy, and correct format.
- Read the text for mechanical correctness: spelling, punctuation, and consistent style (correct expression of numbers; correct use of capitalization and abbreviations).
- Correct any errors.

The following chart shows the symbols used for correcting typed material. A second chart shows the proofreading symbols used by editors to correct galley proofs.

CORRECTION MARKS FOR TYPED ROUGH DRAFTS AND REVISES

Symbol	Meaning	Example
$\wedge$	Insert a word	He did $_\wedge$ say (not)
$=$	Insert a hyphen	Red $_\wedge$ hot metal
$\#$	Insert a space	and then we
$\wedge$	Insert a letter	each book
$\odot$	Make into a period	to me. Then
$\mathcal{A}$	Delete	our first introduction
$\subset$	Close up	ordered copies
$\mathcal{J}$	Delete and close up	was disappointed

Symbol	Meaning	Example
⌣	Join to word	was *in*complete
1#	Single spacing	I know what 1#___
2#	Double spacing	2#___ she'll say.
¶	New paragraph	¶ The writer of
No¶	No new paragraph	No¶ Her answer
[	Move to left	[was one
]	Move to right	] that surprised
][	Center	] FISCAL POLICY [
∾	Transpose	to the the*a*ter
◯	Spell out	(Dept.) has (1)
....	Let stand what is crossed out	no ~~further~~ answer
≡	Make all capitals	Nato treaty
⹀	Make a letter capital	dr. Falk
/	Make a letter lower case	Dr. F/lk
⌒	Change word	if ~~they~~ *you* were
—	Underscore	quoted in the Times
⟨	Move as indicated	had (not) said
═	align horizontally	‖may be *in* town
‖	align vertically	‖ on Wednesday
5]	indent	5] Copiers may
⌒	run-in	vary according
∨	superior figure	Hazelton3

STANDARD PROOFREADING MARKS

Delete ℒ	Let it stand (stet)
Close up ⌒	Lower-case capital letter ℓc
Delete and close up ℛ	Capitalize lower-case letter UC
Insert space #	Set in small capitals SC
Make space between words equal eq#	Set in italic type ital
Make leading between lines equal eq#	Set in roman type Rom
Letterspace ls	Set in boldface type bf
Insert hair (or thin) space th#	Wrong font wf
Begin new paragraph ¶	Reset broken letter Ⓧ
No new paragraph No ¶	Reverse (type upside down) ⊙
Move type one em from left or right [M]	Insert comma ⋀
Move right ⅃	Insert apostrophe ⌄
Move left ⊏	Insert quotation marks ⌄ ⌄
Center ⅃ ⊏	Insert period ⊙
Move up ⌐⌐	Insert question mark ?
Move down ⌊⌋	Insert em dash ⸺
Straighten type; align horizontally ═	Insert en dash ⸺
Align vertically ‖	Insert semicolon ⋀
Transpose ∿	Insert colon ⊙
Spell out (sp.)	Insert hyphen =

(See proofreading example on following page.)

Katharine Gibbs
Business Word Book

This easy to use word book form the prestigous Kathrine Gibbs schools is most up-to-date quick reference of its kind. Especially designed in a compact format, The Katharine Gibbs Business Word Book gives secretaries, typists, witers, editers and executives more than 2,000 words spelled and divided. A concise glossary of business terms, including the newest newest dataprocessing words Practicyal guides for spelling and usage Find-it-fast list of commonly mispelled words abbreviations, and much more

Here's/a/desk/book/that/combines/a/speller-divider and a business glossary with a abundance of practical information. Its really 3 books in one. The speller-divider, based on the prestigious New World Webster's Dictionary, includes all of those words needed for common business use. The glossary section covers fifteen hundred key words related to general bussiness and management, basic accounting and finance, real estate law, and such new business technologies as information processing.

Here you'll find clear, authoritative, brief definitions, based on leading specialized reference books and dictionaries.

BIBLIOGRAPHY

In addition to its own specialized reference sources, every business office should have a desk dictionary, an English handbook, a secretarial handbook, and telephone and ZIP Code directories. The books listed below may be useful to those who wish supplementary reading on topics referred to in the *Katharine Gibbs Handbook of Business English*.

BUSINESS AND TECHNICAL WRITING

Andrews, Deborah C., and Blickle, Margaret D. *Technical Writing (Principles and Forms)*. 12th ed. New York: Macmillan, 1982.

Lannon, John M. *Technical Writing*. 2nd ed. Boston: Little, Brown and Company, 1982.

Londo, Richard J. *Common Sense in Business Writing*. New York: Macmillan, 1982.

Moyer, Ruth; Stevens, Eleanor; and Switzer, Ralph. *The Research and Report Handbook*. New York: John Wiley & Sons, 1981.

Paxson, William. *The Business Writing Handbook*. New York: Bantam Books, 1981.

Treece, Malri. *Effective Reports*. Boston: Allyn and Bacon, 1982.

Turabian, Kate L. *A Manual for Writers (of Term Papers, Theses, and Dissertations)*. 4th ed. Chicago: University of Chicago Press, 1973.

Wilkenson, C. W., and Clarke, Peter B. *Communicating through Letters and Reports*. 8th ed. Homewood, Illinois: Richard D. Irwin, 1980.

GRAMMAR, STYLE, AND USAGE

Bernstein, Theodore M. *The Careful Writer: A Modern Guide to English Usage*. New York: Atheneum, 1965.

Manual of Style, A. 12th ed., rev. Chicago: University of Chicago Press, 1969.

Strunk, William, and White, E. B. *The Elements of Style*. 3rd ed. New York: Macmillan, 1979.

Warriner, John E., and Graham, Sheila L. *English Grammar and Composition: Complete Course*. New York: Harcourt Brace Jovanovich, 1973.

Words Into Type, 3rd ed. Englewood Cliffs, New Jersey: Prentice-Hall, 1974.

U.S. Government Printing Office Style Manual. rev. ed. Washington, D.C.: U.S. Government Printing Office, 1973.

POSTAL INFORMATION

Address Abbreviations. U.S. Postal Service Publication, No. 59. Washington, D.C.: 1972.

Domestic Mail Manual. U.S. Postal Service. Washington: 1979.

Dun & Bradstreet Exporters' Encyclopaedia. Dun & Bradstreet, Inc., New York. (Published annually.)

Five-Digit ZIP Code & Post Office Directory. U.S. Postal Service Publication, No. 65. Washington, D.C.: 1981.

International Mail Manual. U.S. Postal Service. Washington, D.C.: 1981.

International Postal Rates and Fees. No. 51. Washington, D.C.: 1982.

SECRETARIAL HANDBOOKS

Clement, John. *The Grosset Secretarial Handbook.* New York: Grosset & Dunlap, 1980.

Doris, Lillian, and Miller, Besse M. *Complete Secretary's Handbook.* 4th ed. Englewood Cliffs, New Jersey: Prentice-Hall, 1977.

Hutchinson, Lois. *Standard Handbook for Secretaries.* New York: McGraw-Hill Book Co., 1977.

Sabin, William A. *The Gregg Reference Manual.* New York: Gregg Division, McGraw-Hill Book Co., 1977.

Taintor, Sarah A.; Monro, Kate M.; and Shertzer, Margaret D. *The Secretary's Handbook.* 9th ed., rev. New York: Macmillan, 1969.

Thompson, Margaret H., and Janis, J. Harold. *Revised Standard Reference for Secretaries and Administrators.* New York: Macmillan, 1980.

Webster's New World Secretarial Handbook. New York: Simon & Schuster, 1981.

WORD PROCESSING

Bergerud, Marly, and Gonzalez, Jean. *Word Processing Concepts and Careers.* New York: John Wiley & Sons, 1978.

Cecil, Paula B. *Management of Word Processing Operations.* Menlo Park, California: Benjamin Cummings Publishing Co., 1980.

Ellis, Bettie Hampton. *Word Processing: Concepts and Applications.* New York: Gregg Division, McGraw-Hill Book Co., 1980.

Mathews, Anne, and Moody, Pat. *The Word Processing Correspondence Secretary.* Cincinnati, Ohio: South-Western Publishing Company, 1981.

Rosen, Arnold, and Frelden, Rosemary. *Word Processing.* Englewood Cliffs, New Jersey: Prentice-Hall, 1982.

Zarella, John. *Word Processing and Text Editing.* California: Microcomputer Applications, 1982.

INDEX